First World War
and Army of Occupation
War Diary
France, Belgium and Germany

39 DIVISION
116 Infantry Brigade
Royal Sussex Regiment
11th Battalion
4 March 1916 - 30 June 1918

WO95/2582/1

The Naval & Military Press Ltd
www.nmarchive.com
Published in association with The National Archives

Published by

The Naval & Military Press Ltd

Unit 10 Ridgewood Industrial Park,
Uckfield, East Sussex,
TN22 5QE England
Tel: +44 (0) 1825 749494

www.naval-military-press.com

www.nmarchive.com

This diary has been reprinted in facsimile from the original. Any imperfections are inevitably reproduced and the quality may fall short of modern type and cartographic standards.

© Crown Copyright
Images reproduced by permission of The National Archives, London, England, 2015.

Contents

Document type	Place/Title	Date From	Date To
Heading	11th Battalion Royal Sussex Regiment		
Heading	116th Brigade 39th Division France 11th Battalion Royal Sussex Regt. 1916 Mar-1918 Jan Bn Embarked For UK 30.6.18		
Heading	Roy Sussex Regt.		
Heading	116th Brigade 39th Division. Battalion Disembarked Havre 5.3.16. 11th Battalion The Royal Sussex Regiment March 1916		
Heading	War Diary of 11th Service Battalion, Royal Sussex Regt. From 4th March 1916 To 31st March 1916 (Volume I)		
War Diary	Wittey Camp England	04/03/1916	04/03/1916
War Diary	Milford	04/03/1916	04/03/1916
War Diary	Southampton	04/03/1916	04/03/1916
War Diary	Havre	05/03/1916	06/03/1916
War Diary	Steenbecque	07/03/1916	07/03/1916
War Diary	Morbecque	07/03/1916	11/03/1916
War Diary	Estaires	12/03/1916	12/03/1916
War Diary	Fleurbaix	12/03/1916	12/03/1916
War Diary	Estaires	12/03/1916	12/03/1916
War Diary	Fleurbaix	13/03/1916	21/03/1916
War Diary	In Trenches	22/03/1916	23/03/1916
War Diary	Estaires	24/03/1916	25/03/1916
War Diary	Merville	26/03/1916	31/03/1916
Heading	116th Brigade. 39th Division. 11th Battalion The Royal Sussex Regiment April 1916		
Heading	War Diary of 11th Bn Royal Sussex Regiment From 1st April 1916 To 30th April 1916 (Inclusive) (Volume 2)		
War Diary	Merville	01/04/1916	14/04/1916
War Diary	Hingette	15/04/1916	15/04/1916
War Diary	Gorre	16/04/1916	18/04/1916
War Diary	Givenchy Trenches	19/04/1916	22/04/1916
War Diary	Village Line	23/04/1916	25/04/1916
War Diary	Givenchy Village Line	26/04/1916	27/04/1916
War Diary	Trenches	27/04/1916	30/04/1916
Heading	116th Brigade. 39th Division. 11th Battalion The Royal Sussex Regiment May 1916		
Heading	War Diary of 11th (S) Bn Royal Sussex Rgt Volume III From 1st May 1916 To 31st May 1916		
War Diary	Givenchy Trenches	01/05/1916	01/05/1916
War Diary	Hingette	02/05/1916	09/05/1916
War Diary	Le Touret	09/05/1916	13/05/1916
War Diary	Festubert Trenches	14/05/1916	17/05/1916
War Diary	Festubert Village Line	18/05/1916	21/05/1916
War Diary	Festubert Trenches	22/05/1916	25/05/1916
War Diary	Hingette	26/05/1916	28/05/1916
War Diary	Le Quesnoy	29/05/1916	29/05/1916
War Diary	Cuinchy Village Line	29/05/1916	31/05/1916
Heading	116th Brigade. 39th Division. 11th Battalion The Royal Sussex Regiment June 1916		

Heading	War Diary of 11th Bn. Royal Sussex Regt June 1916 Volume IV		
War Diary	Cuinchy Village Line	01/06/1916	01/06/1916
War Diary	Trenches Left Front Line	02/06/1916	05/06/1916
War Diary	Annequin	05/06/1916	05/06/1916
War Diary	Annequin. N.	06/06/1916	08/06/1916
War Diary	Guinchy (Left Sector)	08/06/1916	11/06/1916
War Diary	Hingette	12/06/1916	16/06/1916
War Diary	Croix Barbee	16/06/1916	22/06/1916
War Diary	Ferme Du Bois (New) Left Sector	22/06/1916	28/06/1916
War Diary	Richbourg	29/06/1916	30/06/1916
Heading	116th Brigade. 39th Division. 11th Battalion The Royal Sussex Regiment July 1916		
Heading	War Diary Of 11th Battalion Royal Sussex Regiment From 1st July 1916 To 31st July 1916 (Volume 5)		
War Diary	Richbourg	01/07/1916	01/07/1916
War Diary	Le Touret	01/07/1916	06/07/1916
War Diary	Beuvry	06/07/1916	07/07/1916
War Diary	Auchy	08/07/1916	14/07/1916
War Diary	Kings Road Le Touret	15/07/1916	20/07/1916
War Diary	Ferme Du Bois Left Sect.	21/07/1916	24/07/1916
War Diary	Richbourg St Vaast	24/07/1916	24/07/1916
War Diary	Festubert	25/07/1916	28/07/1916
War Diary	La Touret	28/07/1916	31/07/1916
Miscellaneous	Appendix 1. Plan Of Raid Carried Out By B. Company 11th Bn. Royal Sussex Regiment On The Night 23/24th July 1916	23/07/1916	23/07/1916
Miscellaneous	Appendix 2. Report On Raid Carried Out On Night 23/24th July 1916	23/07/1916	23/07/1916
Miscellaneous	Defence Scheme 11th Bn. Royal Sussex Regiment	09/07/1916	09/07/1916
Operation(al) Order(s)	Operation Order No. 21	20/07/1916	20/07/1916
Operation(al) Order(s)	Operation Order No. 22	24/07/1916	24/07/1916
Miscellaneous	No. 3 AG		
Operation(al) Order(s)	Operation Order No 23 By Major G.H. Harrison, Commanding 11th Royal Sussex Regt.	28/07/1916	28/07/1916
Heading	116th Brigade 39th Division. 11th Battalion Royal Sussex Regiment August 1916		
Heading	War Diary of The 11th Battalion Royal Sussex Regiment From 1st August 1916 To 31st August 1916 (Inclusive) (Volume VI)		
War Diary	Bethune	01/08/1916	06/08/1916
War Diary	Givenchy Rt Subsector	07/08/1916	11/08/1916
War Diary	Auchel	12/08/1916	13/08/1916
War Diary	Monchy Breton	14/08/1916	24/08/1916
War Diary	La Souich	25/08/1916	25/08/1916
War Diary	Bois De Warnimont	26/08/1916	27/08/1916
War Diary	Mailly Wood	28/08/1916	31/08/1916
Operation(al) Order(s)	Operation Order No. 24	01/08/1916	01/08/1916
Operation(al) Order(s)	Operation Order No. 25 Appendix 3	05/08/1916	05/08/1916
Operation(al) Order(s)	Operation Order No. 26 (Appendix 4).	09/08/1916	09/08/1916
Operation(al) Order(s)	Amendment To Operation Orders No. 26	10/08/1916	10/08/1916
Operation(al) Order(s)	Operation Order No. 27. (Appendix 5).	11/08/1916	11/08/1916
Miscellaneous	Night Exercise 17th August 1916. Appendix 6	17/08/1916	17/08/1916
Operation(al) Order(s)	Operation Order No. 29. Appendix 7	23/08/1916	23/08/1916
Operation(al) Order(s)	Operation Order No. 30. Appendix 8	24/08/1916	24/08/1916
Operation(al) Order(s)	Operation Order No. 31. Appendix 9	26/08/1916	26/08/1916

Operation(al) Order(s)	Operation Order No. 30	06/10/1916	06/10/1916
Operation(al) Order(s)	Operation Order No. 40	12/10/1916	12/10/1916
Operation(al) Order(s)	Operation Order No. 41	15/10/1916	15/10/1916
Operation(al) Order(s)	Operation Order No. 43	19/10/1916	19/10/1916
Operation(al) Order(s)	Operation Order No. 47	28/10/1916	28/10/1916
Operation(al) Order(s)	Operation Order No. 48	18/10/1916	18/10/1916
Miscellaneous	A Form. Messages And Signals		
Heading	116th Brigade. 39th Division. 11th Battalion The Royal Sussex Regiment September 1916		
Heading	War Diary From 1st To 30th September 1916 (Inclusive) Volume VII 11th Bn. Royal Sussex Regiment		
War Diary	Mailley Wood	01/09/1916	02/09/1916
War Diary	Beaumont Hamel	03/09/1916	03/09/1916
War Diary	Englebelmer	04/09/1916	06/09/1916
War Diary	Beaussart	07/09/1916	14/09/1916
War Diary	Beaumont Rt Subsection	15/09/1916	30/09/1916
Operation(al) Order(s)	Operation Order No. 30 Appendix 10	14/08/1916	14/08/1916
Operation(al) Order(s)	Operation Order No. 37 Appendix 11		
Miscellaneous	Programme Appendix "A"		
Miscellaneous	Instructions For Smoke Barrage Appendix "B"		
Heading	116th Brigade. 39th Division. 11th Battalion The Royal Sussex Regiment October 1916		
Heading	War Diary of 11st Bn Royal Sussex R For The Month Of Oct 1916		
War Diary	Beaumont Rt Sub Section	01/10/1916	04/10/1916
War Diary	Englebelmer Wood	05/10/1916	05/10/1916
War Diary	Martinsart Wood	06/10/1916	07/10/1916
War Diary	Hamel	08/10/1916	16/10/1916
War Diary	Authville Wood	17/10/1916	19/10/1916
War Diary	Redoubt Sector	20/10/1916	21/10/1916
War Diary	Aveluy Wood	22/10/1916	24/10/1916
War Diary	River Sector Thiepval	25/10/1916	26/10/1916
War Diary	South Bluff	27/10/1916	31/10/1916
War Diary	Schwaben Redoubt	30/10/1916	01/11/1916
Miscellaneous	A Conference 11th Royal Sussex Regt.	12/10/1916	12/10/1916
Miscellaneous	O.C. a Coy E.J.M. 15		
Miscellaneous	O.C. B Coy Urgent. E.J.M. 15/2		
Miscellaneous	Nominal Roll Of Casualties.		
Miscellaneous	Roll of Wounded 11th R Sussex	22/10/1916	22/10/1916
Miscellaneous	Killed. Boswell W. 5628. Snelling R.G. 15295		
Miscellaneous	Nominal Roll of Evacuations Transfers. 11th Sussex	25/10/1916	25/10/1916
Miscellaneous	The Undermentioned Of The Unit Under your Command Been Disposed Of As Follows:-	21/10/1916	21/10/1916
Miscellaneous	132nd Field Ambulance To O.C. 11th Royal Sussex 39th Div.		
War Diary	132nd Field Ambulance To O.C. 11th Royal Sussex 39th Div.		
Miscellaneous	The Undermentioned Of The Unit Under Your Command Been Disposed Of As Follows.	25/10/1916	25/10/1916
Miscellaneous	DRS		
Miscellaneous	Roll of Wounded.	23/10/1916	23/10/1916
Miscellaneous	The Undermentioned Of The Unit Under Your Command Been Disposed Of As Follows:	22/10/1916	22/10/1916
Miscellaneous	C Form (Duplicate). Messages And Signals		
Miscellaneous	A Coy		

Miscellaneous	The Undermentioned Of The Unit Under Your Command Been Disposed Of As Follows:	23/10/1916	23/10/1916
Miscellaneous	Roll of Wounded 11th Sussex	24/10/1916	24/10/1916
Miscellaneous	A Form. Messages And Signals		
Miscellaneous	Nominal Roll Of Evacuations 9 Transfer For Week Ending Oct 26. 1916	26/10/1916	26/10/1916
Miscellaneous	Nominal Roll Of Evacuations 9 Transfer.	25/10/1916	25/10/1916
Miscellaneous	A Form. Messages And Signals.		
Miscellaneous	A Form. Messages And Signals		
Heading	116th Brigade. 39th Division. 11th Battalion The Royal Sussex Regiment November 1916		
Heading	War Diary of 11th Bn Royal Sussex Regt. Nov 1st 1916 to 30th Nov 1916 Vol. IX.		
War Diary	Schwaben Redoubt	01/11/1916	01/11/1916
War Diary	Centre Bluffs	02/11/1916	03/11/1916
War Diary	Senlis	03/11/1916	04/11/1916
War Diary	River Left	05/11/1916	06/11/1916
War Diary	Senlis	06/11/1916	10/11/1916
War Diary	Schwaben Redoubt	10/11/1916	13/11/1916
War Diary	Thiepval	13/11/1916	13/11/1916
War Diary	Pioneer Rd	14/11/1916	14/11/1916
War Diary	Warloy	15/11/1916	15/11/1916
War Diary	Doullens	16/11/1916	17/11/1916
War Diary	M Camp	18/11/1916	30/11/1916
Operation(al) Order(s)	Operation Order No. 50	04/11/1916	04/11/1916
Operation(al) Order(s)	Operation Order No. 51	06/11/1916	06/11/1916
Operation(al) Order(s)	Operation Order No. 52	06/11/1916	06/11/1916
Operation(al) Order(s)	Operation Order No. 53		
Heading	116th Brigade. 39th Division. 11th Battalion The Royal Sussex Regiment December 1916		
Heading	War Diary of 11st Bn Royal Sussex Regt. For The Month Of December 1916 Vol 10		
War Diary	M Camp	01/12/1916	05/12/1916
War Diary	Moulle	06/12/1916	15/12/1916
War Diary	Ypres N. (Canal Bank) (Hill Top Left)	16/12/1916	19/12/1916
War Diary	Canal Bank	20/12/1916	23/12/1916
War Diary	E Camp	24/12/1916	31/12/1916
Heading	11st Bn Royal Sussex Regt War Diary For The Month Of January 1917 Vol X		
War Diary	Boesinghe	01/01/1917	03/01/1917
War Diary	Rossel Fm.	04/01/1917	14/01/1917
War Diary	Ypres	15/01/1917	15/01/1917
War Diary	Potijze	16/01/1917	20/01/1917
War Diary	Ypres	21/01/1917	24/01/1917
War Diary	Potijze	25/01/1917	28/01/1917
War Diary	Ypres	29/01/1917	31/01/1917
Heading	War Diary For The Month of February 1917 11st Bn Royal Sussex Reg. Vol XII		
War Diary	Ypres	01/02/1917	04/02/1917
War Diary	A Camp.	05/02/1917	15/02/1917
War Diary	Bollezeel	16/02/1917	23/02/1917
War Diary	Winnipeg Camp	24/02/1917	25/02/1917
War Diary	Ypres	26/02/1917	28/02/1917
Heading	War Diary of 11st Bn Royal Sussex Reg. For March 1917 Vol 13		
War Diary	Observatory Ridge	01/03/1917	02/03/1917

War Diary	Winnipeg Camp	03/03/1917	09/03/1917
War Diary	Zillebeke Bund	10/03/1917	13/03/1917
War Diary	Observatory Ridge Right Sector	14/03/1917	17/03/1917
War Diary	Krusstraat (Divisional Reserve)	18/03/1917	21/03/1917
War Diary	Winnepeg Camp	22/03/1917	27/03/1917
War Diary	Observatory Ridge Sector	28/03/1917	31/03/1917
Heading	War Diary of 11st Bn R Sussex Regt For April 1917. Vol 14		
War Diary	S. of The Bund Zillebeke	01/04/1917	04/04/1917
War Diary	Observatory Ridge Left Sector	05/04/1917	07/04/1917
War Diary	Brandhoek	08/04/1917	11/04/1917
War Diary	Ypres	12/04/1917	15/04/1917
War Diary	Brandhoek	16/04/1917	17/04/1917
War Diary	Hill Top. Sector Left Section	18/04/1917	30/04/1917
War Diary	M Camp	01/05/1917	01/05/1917
War Diary	Hallines & Zudausques	02/05/1917	02/05/1917
War Diary	Zudausques	03/05/1917	16/05/1917
War Diary	Longuenesse	17/05/1917	17/05/1917
War Diary	Zermezeele	18/05/1917	18/05/1917
War Diary	Wormhoudt	19/05/1917	28/05/1917
War Diary	D Camp.	29/05/1917	31/05/1917
Heading	11th Battalion Royal Sussex Regiment War Diary From 1st June To 30th June 1917 Volume 16		
War Diary	Hill Top Left Sub Sector	01/06/1917	05/06/1917
War Diary	Canal Bank East	06/06/1917	10/06/1917
War Diary	Hill Top. Left Sub Sector	11/06/1917	17/06/1917
War Diary	E. Camp.	18/06/1917	20/06/1917
War Diary	Houlle	21/06/1917	30/06/1917
Miscellaneous	C Company. 11th Bn. Royal Sussex Regt., 116th Inf. Bde.	07/06/1917	07/06/1917
War Diary	C Company, 11th Bn., Royal Sussex Regt., 116th Inf. Bde.	07/06/1917	07/06/1917
Map			
War Diary	Houlle	01/07/1917	15/07/1917
War Diary	C. Camp.	16/07/1917	28/07/1917
War Diary	Hill Top	29/07/1917	31/07/1917
Miscellaneous	O.C. 11st Battn. Royal Sussex Regt.	23/07/1917	23/07/1917
Operation(al) Order(s)	Operation Order 12th Bn. Royal Sussex Regt.	19/07/1917	19/07/1917
Miscellaneous	Time Table To Accompany Order No.		
War Diary	3rd Battle Of Ypres	01/08/1917	03/08/1917
War Diary	School Camp	04/08/1917	08/08/1917
War Diary	Meteren	09/08/1917	13/08/1917
War Diary	Spoil Bank	13/08/1917	13/08/1917
War Diary	Support Left Sub Sector Hollebeke	14/08/1917	17/08/1917
War Diary	Hollebeke Left Sub Sector	18/08/1917	21/08/1917
War Diary	Support Left Sub Sector Hollebeke	22/08/1917	23/08/1917
War Diary	Ridge Wood Camp	24/08/1917	27/08/1917
War Diary	Right Batn Left Bde	28/08/1917	31/08/1917
War Diary	Cordon Tr Voormezeele	01/09/1917	02/09/1917
War Diary	Ridge Wood Camp	03/09/1917	08/09/1917
War Diary	Mt. Sorrel	09/09/1917	12/09/1917
War Diary	Voormezeele	13/09/1917	14/09/1917
War Diary	Shrews Bury Forest Sector	15/09/1917	18/09/1917
War Diary	Ascot Camp	19/09/1917	22/09/1917
War Diary	Beggar's Rest	23/09/1917	23/09/1917
War Diary	Menin Road	24/09/1917	27/09/1917

War Diary	Nr. Berthen	28/09/1917	30/09/1917
Miscellaneous	Time Table To Accompany Order No.		
Heading	11th Bn Royal Sussex Regt. War Diary For 1st October 1917 To 31st October 1917. Volume 20		
War Diary	Kokereele (Stafford Camp)	01/10/1917	15/10/1917
War Diary	Canada Street	16/10/1917	16/10/1917
War Diary	Tunnels Near Zillebeke	17/10/1917	17/10/1917
War Diary	Tower Hamlets Right	18/10/1917	19/10/1917
War Diary	Near Vierstraat	20/10/1917	22/10/1917
War Diary	Carnarvon Camp	23/10/1917	23/10/1917
War Diary	Near Reninghelst	23/10/1917	27/10/1917
War Diary	Chippewa Camp	28/10/1917	31/10/1917
Miscellaneous	11th Service Battalion Royal Sussex Regiment. Appendix A	26/10/1917	26/10/1917
Miscellaneous	11th Service Battalion Royal Sussex Regiment. Appendix B	28/10/1917	28/10/1917
Heading	11th Battalion Royal Sussex Regiment War Diary For 1st November To 30th November 1917. Volume 21		
War Diary	Chippewa Camp	01/11/1917	03/11/1917
War Diary	Tower Hamlets Rt Sub Sector	04/11/1917	06/11/1917
War Diary	Support Bodmin Copse	07/11/1917	07/11/1917
War Diary	Godezonne Camp	08/11/1917	08/11/1917
War Diary	Chippewa Camp.	09/11/1917	13/11/1917
War Diary	Bedford House	14/11/1917	19/11/1917
War Diary	Scottish Wood CP	20/11/1917	25/11/1917
War Diary	Winnezeele	26/11/1917	29/11/1917
War Diary	Potijze	30/11/1917	30/11/1917
Heading	11th Battalion Royal Sussex Regiment War Diary For 1st December To 31st December 1917 Volume 22		
War Diary	Potijze	01/12/1917	08/12/1917
War Diary	Winnezeele	09/12/1917	10/12/1917
War Diary	Seninghem	11/12/1917	30/12/1917
War Diary	Siege Camp	31/12/1917	31/12/1917
War Diary	11th Service Battalion, Royal Sussex Regiment. War Diary For January 1918 (Volume 23)		
War Diary	Siege Camp	01/01/1918	07/01/1918
War Diary	Irish Farm Camp	08/01/1918	08/01/1918
War Diary	L Moracco Camp	09/01/1918	14/01/1918
War Diary	Irish Farm Camp	15/01/1918	15/01/1918
War Diary	Trenches	16/01/1918	18/01/1918
War Diary	Hill Top Farm Camp.	19/01/1918	21/01/1918
War Diary	School Camp.	22/01/1918	26/01/1918
War Diary	Cherisy Gailly	27/01/1918	30/01/1918
War Diary	Haut. Allaines	31/01/1918	31/01/1918
Miscellaneous	Estimate 1 HR		
Heading	11th Bn. Royal Sussex Regt. War Diary From 1st February To 28th February 1918 (Volume 24)		
War Diary	Haut Allaines	01/02/1918	01/02/1918
War Diary	Revelon Farm	02/02/1918	03/02/1918
War Diary	Line	04/02/1918	09/02/1918
War Diary	Revelon Farm	10/02/1918	13/02/1918
War Diary	Line	14/02/1918	22/02/1918
War Diary	Revelon Farm	23/02/1918	26/02/1918
War Diary	Line	27/02/1918	28/02/1918
Heading	116th Inf. Bde. 39th Div. 11th Battn. The Royal Sussex Regiment March 1918		

Heading	War Diary 11th Battn Royal Sussex Regiment Volume 25		
War Diary	Gouzeacourt	01/03/1918	06/03/1918
War Diary	Revelon Farm	07/03/1918	10/03/1918
War Diary	Gouzeacourt	11/03/1918	12/03/1918
War Diary	Gurlu Wood	12/03/1918	14/03/1918
War Diary	Hem	15/03/1918	21/03/1918
War Diary	Villers Faucon	22/03/1918	23/03/1918
War Diary	Bussu	23/03/1918	23/03/1918
War Diary	Hem	24/03/1918	25/03/1918
War Diary	Chuignolles	26/03/1918	31/03/1918
Heading	2/L G. A Davidson 11st R. Sussex Rgt. 1918		
Miscellaneous	Extracts from Diary of 2/Lieut. J.A. Davidson, "B" Coy. 11th R. Sussex Regiment, 116th Brigade (Br. Gen. Montague Hornby), 39th Division, Fifth Army.		
Miscellaneous	11th Royal Sussex Regt.	21/03/1918	21/03/1918
Miscellaneous	11th Royal Sussex Regt.	22/03/1918	22/03/1918
Miscellaneous	11th R. Sussex Regt.	23/03/1918	23/03/1918
Miscellaneous	11th R. Sussex	23/03/1918	23/03/1918
Heading	39th Division. Composite Brigade Became "A" & "B" Cos. No. 1 Composite Battalion 11.4.18 11th Battalion Royal Sussex Regiment April 1918		
Heading	War Diary 11th (S) Bn Royal Sussex Regt. Volume XXVI April 1918		
War Diary	Cleary	01/04/1918	02/04/1918
War Diary	Aumont	03/04/1918	03/04/1918
War Diary	Amatre	04/04/1918	07/04/1918
War Diary	Embleville	08/04/1918	09/04/1918
War Diary	Tatinghem	10/04/1918	11/04/1918
War Diary	Toronto Camp	12/04/1918	12/04/1918
War Diary	Otago Camp	13/04/1918	15/04/1918
War Diary	Voormezeele	16/04/1918	21/04/1918
War Diary	Elzenwalle Chateau (Front Line)	22/04/1918	27/04/1918
War Diary	Support Line	28/04/1918	29/04/1918
War Diary	Devonshire Camp	30/04/1918	30/04/1918
Heading	11th Battalion Royal Sussex Regiment War Diary For May 1918 Volume 27		
War Diary	Devonshire Camp	01/05/1918	04/05/1918
War Diary	M. Camp	05/05/1918	05/05/1918
War Diary	Nielles Les. Ardres	06/05/1918	23/05/1918
War Diary	Licques	24/05/1918	31/05/1918
Miscellaneous	The Military Medal	03/06/1918	03/06/1918
Heading	11th Battalion Royal Sussex Regiment War Diary For 1st To 30th June 1918 (Volume) 28		
War Diary	Licques	01/06/1918	16/06/1918
War Diary	Listergaux	17/06/1918	21/06/1918
War Diary	Grasse Payelle	22/06/1918	29/06/1918
War Diary	Boulogne	30/06/1918	30/06/1918

11TH BATTALION ROYAL SUSSEX REGIMENT

116TH BRIGADE
39TH DIVISION

FRANCE
11TH BATTALION
ROYAL SUSSEX REGT.
~~MAR — DEC 1916~~

1916 MAR — 1918 JUN

ON EMBARKED FOR UK 30.6.18

June 18

Roy Lucian Roy

March – Dec 1916

116th Brigade
39th Division.

Battalion disembarked HAVRE 5.3.16

11th BATTALION

THE ROYAL SUSSEX REGIMENT

MARCH 1916

Original

Army Form C. 2118

WAR DIARY
or
INTELLIGENCE SUMMARY
(Erase heading not required.)

11 Sussex Vol I

Confidential

War Diary
of
11th Service Battalion, Royal Sussex Regt.

From 4th March 1916 to 31st March 1916

(Volume I)

Army Form C. 2118

WAR DIARY
or
INTELLIGENCE SUMMARY
(Erase heading not required.)

Instructions regarding War Diaries and Intelligence Summaries are contained in F. S. Regs., Part II. and the Staff Manual respectively. Title Pages will be prepared in manuscript.

Place	Date	Hour	Summary of Events and Information	Remarks and references to Appendices
Witley Camp England	4.3.16	3.30am	The Battalion marched out of camp to entrain at Milford for active service.	
Milford	4.3.16	6am 7am 7.55am	Three Trains left MILFORD for Southampton.	
Southampton	4.3.16	7.30pm	The Battalion embarked, split up into 3 ships.	
HAVRE	5.3.16	7am	The Battalion disembarked at HAVRE.	cont.
HAVRE	5.3.16	8.30am	The Battalion arrived at No 5 Docks Rest camp.	
HAVRE	6.3.16	3.45am	The Battalion left the Rest camp & entrained at La GARE MERCHANDISES. HAVRE.	cont.
"	6.3.16	8.30am	Halts were made at MONTEROLIER BUCHY & ABBEVILLE.	cont.
STEENBECQUE	7.3.16	6.30am	The Battalion detrained & march to Brielle at MORBECQUE	

1875 Wt. W593/826 1,000,000 4/15 J.B.C. & A. A.D.S.S./Forms/C. 2118.

Army Form C. 2118

WAR DIARY
or
INTELLIGENCE SUMMARY

(Erase heading not required.)

Instructions regarding War Diaries and Intelligence Summaries are contained in F. S. Regs., Part II. and the Staff Manual respectively. Title Pages will be prepared in manuscript.

Place	Date	Hour	Summary of Events and Information	Remarks and references to Appendices
MORBECQUE	7.3.16	9 am	The Billets consisted of Farm houses, Barns, Schools & & huts & various houses in the village	
"	7.3.16	4.30	Telephone communication established between Battalion & Bde Hqrs.	clay
"	8.3.16		The Battalion remained in Billets	clay aay
"	9.3.16		" "	clay
"	10.3.16		" "	clay
"	11.3.16	10 am	The Battalion marched to ESTAIRES & were accommodated in Billets	
ESTAIRES	12.3.16	6 am	A & B coys marched to FLEURBAIX & were attached to the 8th York & Lancs for instruction	
FLEURBAIX	12.3.16	6.15 pm	A & B coys marched up to the trenches & were distributed amongst the York & Lancs in Trench. N52 N53 N54 N55. 1 OR was killed entering the trench	

1875 Wt. W593/826 1,000,000 4/15 J.B.C. & A. A.D.S.S./Forms/C. 2118.

WAR DIARY or INTELLIGENCE SUMMARY

Army Form C. 2118

Place	Date	Hour	Summary of Events and Information	Remarks and references to Appendices
ESTAIRES	12.3.16	7 pm	C & D coys marched to FLEURBAIX & were attached to the 9th York & Lancs Regt & accommodated in Billets for instruction. Major HARRISON was in command of the party.	
FLEURBAIX	13.3.16	4-5 pm	FLEURBAIX was shelled by enemy artillery about 12 5.9 shells exploded. One shell struck C coy's billets. Major The Hon NEVILLE LYTTON & Capt H TYLER wounded. OR 4 killed 9 wounded, 1 died of wounds. Company commanders of C & D coys visited Batteries covering our portion of the front.	
"	14.3.16	6.30 pm	9th York & Lancs with M.G. corps of this Battalion relieved 8th York & Lancs & MG corps of this Battalion the latter marching	

WAR DIARY
or
INTELLIGENCE SUMMARY
(Erase heading not required.)

Army Form C. 2118

Place	Date	Hour	Summary of Events and Information	Remarks and references to Appendices
			back to the billets occupied by the former.	Ceay.
			Capt C PENRUDDOCKE took over command of C coy vice Major The Hon NEVILLE LYTTON wounded 1 OR (reported wounded) died of wounds in hospital	
FLEURBAIX	15.3.16		CO & Adjutant visited 32nd Battery R.F.A. at 9am this battery was shelled by enemy 5.9's. 13 shells were counted & trifling damage only was done A & B coys were in billets C & D coys were in the trenches The front was quiet throughout the day, the weather very fine & bright.	Ceay

WAR DIARY
or
INTELLIGENCE SUMMARY
(Erase heading not required.)

Army Form C. 2118

Place	Date	Hour	Summary of Events and Information	Remarks and references to Appendices
FLEURBAIX	16.3.16		FLEURBAIX was shelled A & B coys returning into dug outs & shelter trenches. 1 O.R wounded. C & D coys had a quiet day in front line trenches 1 O.R wounded.	coy
"	17.3.16		Quiet day in both trenches & billets 1 O.R wounded.	
"	18.3.16	6.30 pm	8th York & Lancs with A & B coys attacked & relieved 9th York & Lancs in the trenches (with C & D coys attached) the latter marched back to their billets in FLEURBAIX. 1 O.R (reported wounded) died of wounds.	coy

Army Form C. 2118

WAR DIARY
or
INTELLIGENCE SUMMARY
(Erase heading not required.)

Instructions regarding War Diaries and Intelligence Summaries are contained in F.S. Regs., Part II. and the Staff Manual respectively. Title Pages will be prepared in manuscript.

Place	Date	Hour	Summary of Events and Information	Remarks and references to Appendices
FLEURBAIX	19.3.16		Quiet day. 1 OR (reported wounded) died of wounds	diary
FLEURBAIX	20.3.16	7 pm.	C & D coys march up to the trenches & relieve 8th York trenches. line held by 8th York trenches now entirely held by this battalion. Lieut R.H. Septon takes over command of D coy vice Capt E. Cassels (trek)	
FLEURBAIX	21.3.16		Quiet day in the trenches. Parapet improved. Parados built up. Trenches drained by night. Numerous patrols went out.	diary
TRENCHES	22.3.16		Quiet day in Trenches, very wet day, usual work carried on by night. Numerous patrols went out.	diary

WAR DIARY or INTELLIGENCE SUMMARY

Army Form C. 2118

(Erase heading not required.)

Place	Date	Hour	Summary of Events and Information	Remarks and references to Appendices
In Trenches	23.3.16	8pm	The Battalion was relieved by the 15th Royal Scots & marched to ESTAIRES & occupied billets.	ccay
ESTAIRES	24.3.16		Quiet day in billets. Lieut P. Campbell-Harris takes over the duties of Transport officer from Lt L.E. Phoggin (tick)	ccay
"	25.3.16	10pm	The battalion marched to took over billets at MERVILLE & REGNIER LE CLERC.	ccay
MERVILLE	26.3.16		In billets. Coys clean up generally. Capt T Wallace takes command coy. & B Coy Vice Capt S. Pinewood (tick.)	ccay
"	27.3.16		In billets. Coys carry out wood infections, & perform drill, bayonet fighting & physical training. Capt J. Pinewood died in Hospital	ccay

Army Form C. 2118

WAR DIARY
or
INTELLIGENCE SUMMARY

(Erase heading not required.)

Instructions regarding War Diaries and Intelligence Summaries are contained in F. S. Regs., Part II. and the Staff Manual respectively. Title Pages will be prepared in manuscript.

Place	Date	Hour	Summary of Events and Information	Remarks and references to Appendices
MERVILLE	28.3.16		Companies carry on with baths, drill, Physical Training, etc in their billets.	
			Capt C E A TERRY took over duties of Adjutant vice	copy
			Major G. H. HARRISON (sick)	
			Capt T. WALLACE took over duties of Adjutant from Capt	
			C E A TERRY.	
			Lt F Canada took over command of B Coy vice Capt T	
			WALLACE.	
MERVILLE	29.3.16.		Mr Willets. Major the NEVILLE LYTTON. Returned to duty from Hospital.	copy
"	30.3.16.		No billets, companies carry on with baths, drill etc.	copy

WAR DIARY
INTELLIGENCE SUMMARY

Place	Date	Hour	Summary of Events and Information	Remarks and references to Appendices
MERVILLE	31.3.16	10.30am	The Battalion left their billets & occupied fresh billets at the west end of MERVILLE.	Clery

M.S.Jiverson Lt Col.
11 R. Suss R.

31/3/16

116th Brigade.
39th Division.

11th BATTALION

THE ROYAL SUSSEX REGIMENT

APRIL 1 9 1 6

XXXIX

CONFIDENTIAL

War Diary

of

11th Bn. Royal Sussex Regiment

From 1st April 1916 to 30th April 1916 (inclusive)

(Volume 2)

Army Form C. 2118

WAR DIARY
or
INTELLIGENCE SUMMARY
(Erase heading not required.)

Instructions regarding War Diaries and Intelligence Summaries are contained in F. S. Regs., Part II. and the Staff Manual respectively. Title Pages will be prepared in manuscript.

Place	Date	Hour	Summary of Events and Information	Remarks and references to Appendices
MERVILLE	1/4/16		B'n in Billets. Weather fine. Training carried on	TW
do	2.4.16		do Divine Service	TW
do	(Sunday) 2/4/16			TW
			MAJOR. HON. N. LYTTON returned from hospital. Took over duties of 2nd in Comd. vice CAPT. TERRY CAPT. T. WALLACE took over Comd. of "A" Coy vice LIEUT. F. CASSELS. CAPT. TERRY took over duties of ADJT.	
do	3.4.16	10 a.m.	B'n was inspected by G.O.C. XI CORPS. BRIG. GEN. 116th BDE (Th'd Batt: Grena) congratulated the units of B'one on their excellent turnout on inspection. Weather fine.	TW
do	4.4.16		Quiet day in Billets. Drill etc. Weather fine	TW
do	5.4.16		do	TW
do	6.4.16		B'n had use of Rifle Range at LES LAURIERS. Night operations.	TW
do	7.4.16		Training proceeds with weather fine. Night operations	TW
do	8.4.16		do	TW
do	9.4.16		do Divine Service	TW
do	10.4.16		do	TW
do	11.4.16		B'n had use of Rifle range. Weather dull, wet at times. Rain	TW
do	12.4.16		do	TW
do	13.4.16		do	TW
do	14.4.16	9.30 a.m.	B'n marches to LOCON AREA (HINGETTE) via PACAUT. Changing {Draft of 30 men} arrived from England.	TW
HINGETTE	15.4.16	8 a.m.	B'n " " trench in GORRE, via AVELETTE, LES CHOQUAUX, LOCON, MESPLAUX + LE HAMEL. Control posts on CANAL towing way.	TW
GORRE	16.4.16		B'n in Billets. Divine Service. Rain	TW
do	17.4.16		do Dull. Working parties to R.E. Rainy	TW
do			CO very Musan wants inspected trenches to be taken over	TW

1875 Wt. W593/826 1,000,000 4/15 J.B.C. & A. A.D.S.S./Forms/C. 2118.

WAR DIARY / INTELLIGENCE SUMMARY

Army Form C. 2118

Place	Date	Hour	Summary of Events and Information	Remarks and references to Appendices
GORRE	18/4/16		Participated trenches at GIVENCHY. An Officer mostly arrived – R.G.A. – who handed over by Adjutant 116th BDE. CAPT. T. WALLACE took over duties of ADJT vice CAPT. C.E.A. TERRY appointed Acting Staff CAPT. 116th BDE. CAPT. T.H. COTLING took over cmd of 'A' Coy vice CAPT. T.D. PAGET appointed O.C. BDE. workshop 116th BDE. LIEUT. F. CASSELS took over cmd of 'D' Coy vice CAPT. T. WALLACE. Spy seen at 12 m.n.	TW
GIVENCHY TRENCHES	19/4/16	8am	Bn marched to trenches at GIVENCHY on relief of 13th R. St.	TW
		11.20am	Relief completed. Bn hold at WINDY CORNER. Artillery attack rather active during night. 5 casualties in 'C' Coy from shell. Rain during night	
do	20/4/16		Bn in trenches. 1 casualty in 'A' Coy from snipers at DUCKS BILL. Artillery shell dump. Afternoon and between 9/10 am 12 m.n. Grenade parties went into action. Patrols during night under LIEUT. BATTLEY bombed enemy trench opposite DUCKS BILL and brought in French Sergeant. 3 Germans safe. Patrol under LIEUT. J.C. KELIHER brought in GERMAN forage cap. These trespasses were sent to 116th BDE.	TW
do	21/4/16	4pm	There was unprecedented artillery duels throughout the day. 2 LIEUT F.W. BATTLEY and 2 men were about by rifle grenade at DUCKS BILL and mortally wounded.	TW
do	22/4/16	10am	2 LIEUT. F.W. BATTLEY died in GIVENCHY cemetery by C.O.E. Chaplain. Artillery on both sides active. Casualties – 1 man killed, 2 wounded	TW
		8pm	LIEUT. C.A. VORLEY 10th R. St. Regt joined from ENGLAND	
VILLAGE LINE	23/4/16	5am	Relieved by 13th R. St. Took over VILLAGE LINE from 14th Hants. Easter Sunday. Weather fine.	TW
do	24/4/16		Weather fine. Working parties supplied to R.E.'s. Shelling during day by 70th Sector do.	TW
do	25/4/16	2pm	O/c Coy successfully wounded in GIVENCHY KEEP. Bangalore Torpedo experiment by R.E.'s. Great success. Huge Crater on right of CANAL. A Willy bombing trench erected April 12 m.n. 1 man wounded in 'A' Coy	TW

WAR DIARY
or
INTELLIGENCE SUMMARY
(Erase heading not required.)

Army Form C. 2118

Instructions regarding War Diaries and Intelligence Summaries are contained in F.S. Regs., Part II. and the Staff Manual respectively. Title Pages will be prepared in manuscript.

Place	Date	Hour	Summary of Events and Information	Remarks and references to Appendices
GIVENCHY VILLAGE LINE	26.4.16		Neubois line. Aeroplanes and some artillery activity. CAPT. MILLWARD joined Batt: at 8 pm F.G. Court Martial on C.S.M. COLEMAN in GORRE.	TW
	27.4.16	5 a.m	Great artillery activity on our right towards LOOS. Lasted until 8 am. Trace of gas in GORRE during this. Men all warned.	TW
TRENCHES		9 am	Relieved 13th R Sx in trenches. 13th R Sx took over the VILLAGE LINE. CAPT. MILLWARD posted to "D" Coy.	
do	28.4.16		German attack near LOOS. Artillery Active 8.30 pm – 10 pm. Gas alarm. HQs moved to GUNNERS SIDING at 8.45 pm & returned about 10.15 pm 2 ORs wounded LT C.A.G. BURGESS wounded 2 ORs killed and 8 OR s wounded (including 4 shell shock) 1 missing	TW
do	29.4.16		Artillery active on both sides. Enemy's artillery caused 2 breaches in Rt Coy parapet. M.Gs active on breaches. Our howitzers did considerable damage on enemy wires & parapets. Officers of 1/6th CHESHIRES shown round trenches.	TW
do	30.4.16		Artillery quiet. Runs jam on WOLFE RD. and at DUCKS BILL. No Damage. 1 OR previously reported wounded, died of wounds. Breaches in parapets repaired and parapets strengthened. Entrance to new Sap discovered facing Sap A at DUCKS BILL	TW

M Millward
Lieut Colonel
Commdg 11th R Sussex Regt

116th Brigade.
39th Division.

11th BATTALION

THE ROYAL SUSSEX REGIMENT

MAY 1916

Confidential

War Diary of
11th (S) Bn. Royal Sussex Regt.

Volume III

From 1st May 1916 to 31st May 1916

WAR DIARY
or
INTELLIGENCE SUMMARY
(Erase heading not required.)

Army Form C. 2118

Instructions regarding War Diaries and Intelligence Summaries are contained in F.S. Regs., Part II. and the Staff Manual respectively. Title Pages will be prepared in manuscript.

ORDERLY ROOM — 11th SERVICE BATTN. ROYAL SUSSEX REGT.

Place	Date	Hour	Summary of Events and Information	Remarks and references to Appendices
GIVENCHY TRENCHES	1.5.16	8 a.m.	Advance party moved off to take over billets at HINGETTE	TW
		8 p.m.	Battalion was relieved by 1/6 CHESHIRES. Relief completed at 11.30 p.m.	TW
HINGETTE	2.5.16	4.30 a.m.	Last Coy arrived at billets.	TW
do	3.5.16		Day spent in cleaning up billets, clothing etc. Inspection of Bn. by C.O. Weather delightful.	TW
do	4.5.16		Bn. in training. Weather fine. Bathing in CANAL. Band plays in evening.	TW
do	5.5.16		Bn. on Range at PONT L'HINGES. Bayonet fighting, musketry returns. Weather fine.	TW
do	6.5.16		Route march → HINGETTE – HINGES – BETHUNE – HINGETTE. Weather fine.	TW
do	7.5.16	9 a.m.	Divine Service. Showery. 2 Lieut: A. CHALK joined Bn from H.A.C. Posted to 'C' Coy.	TW
do	8.5.16		Practice on range during morning. GEN: BARNADISTON inspected billets. Advance party marches off to LE TOURET to take over billets. Draft of 47 men arrived from ENGLAND.	TW
			CAPT. E. CASSELS arrived from hospital. 2 LIEUT. VIDLER returned from Base & ENGLAND.	
do	9.5.16	9.30 a.m.	Bn marched via LOCON & MESPLAUX to LE TOURET. Weather wet.	TW
		11.45	Bn arrived at LE TOURET. Weather wet.	
LE TOURET			C.O. & Officers reconnoitred VILLAGE LINE.	TW
do	10.5.16	10 a.m.	Fatigue parties for R.E.S. 1 O.R. reced in O.R. wounded. Weather fine. 2 officers attached to R.A.	TW
do	11.5.16		do. 1 O.R. self inflicted wound. 2 O.Rs. accidentally wounded by detonator.	TW
			LT. E. C. KELIHER joined from 13th R.Sx. 2 officers attached to R.A.	
do	12.5.16		Fatigue parties. 2 officers attached R.A. Weather wet. Enemy M.Gs active during	TW
			night. 1 O.R. killed 1 O.R. wounded. M.G.S. Coy & FESTUBERT LINE.	
do	13.5.16	8.30 p.m.	Bn took over FESTUBERT LINE from 13th Bn., the 13th Bn taking over 11th Relieved.	TW

1875 Wt. W593/826 1,000,000 4/15 I.B.C. & A. A.D.S.S./Forms/C. 2118.

WAR DIARY or INTELLIGENCE SUMMARY

Army Form C. 2118

Place	Date	Hour	Summary of Events and Information	Remarks and references to Appendices
FESTUBERT TRENCHES	14.5.16	1 pm	Relief completed. 1 O.R. killed at "Stand to". 8 Wiring parties Tyler near R.H. Oc	T.W.
		6 p.m.	Heavy Shrapnel fire. Enemy artillery on Wright. Work done in parapets. Wire 70 coils D. wire put out	T.W.
do	15.5.16		2nd LTS. G.W. DOOGAN & E.C. BLUNDEN joined Bn. from 10th R. Sx. 2 O.R. wounded. Enemy Aerial quiet. Sniper in SHETLAND RD. Enemy M.G. active. Work in SHETLAND RD. 4 O.Rs wounded (1 died) from M.G. fire whilst working on parapets at Island 34. Plt of 13th Batt. crawled from "NO MAN'S LAND" into 30 yards after being wire were down for 4 days	T.W.
do	16.5.16		Artillery active at times. Sweeping the ridges. SHETLAND RD + at Island 14. No aeroplanes. Snipers claimed 3 victims. Wiring fire. 1 O.R. wounded overhead aeroplanes at night. Moonlight.	T.W. T.W.
do	17.5.16		Div. Gen. visited trenches. Work in parapets, SHETLAND RD more. Enemy artillery active on our front/support & lines of Island 38. Batt. relieved by 13th Battn & marches to VILLAGE LINE. 1 O.R. wounded	T.W.
		9 pm		
FESTUBERT VILLAGE LINE	18.5.16		Reconnaissance of Kupps & Route to O.P.L. Quiet day. Fatigues in R.E. work. Weather fine.	T.W.
do	19.5.16		Enemy aeroplanes active. 'Short Horns', Shells. R.E. work trench in Kupfer. Draft of 99 men from Cyclist Corps	T.W.
do	20.5.16		Our artillery and aeroplane active. White smell. R.E. fatigues. Weather fine. 2 O.Rs wounded (one since died) by M.G.	T.W.
do	21.5.16		Enemy artillery active. Shells in FESTUBERT EAST + School House. Division GAR. Our artillery fire with effect on enemy M.G. emplacements. Work in Kupfer in VILLAGE LINE. Gas attack practice. Mine explosion at GIVENCHY.	T.W.
		10 am 11 am	Enemy aeroplane active. Battn moves to Trenches relieving 13th R.Sx.	T.W.
FESTUBERT TRENCHES	22.5.16	9 pm	Artillery quiet. Enemy Trench Mortars active on SHETLAND RD. Front & Support. Enemy Trench Mortar Bombs continued. Work in SHETLAND RD. Patrol and Working party through neumontries. "NO MAN'S LAND". LIEUT. KAPP wounded.	T.W.

1875 Wt. W593/826 1,000,000 4/15 J.B.C. & A. A.D.S.S./Forms/C. 2118.

WAR DIARY or INTELLIGENCE SUMMARY

Army Form C. 2118

(Erase heading not required.)

Instructions regarding War Diaries and Intelligence Summaries are contained in F.S. Regs., Part II. and the Staff Manual respectively. Title Pages will be prepared in manuscript.

ORDERLY ROOM
11th SERVICE BATTN.
ROYAL SUSSEX REGT.

Place	Date	Hour	Summary of Events and Information	Remarks and references to Appendices
FESTUBERT TRENCHES	23.5.16	5pm	Enemy artillery active. Whizzbangs on RICHMOND TERRACE and on OTL. Shells on SHETLAND RD.	TW.
		7pm	Our artillery shells enemy front line. Patrols entered enemy lines in NO MANS LAND	TW.
do	24.5.16	3pm	Sniping down to minimum. (15th Div) Weather fine.	
		10pm	Our artillery ruptured an enemy's trench opposite ISLAND St. 10 rnds rapid in this spot. 1st HERTS. MAJOR G.H. HARRISON found from M.G. detachment relieved by 1st HERTS.	TW.
do	25.5.16		ENGLAND. Relieved by 1st HERTS at 10 pm. Batt. marched back to HANGETTE. Weather wet.	TW.
HINGETTE	26.5.16	4pm	Bn all in billets. Day of rest. CR. GRISEWOOD proceeded on leave.	TW.
do	27.5.16		MAJOR HARRISON took over as 2nd in Comd of Regt: during absence of CR. GRISEWOOD. MAJOR LYTTON went on leave. Day of inspections. Weather fine. Band service during morning.	TW.
do	28.5.16	2.30pm 7.30pm	Went for march. Proceed to LE QUESNOY as Battn in Reserve of CUINCHY Section. Took over from 4th KINGS LIVERPOOLS	TW.
LE QUESNOY	29.5.16	3am 7am 2.30pm	Going to move to VILLAGE LINE, CUINCHY B'n moved to do do do Relief completed.	
CUINCHY VILLAGE LINE		10pm	Our artillery rattling active. Enemy bombardment of ESPERANTO TERR: and CUINCHY SUPPORT PT. Orbat two shells trD. No damage done. 1 otr. killed shock. Rum at night.	TW.
		11.45pm	Much sniping on our front by enemy.	
do	30.5.16	9pm	Shrapnel on CAMERON POST. Our artillery active. B	TW.
			R.E. fatigues took on keeps trenches.	
do	31.5.16	4pm 7.45pm	Enemy T.M.'s + Whizzbangs active on BRICKSTACKS. CUINCHY SUPPORT PT. SHELD. 2 Whizzbangs on CAMERIN POST. Working parties with RES. Repairs to trenches etc etc	TW.

W Winwood Lt Col

116th Brigade.
39th Division.

11th BATTALION

THE ROYAL SUSSEX REGIMENT

JUNE 1916

11 Sussex

ORDERLY ROOM
11
ROYAL SUSSEX REGT.

Vol 4
June

11/39

XXXIX

H.E
6 sheets

Confidential

War Diary
of
11th Bn. Royal Sussex Regt
June 1916.

VOLUME IV.

WAR DIARY or INTELLIGENCE SUMMARY

Army Form C. 2118

Place	Date	Hour	Summary of Events and Information	Remarks and references to Appendices
GUINCHY VILLAGE LINE.	1.6.16		2/LIEUT. E.K. KAPP left Batt to report to 29th DIV as 3rd Class Intelligence Officer. 2/LIEUT. G. MICHELL proceeded on leave. LIEUT. NO.S. LEWIS awarded Military Cross for gallantry at GIVENCHY 27.4.16	P.u.
		2.2pm	Relieved 13th BATTN in front line trenches. Quiet night. Work on mine.	P.u.
TRENCHES Left Front line	2.6.16	5.45pm 7am	ESPERANTO TERR: + BERKS: LANE shelled 2 O.Rs killed	P.u.
		3.15pm	Enemy Cay mortared + BRICKSTACK TERR: by whizzbangs and minenwerfer in trench line. LIEUT. G. COMPTON relieved W. BOOTH owing to Military Cross for gallantry at GIVENCHY 27.4.16.	P.u.
do	3.6.16	1am	"LIEUT RICHARDS" killed. Enemy attempt a raid on our crater front. Bombardment of trenches with rifle grenades. Patrol "C" "D" Cays met Sgt GREEN who were repulsed with rifle fire. Three wounded.	
		2am	Sap. 15 blown in 3. O.R.s killed	
		4am	Snipers shot 2 O.Rs 5 O.R.s wounded	
			S.O.R.s killed, 5 O.R.s wounded. True casualties.	
		7.45am	Whizzbangs on left Coys. Comm:Trench. Some damage. Weather fine. Wind unfavourable to enemy.	
			1.O.R. killed believed by 33 Div. Artillery	Sy.
	4.6.16	5.15pm	Enemy Artillery.	Sy.
		8.25pm	Mine exploded by enemy 25 yds. from front between Saps. 5+6. Heavy Enemy Artillery bombardment. Our Bombers immediately occupied new Lip of crater. This was commenced to 9 right half Coy. Our Comrs attempted to locate enemy party. No 7 Comrd.
We expended a mine in enemy front. No 7 Comrd.
		10 pm	6 O.R. killed 37 wounded (17 returned to duty). Weather fine.
	5.6.16	9am	2/Lt E. B.T. Jones took on duties of Intelligence + Assist: Clothing officer.
Bn relieved by 13th R. Sussex in trenches located NORTH MIDDLE LINE.
		3 pm	Bn relieved 12th R. Sussex arrived at ANNEQUIN NORTH.	Sy.
ANNEQUIN.		5.45pm	ACI in bulles It. R. H. Dw/km went in Camp. Lt. E. C. Kelcher took over command of B. Co.
			Rain at intervals.

WAR DIARY or INTELLIGENCE SUMMARY

Army Form C. 2118

(Erase heading not required.)

Place	Date	Hour	Summary of Events and Information	Remarks and references to Appendices
ANNEQUIN. N.	6.6.16		B'n in billets. Weather cold & fine. 2nd Lieut. J.T. Lyon resumed command from Lieut Redmond. Capt. Terry reported to England. 2/Lt. E.K. Kapp appt'd 3rd Grade Intelligence Officer at B.H.Q. Command of "C" Coy. 2/Lt. E.K. Kapp appt'd 3rd grade Intelligence Officer at G.H.Q.	J.G.
"	7.6.16		B'n in billets. Rain in morning. Working parties.	J.G.
GUINCHY (Southern)	8.6.16	7.30 a.p.	B'n marched in sections to relieve 13th Bn R.S.R. in the trenches at GUINCHY. left. Relief complete. Speed 18 " "C" Coy 8th Hussars is arrived. Enemy artillery & minnen activ. Our artillery, knows T.M's replied promptly, divided by our bombers.	J.G.
		12.30		
		3-5 p.m.		
		11 p.m.	Enemy bombed Sap. 16. recaptured but our prompt dispersed by our bombers.	
"	9.6.16		Enemy artillery quiet during day. Rifle grenades & T.M's active in afternoon. 2/Lt. Mitchell returned from Cleaus. Weather wet.	J.G.
	10.6.16	1 a.m.	Order for warrants att'd to murnour.	
		1.95 a.m	Interchange of Bombs at Sap. 7. Rifle Fire T.M's during day.	
		12 noon	2/P warrants moved up to join Bn.	J.G.
		5.30 p.m.	Enemy blew up smell mine S.E. of JERUSALEM CRATER.	
		11.45 p.m	Our bombers bombed Saphead left of JERUSALEM CRATER. Weather wet.	
	11.6.16	6 a.m.	Advance party proceeded to HINGETTE.	J.G.
		5 p.m.	Mine exploded by us opposite Sap. no. 13.	
		7 a.m.	Bn relieved by 2 R'd Inf. Hiberiers. Batt'n marched to HINGETTE. Weather wet.	J.G.
HINGETTE	12.6.16		All in billets. Weather wet.	J.G.
	13.6.16	11 a.m.	4 Officers & 20 N.C.O's & men attended Memorial service for 2/Lt. Kitchener at LOCON. Weather wet. Lt. Bolton returned from leave & assumed command C. D. Coy.	R.L.G.
	14.6.16		Weather wet. Lt. Bolton returned from leave & assumed command C. D. Coy	
	15.6.16		Orders from Brigade to march to CROIX BARBEE	

WAR DIARY or INTELLIGENCE SUMMARY

Army Form C. 2118

(Erase heading not required.)

Place	Date	Hour	Summary of Events and Information	Remarks and references to Appendices
CROIX BARBEE	16.6.16	6.30 a.m	Bn. marched to CROIX BARBEE. Took over Billets from 14th GLOS. 72nd Bde is in reserve.	RHA
"	"	10.15 a.m	All in Billets. Found billets in very dirty condition. Weather fine.	RHA
	17.6.16		Weather fine. Light winds blowing. Dug ways parties.	RHA
	18.6.16		Weather fine. Light winds. Dug ways parties.	RHA
	19.6.16		Weather fine. Large working parties.	RHA
	20.6.16		Bn moved to Rebuts to relieve 1/5 R.B. Northumb. in FERME du BOIS (NEW). RCAD attached.	RHA
	21.6.16	9.30 pm	A Coy (Capt.) B (Cy) Centre. B (Cy) right. D Cy in support. Weather fine & hot.	RHA
Ferme du Bois (New)	22.6.16	10 a.m	Relief Completed. Orders in line.	RHA
W Section			Enemy fairly quiet. Aeroplane activity on both sides; enemy aeroplanes being driven back at 1 p.m. 6 of m. Snipers active throughout the day. At night enemy H.Qs active, specially around 7 Sisters. Silenced for some time at 11 p.m. by our howitzers. 1 O.R. killed. Weather fine.	RHA
	23/6/16	6 a.m	Enemy's 5.9s fell on Hill's Post. 4 direct hits. Little damage.	RHA
		8 a.m	" " " " " " " 2 O.Rs wounded. Heavy rain in afternoon & evening.	RHA
		3 p.m	5.9s on Neuve Chapelle ruins. Artillery retaliated.	
	24/6/16	12.30 am	T.M. shells well behind right Coy. Own Artillery retaliated with nothing damage.	RHA
		11.55 am	Comm. Trenches shelled. 4 casualties.	
		12 noon	Hill's Post & Port Arthur lightly shelled.	RHA
		7 p.m	Artillery & aeroplanes active during day. Enemy quiet during night.	
		10-60 pm	Observation balloon returned drifting in N.E. direction on left of our line.	
			Lt. Colonel A.J. Griswood relinquished command of Battn.	
	25/6/16		1 O.R. killed. Enemy H.Q. shelled. HUN ST. HILLS POST & PORT ARTHUR also howitzers near LANSDOWN POST. Enemy M.G. emplacement at S.II a 6.3 destroyed by artillery.	RHA
			Own artillery active day & night. Weather fine.	
	26/6/16	11.40 p.m	HUN POST shelled intermittently during morning. Own Artillery active. Heavy rain during evening & night. Supports breaching left Coy's line no 3. We shelled front line on left. Enemy retaliated on own front line. No casualties.	RHA
			Little damage done. M.Gs active on both sides.	
	27/6/16		A quiet day, weather wet.	RHA
	28/6/16	afternoon	Enemy quiet. Support Trench & Copse Conn TRENCH lightly shelled. No damage. Relieved by 1/1st Cambs. marched to Richebourg, taking over Billets & Support Posts from 1/1st Herts.	RHA

WAR DIARY or INTELLIGENCE SUMMARY

Army Form C. 2118

(Erase heading not required.)

Place	Date	Hour	Summary of Events and Information	Remarks and references to Appendices
RICHEBOURG	29/6/16	2-5:30pm	1 m. Willets shots. Artillery bombarded enemy front line. Enemy retaliated on Factory Post. No damage. 1 O.R. killed. Not of the Batt. went as carrying parties to 12th & 13th R. Sussex Regt. Also formed stragglers posts etc.	R.O.R. R.O.3.
	30/6/16	2:30AM	Intense bombardment by our Artillery & enemy retaliation. Our carrying parties followed 12th & 13th Batt ms to enemy's front line with R.E. material & S.A.A. Casualties. Wounded. Capt. E.G. Cassels, Lt H.S. Lewis, 2nd Lt E.B.T. Jones, 2nd Lt A. Chalk. Missing believed killed 2nd Lt F. Grisewood. 2nd Lt A.C. Cushen. O.R. aftross. Killed 4 Wounded 80. Missing 32. Burial parties & salvage parties for front line.	R.177. W.D.

30/6/16

A.W.Warren
Major
Comdg 11th Royal Sussex Regt

116th Brigade.
39th Division.

11th BATTALION

THE ROYAL SUSSEX REGIMENT

JULY 1916 :::::::

CONFIDENTIAL

WAR DIARY. Vol 5

OF

11TH. BATTALION ROYAL SUSSEX REGIMENT

FROM 1ST JULY 1916 TO 31ST JULY 1916.

(VOLUME 5)

Army Form C. 2118

WAR DIARY
INTELLIGENCE SUMMARY
(Erase heading not required.)

Instructions regarding War Diaries and Intelligence Summaries are contained in F. S. Regs., Part II. and the Staff Manual respectively. Title Pages will be prepared in manuscript.

Place	Date	Hour	Summary of Events and Information	Remarks and references to Appendices
RICHEBOURG.	1/7/16.		Burial & collecting parties for Front Line. Relieved by 1/6th Cheshires whose billets at KINGS ROAD LETOURET we took over with attached posts.	RHA
LE TOURET		11 PM to 2 AM.	Battn stood to in support to 118th Infantry Brigade. Heavy bombardment on our left.	RHA
	2/7/16.		Cleaning up billets.	RHA
	3/7/16.		Arms dntl. Physical Exercises. Men engaged on June 30th inspected by G.O.C. 10.15 A.M. C.Os inspection in the evening.	RHA
			2nd Lt. LAWRENCE BARROW joined the Battn on transfer from 10th R.Sus.R. by Corps Comm. 10.30 A.M.	RHA
	4/7/16		Route march to LA PANNERIE. 3 Coys moved to support of 118th HANTS in support of Village line.	RHA
			Baths at VIEILLE CHAPELLE. Coys drill under O.C. Coys.	
	5/7/16		Route March to LA PANNERIE & firing on range. A & D Coys moved to FESTUBERT RESERVE LINE in support of 14th HANTS, returning next morning midday. 2 O.Rs wounded.	RHA
	6/7/16		Lt. G. MAYCOCK joined B.M vice Lt. Pharazyn sick. B & C Coys proceeded on Divisional Training Ground PACAUT. Orders to move other Coys did not proceed to PACAUT.	
BEUVRY.		10 PM	Battn moved to BEUVRY, handing over their billets to 1/6th CHESHIRES. Occupied billets at BEUVRY.	RHA
		12 NN.	Maj. Hon N.S. Lytton appointed Bde Sniping Officer.	
	7/7/16.		Lt. E.S. Northcote took over command of C Coy. vice Major Lytton. Battn in billets. Ravin.	RHA
			B.N. marched to AUCHY Sectr. Right Subsection & relieved 4 Kings Liverpools in the Trenches	

WAR DIARY or INTELLIGENCE SUMMARY

Army Form C. 2118

(Erase heading not required.)

Place	Date	Hour	Summary of Events and Information	Remarks and references to Appendices
AUCHY.	8/7/16	1:50 AM	Relief complete. Enemy quiet. 3 O.Rs wounded.	
		8.30-9.30 AM	Support line & Comm Trenches lightly shelled, our artillery retaliated.	RHA.
		11.50 PM	Rifle grenades fired intermittently during day. Our aeroplanes active. T.M.Bs fired in enemy's front line.	
	9/7/16.	12 MN	We blew a mine in front of night Sap at MINE POINT.	
		12-12.15	Artillery bombarded enemy front line. Retaliation feeble. Weather fine. We sapped out to near lip of the crater. 2 Lts. GANNON & LINTOTT joined the Bn. Enemy rifle grenades fired intermittently during day & night. Artillery inactive on either side.	RHA.
			Casualties 1 O.R killed	
			2 Lt DOOGAN wounded	
			7 O.Rs wounded	
	10/7/16		Our rifle grenades & M.Gs active by day & night. Our Artillery in conjunction with Bn on our right bombarded enemy front line near MAD POINT. Enemy retaliated on our Right front line doing some damage to our parapet. Our Lewis Guns traversed enemy's parapet during the night. A patrol examined Railway across No Man's Land.	RHA
	11/7/16.	11.20 PM	Rifle grenades active on both sides during day & night. Minenwerfer fell on Left Coy between front & support lines. Our aircraft active. 2nd Lts. H.P.Mole & W.C.7.Caldwell joined Bn on transfer from 3rd R.Sx Regt.	RHA.
	12/7/16.		Enemy artillery active. Enemy snipers active. Artillery quiet. 2 Lt W.C.7.Caldwell appointed M.G.O vice 2 Lt Doogan (wounded).	RHA.

Army Form C. 2118

WAR DIARY
INTELLIGENCE SUMMARY
(Erase heading not required.)

Instructions regarding War Diaries and Intelligence Summaries are contained in F. S. Regs., Part II. and the Staff Manual respectively. Title Pages will be prepared in manuscript.

Place	Date	Hour	Summary of Events and Information	Remarks and references to Appendices
AUCHY.	13/7/16	12.30 a.m.	Demonstration on MINE POINT CRATER & lip of the old crater A.27.B.65. Artillery Trench mortars rifle grenades & cup rifle bombs cooperating. Enemy's retaliation weak.	RHL
		8.56 p.m.	During afternoon artillery registered on their front line & MINE POINT. Enemy blew a mine at A.27.B.74.42. about 40 yds from our right sap to TWIN CRATERS. Very slight damage to saps & front line. Considerable damage to enemy front line. At same time he shelled our Support line with T.M.S., rifle grenades, stokes-bombs. We extended sap to near lip of new crater & occupied it. 1. O.R. killed. 5 O.R. wounded.	RHL
	14/7/16	12.15 to 12.30 a.m.	Combined demonstration of artillery, T.M.S. rifle grenades, L.G.s on enemy craters & MINE POINT. Enemy actuated.	RHL
		1 a.m. 12 m	Enemy sawing party at RAILWAY CRATER twice dispersed.	
			In afternoon some heavy shells fell behind Bn HQRS.	RHL
RINGS ROAD LE TOURET.	15/7/16	12 m.n.	Bn relieved by 2nd Scottish Rifles & marched to BEUVRY, proceeding thence by motor bus to billets at KINGS ROAD, LE TOURET.	RHL
		5 a.m	Bn settled in billets. Rest & cleaning up.	
	16/7/16		In billets. Divine Services, Inspections, Drill, working parties. Weather wet.	RHL
	17/7/16		2nd Lt Dogan returned to duty.	RHL
			Inspections, drill etc Working parties by day & night.	
	18/7/16		2nd Lieuts. E.C. Kelcher & 2nd Lt A. Rath reported to England. 2nd, 3rd & 4th July.	RHL
			Drill, Inspection & working parties, weather fine	
			2nd Lts V.M.B. D'IVERNOIS, O. HOOD, A. FRENCH, J.S. CASSELS joined Bn on transfer from 10th R Suss R.	
	19/7/16	11 a.m. 2 p.m.	Coys 3.6 & 7 by under orders from 116th Brigade. Weather fine	RHL

1875 Wt. W 593/826 1,000,000 4/15 J.B.C. & A. A.D.S.S./Forms/C. 2118.

WAR DIARY
INTELLIGENCE SUMMARY
(Erase heading not required.)

Army Form C. 2118

Instructions regarding War Diaries and Intelligence Summaries are contained in F.S. Regs., Part II. and the Staff Manual respectively. Title Pages will be prepared in manuscript.

Place	Date	Hour	Summary of Events and Information	Remarks and references to Appendices
INQ ROAD LE TOURET	20/7/16	2.P.M 9.30 P.M.	Preparation for return to trenches. Advance party left. B.2 marched to trenches FERME DU BOIS LEFT SECTION to relieve 17 N.R.R.C. Weather fine. Lt. Charnwood transferred to R.F.C. Lt. C. Campbell-Harris reported to England (sick) 20.7.16.	RHK
FERME DU BOIS Left Sect.	21.7.16	12.10 AM	Relief Complete. 2 O.R. wounded during relief. M.Gs active on both sides during night. Enemy working party dispersed. Front & Support line shelled during day, little damage. Our Artillery & L.T.M's registered on enemy Front line. — 2nd Lt. C.L. MICHELL takes over command of D Co vice Lt. Charnwood transferred to R.F.C. Capt Wallace + 2 O.Rs wounded during afternoon. Patrols went out for purpose of locating Gaps in enemy's wire & selecting points of entry for proposed Raid. 2nd Lts. C.A. Allen + W.R. Redway join the Battalion on transfer from R. Fusiliers	RHK
do	22-7-16	12.30PM 12.30" 2.45pm	Artillery, Howitzers, 18pdrs, TMs MGs Rifle Grenades carried out effective demonstration. Enemy's front trenches touchlying works in vicinity of SISTERS. Enemy's retaliation weak. 4 O.Rs wounded. Our Howitzers registered on Enemy Parapet.	JL JL
do	23-7-16	11.30am 15 1.50" 4 pm	Special Fire operations carried out - V.M.Gs L.M.Gs + L.T.Ms in cooperation with Grenades rifle fire on selected points. Enemy retaliation weak - 2 O.Rs wounded. Artillery on both sides active during day. Raid on Enemy Trenches 2nd Bn Gordons O.R wounded. OR 2 killed, 3 wounded 1 missing (Report attached)	JL APPENDIX 1 JL 2
RICHBOURGE ST VAAST	24/7/16 "	3.30pm	Quiet day, colder — Shelling Artillery activity. Battalion relieved by 13th Y.L. Bn and marched to RICHBOURGE ST VAAST. Battalion noted on outskirts. Relief completed.	JL JL

Army Form C. 2118

WAR DIARY or INTELLIGENCE SUMMARY

(Erase heading not required.)

Instructions regarding War Diaries and Intelligence Summaries are contained in F. S. Regs., Part II. and the Staff Manual respectively. Title Pages will be prepared in manuscript.

Place	Date	Hour	Summary of Events and Information	Remarks and references to Appendices
RICHBOURG ST VAAST	24-7-16	9. pm	Battalion marched to FESTUBERT left our section and relieved the 1/7th Hants in the firing line.	h
FESTUBERT	25-7-16	1. am	Relief complete.	h
			Enemy very quiet. a little trench rifle fire. Enemy's snipers active during day, much use being apparently made of fixed rifles.	h
do	do	3 pm	Our Artillery active breaching enemy's parapet in two places.	h
		6 am	Enemy retaliated shells falling near ROPE WALK and beyond O.B.L.	
do	do		Enemy mg fire very quiet. Inspection by Corp of wire. Lt. Mole + 4 O.R. Patrolled Normans-Round on Battalion Left Front.	h
			Weather fine - coldish	
do	26-7-16		Enemy Snipers fairly active during day.	h
		1.20 pm	Enemy shelled Left Corp parapet - with whizbangs breaching parapet in one place	h
		4.45 pm	Our Artillery shelled CT's during afternoon	h
		5 pm	Enemy retaliated on Islands & Communication trenches	h
			M.G. active during night. Enemy very quiet	h
do	27-7-16		2nd Lt A.M. Foley joins the Battalion on Transfer from the 10th R. Sussex Regt.	h
		9.35 pm	Enemy Artillery active throughout day particularly on RICHMOND TERRACE & SHETLAND RD. Our Artillery put up a Barage across No mans Land on account of Hostile raid on our extreme Left but nothing on our area. 2 O.R. wounded by the side 2nd Lts J.S. Casels + H.O. Mole took out a patrol accompanied by 2nd Lt. Caldwell + a Lewis Gun team. Hostile patrol encountered & dispersed	h h
do	28-7-16		Very quiet all day.	
		10.0 pm	Relieved by the 13th R. Sussex Regt. who suffered 1 O.R. Killed during relief afterwards it was quiet	h
LA TOURET		12.15 AM	Relief completed	h
			March to Billets at LA TOURET	

1875 Wt. W593/826 1,000,000 4/15 J.B.C. & A. A.D.S.S./Forms/C.2118.

WAR DIARY
INTELLIGENCE SUMMARY
(Erase heading not required.)

Army Form C. 2118

Place	Date	Hour	Summary of Events and Information	Remarks and references to Appendices
LA TOURET.	29-7-16		Inspections by Coys of Kits raws, Bathing Parades. Regimental Course of Instruction organised. "B" Coy supply 60 men + officers for reserve in the O.B.L. for the 13th R Suss Regt. Working party also supplied by "D" for carrying T.M. ammunition	JL
do	30-7-16		Divine Service. Working parties for carrying R.E. material ammunition etc to Front Line. Regimental Instruction commenced. (Batt. stand to) Lewis Guns + Bombing. Weather - sultry, very warm.	JL
		6.0 PM		JL
do	31-7-16	6.0 AM	Weather - Very warm + little breeze. Riding lesson for officers. H.Q. Staff. Physical Exercises Run.	JL
		9.00 AM	"D" Coy rehearse proposed raid. Regimental Course of Instruction + Training carried out throughout today. Working parties sent to front line, carrying rations R.E. Material etc. Situation quiet all day.	JL JL JL

1st August 1916

JMWarren
Major
Commanding 11th R Sussex Regt.

APPENDIX 1.   SECRET.

Plan of RAID carried out by B.Company 11th Bn. Royal Sussex
Regiment on the night 23/24th July 1916.

INFANTRY ACTION.

Objective.   (i) To capture one of the enemy alive, or, failing
                   this, to obtain some identification of him.
              (ii) To kill as many as possible.

PRELIMINARIES.

Wire-cutting. The Artillery will cut wire at points S.11.a.1.1½
and S.11.a.4.3. during daylight 23rd July.

Reconnaissance. Patrol NO MAN'S LAND on night 22/23rd July with a
           view (1) To locating exact positions of gaps in
                    hostile wire near S.10.d.7¾.8.
                (2) To discovering enemy's defensive dispositions
                    at that point with a view to selecting cover
                    points near that point and to enable raiding
                    party to act in such a manner as to ensure
                    an entry into enemy's trenches.

THE PLAN ON THE NIGHT.

                ZERO 11 p.m.

                TIME   TABLE.

5 Mins. before   Raiding Party in position of assembly behind the
   ZERO.   parapet at S.10.b.7.0

ZERO.   Infantry leave the Trenches and take up positions
                  in NO MAN'S LAND that have been previously decided
                  upon. The Raiding Party being hidden in the long
                  grass close up to the enemy's wire.

ZERO 7.   Artillery opens on Enemy's works near the SEVEN
                  SISTERS between S.11.a.7¾.5. and S.11.a.8.8½.
                  This fire will be kept up until the end of the
                  operations.

ZERO 12.   Artillery box barrage on trenches leading round
                  section of trench between S.10.d.6.7½ and
                  S.11.c.1.9¾.
                  Special fire on enemy's second line trench behind
                  these points and at M.G.Emplacements near
                  S.10.d.5.5½ and S.11.a.1.1.
                  6 White lights will be fired from S.11.a.2½.7½.
                  At this signal V.M.G's. and Lewis Guns will open
                  fire between points S.10.d.9¾.8½. and S.11.a.8.8.
                  and S.10.d.5½.6½. and S.10.d.4.5.

ZERO 12 - 17.   Trench Mortars fire on enemy's Support Trench between
                  S.10.d.6½.5. and S.11.c.½.8.

BETWEEN ZERO 12 AND ZERO 17 INFANTRY WILL ENTER THE ENEMY'S TRENCHES.

ZERO 27.   Infantry leave the trenches, the signal for the
                  withdrawal will be the cry "PENRUDDOCKE".

ZERO 32.   Artillery barrage ceases and the bombardment of
                  SEVEN SISTERS ceases. V.M.G's cease fire.
                  Lewis Guns will only cease fire under orders of
                  O.C.Companies.

     During operations all men in the Front Line will Stand To.
Only sentries will fire, they will not fire on zone of operations.

COMPOSITION OF RAIDING PARTY.

1 Officer. 2nd Lt. K.W. Gammon.
2 Bombing Parties. 1 N.C.O. & 5 men each.
1 Liaison Party of 1 N.C.O. & 5 men. To remain on parapet at point of entry.
2 Covering Parties of 1 N.C.O. & 6 men each. To lie out on flanks in selected places in NO MAN'S LAND.

DRESS OF RAIDING PARTY.

Men actually entering trenches.

Revolver.
Knob-kerry.
30 Bombs. Carried in Bombing waistcoat.
Wire Cutters.
Torches.

Liaison Party.

Rifles.
Bucket with Bombs.
Wiring Gloves.

Covering Party.

Drill order. Rifles, ammunition and 6 bombs each.

Watches will be synchronised at 8 p.m.

(Signed) C.P. PENRUDDOCKE.
O.C. B. Company.
19/7/16.   11th Royal Sussex Regiment.

APPENDIX 2.

REPORT ON RAID CARRIED OUT ON NIGHT 23/24th JULY 1916.

GENERAL NARRATIVE.

The raiding party left our trenches at 10.55 p.m. and collected into their proper formation after crossing the ditch that runs parallel to our line and advanced right on towards the gap in Enemy's wire at S.10.d.8.2½. Noises of working parties were heard whilst crossing the ditch but ceased as soon as the advance began.

On arriving at Gap it was found to be only 3 or 4 feet wide with a large shell hole in between which had been filled with loose wire. A Plank which had been brought for crossing obstacles was thrown across this and the raiders got through to the Enemy parapet but not without being observed. The Gap being so small the advance on to their parapet was slow and the chances of surprise lessened. It was evident however that the enemy had been warned, probably by the returning Working Party, as they immediately opened up with a fusilade of grenades, these were thrown not only from their trench but from their parados which he was holding. The raiders, however, went straight on and manned their parapet and bombing down their trench to a distance of at least 2 or 3 bays either side of the Gap. Much groaning and shouting was heard and it is assumed that many casualties were inflicted. 2nd Lieut. Gammon shot two Germans himself and was himself hit in the leg and wrist. At this juncture it was deemed advisable to retire as the party was small and the enemy was extremely strong and were every minute increasing, being reinforced from their flanks. Owing to these circumstances it was wholly impossible to get into his trench, although two men were successful in getting in, but immediately returned on hearing the catchword "PENRUDDOCKE" being shouted from the Parapet. The whole operation was carried out without a hitch, each party knowing and doing their particular duty.

It is regretted that on the return two of the party were hit and killed. These men were brought into our lines. Two men were slightly wounded by bombs and were able to get back without assistance. 2/Lt.Gammons wound was dressed by the Stretcher Bearers in a shell hole in NO MAN'S LAND and brought in after the retaliation had died down.

The Smoke Bombs and Artillery bombardment at SEVEN SISTERS was successful in diverting the enemy's fire for several minutes.

ENEMY'S WIRE.
It was noticed that the enemy had very thick wire on either side of the Gap, mostly knife rests with staked wire in front. Iron staked wire was also noticed on the flanks. Much loose wire has been distributed well out in front of his main wire, but this may have been blown out as the result of Artillery. The grass in front of his main wiring system has been cut.

ENEMY'S TRENCHES.
There was little opportunity for examining their Trenches, but it was noticed that they were extremely deep and narrow, 8 to 10 feet deep and 3 feet wide at top, all well revetted with planks.

He appears to have an island traversed system and from the rear of these islands he was effective in throwing his grenades without exposing himself.

SECRET.

DEFENCE SCHEME

11th Bn. Royal Sussex Regiment.   CUINCHY "Right".

BOUNDARIES. Boyau 1 (inclusive) to Boyau 20 (inclusive).

DISPOSITIONS OF BATTALION.

Coy.	Extent.
Right Company.	No. 1. Boyau to a Point between Nos 5. & 6. Boyaux.
Right Centre Company.	Point between 5 & 6 Boyaux to No. 9. Boyau.
Left Centre Company.	No.9.Boyau to No.16.Boyau.
Left Company.	No.16.Boyau to No.20.Boyau.
Lewis Guns.	2 at Right Coy; 2 at Right Centre Co; 2 at Left Centre Coy.

Headquarters:

Brigade.	LE PREOL.
Battalion.	No.2.Siding. A.27.a.2.3½.
A. Company.	No.16 Boyau.
B. Coy.	no. 8 Boyau
C. Coy.	No.4. Boyau.
D. Coy.	A.27.b.23.61.
M.G. Company.	OLD BOOTS. A.27.c.9.4.
T.M.Battery.	KINGSWAY. A.27.a.2.7½.

Artillery: The Battalion is in telephonic communication with supporting batteries. *from Bn HQS*

Medical. Aid Posts 2.   One at RAILWAY ALLEY E. of 2nd. Railway Crossing.
One at WIMPOLE ST. A.2c.b.c.1p.
Advanced Dressing Station: CAMBRIN CHURCH.

S.A.A. & BOMB STORES.

S.A.A.   Amounts already in possession of Companies is to be kept up to establishment.
Each Platoon should have one unbroken box in Platoon Reserve.
Sentries will be provided with extra bandoliers of S.A.A. for observation and night firing work.

Bombs.   Distribution of Bombs in Company Areas will be checked by Battalion Bombing Sergeant and list handed to O.C. Companies.

ACTION IN CASE OF XXXXXX ATTACK.

Companies will immediately inform Battalion Headquarters by telephone as to nature of attack. One Officer per Company will remain at the telephone during the action.

Companies will each send 3 orderlies, previously detailed, to Battalion Headquarters.

Tunnellers will be informed at once.

The front line and saps will be held at all costs and in the event of the enemy entering our trench at any point the senior Officer or N.C.O. will immediately organise a counter attack and drive him out.

O.C.Companies will reconnoitre ground between front line and support lines with a view to counter attack over the open.

(2)

Bombers not employed in Saps will be organised into Groups.

CODE SIGNALS. To be telephoned to Battⁿ H.Q.

   S. O. S.   " C ".
 G. A. S. S. O. S. " C ".

Copies of these to be in possession of all Officers.

A GREEN Rocket fired is the signal that an Artillery barrage is required to check enemy's advancing infantry.

ENEMY ATTACKS.

1. <u>After heavy bombardment</u> collect all available men in nearest Support Trench and prepare for counter attack over the open.

2. <u>Under cover of Gas</u>. Put on helmets; sentries will sound gongs; all ranks will man fire steps; oil all metallic parts of rifles and lewis guns and prepare for enemy Infantry Attack.

3. <u>Following explosion of series of mines</u>. All men will be collected in Support Trenches and senior Officer present will immediately launch a counter attack across the open.

4. <u>Explosion of Mine</u>. The near lip will be immediately occupied and a sap dug out from trench to lip.

5. <u>A Raid by Night</u>. Inform Battalion Headquarters giving section of trench raided.
All men in section not raided will man fire step and open rapid fire on enemy trenches.
Bombing parties will immediately advance inwards from flanks of raided area.
If raid in considerable force a counter attack over open will be made by supporting platoons.

             G H Harrison

9/7/16.   Major.

SECRET.

OPERATION ORDER No. 21.

Copy No. .....

Relief. 1. The Battalion will relieve the 17th. Bn. K.R.R.C. today Thursday 20th July 1916 in the Trenches, FERME DU BOIS Left Sub-section - PLUM ST to OXFORD STREET inclusive.

The relief will take place as follows:-

B.Coy. & 11th Bn. relieve Right Coy K.R.R.(No.1 Coy).
1 Platoon
of C.Coy.

D.Coy. & 11th Bn. " Left Coy K.R.R.(No.2 Cy)
1 Platoon
of C.Coy.

Remainder 11th Bn. " PORT ARTHUR (1 Platoon)
of C.Coy. " HUN STREET (1 Platoon)

Headquarters 11th Bn. will be at HUN STREET.

A.Coy. 11th Bn. relieve LANSDOWNE POST.

Advanced Parties. 2. Specialists, and Advanced Parties of 1 Officer per Company & 1 N.C.O. per Platoon will proceed to LANSDOWN POST where guides will meet them at 3 p.m. Parties will parade at Bn. H.Q. at 2 p.m.

Main Body. 3. The Main Body will move off from Bn.H.Q. at 2-30 p.m. in the following order: Bn.H.Q., B.Coy.& 1 Platoon of C.Coy., 1 Platoon of C.Coy. & D.Coy., Remainder of C.Coy., A.Coy.
Route: X11.b.- KING GEORGES RD- to S.2.c.3.2.- S.8.a. S.8.b.5.4.- WINDY CORNER- LANSDOWN POST (~~~~~~~~.)
Movement to be by Platoons to S.2.c.3.2. and then by Sections with intervals of 100 yards in both cases.

Guides. 4. Guides from K.R.R.'s will be at LANSDOWN POST as follows:
4 from Right Coy. 4 from Left Coy.
1 from PORT ARTHUR & 1 from HUN STREET.

Dress. 5. Dress Full Marching Order, water bottles will be filled.

Transport. 6. Coy. Stores, Officers Kits etc., not to be taken to Trenches will be stacked outside Orderly Room by 8 p.m.
Stores for the Trenches will be stacked outside Company Billets by 8 p.m.

7. Trench Standing Orders on Reliefs will be strictly complied with.

Rations. 8. Rations will be issued to Companies before marching off.

(Signed) R.H.LUPTON,
Lieut. & A/Adjutant,

20/7/16.

Issued to:

Copy No. 1. O.C. A.Coy.
2. B.Coy.
3. C.Coy.
4. D.Coy.
5. Transport Off.
6. K.R.R.'s. 7. Office Record.
8. C.O.

SECRET.

OPERATION ORDER No. 22.

Copy No.......

Relief. 1. The Battalion will be relieved by the 13th. Bn. Y.&.L. Regt. in the Trenches today 24/7/16 at about 1-30 p.m.
The Relief will take place as follows:

D.Coy. & 1 Platoon C.Coy.	relieved by	No.1.Coy. 13th. Y.&.L. Regt.
B.Coy. & 1 Platoon C.Coy.	relieved by	No.2.Coy 13th. Y.&.L. Regt.
PORT ARTHUR HUN STREET LANSDOWN POST	relieved by	No.3.Coy 13th. Y.&.L. Regt.
HILLS POST.	relieved by	14th. Y.&.L.Regt.

Advanced 2. Advanced parties as already detailed.
Party.

TRENCH 3. Trench Stores will be handed over and the usual
Stores.   receipts obtained.

COY. 4. Coy. Stores, Officers' Kits etc., to be carried
Stores.   by Transport will be dumped at Railhead HUN ST
by 1 p.m. to be conveyed at night to ST VAAST
Dump.
Pushing Parties of 1 N.C.O. & 4 men per Company
will remain behind at HUN ST Railhead for this
purpose.

N.B. Arm Racks, Rifle Grenade Batteries, and all
Stores not handed over to us are included in this
heading.

ROUTES. 5. On completion of Relief Companies will move
independently to RICHEBOURG ST VAAST and await
further orders. The usual traffic regulations
will be observed.
The following will be the routes taken by Coys.
to RICHBOURG.-

B.Coy. & 1 Plat.C.Coy. will proceed by
LANSDOWN COMM. TRENCH to LANSDOWN POST thence
by WINDY CORNER to RICHBOURG.
D.Coy. & 1 Plat.C.Coy. will proceed by HUN ST-
SANDBAG ALLEY-LANSDOWN POST- thence by WINDY
CORNER.
The Remainder of C.Coy. will follow in rear of
D.Coy.
A.Coy. will move in rear of remainder of C.Coy.
via WINDY CORNER to RICHEBOURG.

Rations. 6. Quartermaster will arrange to issue rations in
RICHEBOURG by 5.p.m tonight. Rations will be
carried on the men up to the Trenches.

2nd. Relief. The Battalion will relieve 1/1st Herts in the
FESTUBERT L. Sub.Sect. tonight. Advanced Parties
will meet CAPT. MILLWARD at Bn. H.Q. HUN ST. at
12.30 p.m. today. Further details will be issued
later.

(Signed) R.H.LUPTON,

24/7/16. Lieut. & A/ADjutant.

Transport for Officers Kits, Stores etc will be at ST VAAST Dump
at NINE p.m. tonight.

No 3 A Coy
No 2 B Coy
No 1 C Coy
No 4 D Coy
No 5 Yoh
No 6 Waida
No 7 Qui

SECRET.

OPERATION ORDER NO 23
By
Major G.H.Harrison,
Commanding 11th Royal Sussex Regt

Copy No

RELIEF. 1. The 11th R.Sussex Regt will be relieved by the 13th R. Sussex Regt on the night of the 28th July 1916. On relief they will proceed to Billets at LE TOURET.

ADVANCE PARTIES. 2. One Officer per Company and 1 N.C.O. per platoon will proceed to LE TOURET at 3 p.m. and take over the same billets as before.

SPECIALISTS. 3. Specialists (Signallers, Lewis Gunners, Bombers, Snipers) will proceed to billets as soon as relieved by the incoming Unit.

GUIDES & ROUTES. 4. One Guide per Platoon and one for Headquarters will be sent to the Hdqrs of the 13 Battn in the VILLAGE LINE at 8.15 p.m. ready to move off at 8.45 p.m. They will guide the incoming Unit by the following routes.

A.Coy will guide No 1 Coy (Left Via TRAMWAY and ROPE
                         Front Coy)   WALK
C.Coy   do   No 2 Coy (Right Via RUE DESAILLEUX &
                         Front Coy)   PIONEER TRENCH.
Hdqrs.   do   Hdqrs, No 3 Coy By TRAMWAY to O.B.L. (L.Coy HQs)
D. & B   (Rt O.B.L.) & No   By RUE du CAILLOUX to O.B.L. (R.Coy HQ)
Coys.   4 Coy (Lt O.B.L.)

Companies when relieved will proceed out of trenches by these routes, and march to billets independently.

HANDING OVER LISTS. 5. These will be given as laid down in Standing Orders. Copy of list of trench stores etc to be handed over to be sent to Battn Hdqrs by 6 p.m.

TRANSPORT. 6. All Stores for conveyance by Transport will be at the Railhead Battn Hdqrs by 7.30 p.m., and a pushing party of 1 N.C.O. and 4 men per Coy will be detailed to accompany them. They will be picked up by Transport at 9.p.m. and conveyed to Coy billets at LE TOURET.

REPORTS. 7. Relief complete will be wired to Battn Hdqrs by the Code Word "COOPER". Companies in Billets will be reported to Battn Hdqrs at LE TOURET.

(Signed) R.H.Lupton,
Lieut. & Adjutant,
11th R. Sussex Regt

28th July 1916.

Issued to A. Coy.   Copy No 1.
           B. Coy.   Copy No 2.
           C. Coy.   Copy No 3.
           D. Coy.   Copy No 4.
     Commdg Officer.   Copy No 5.
     Quartermaster.   Copy No 6.
     Transport Officer.   Copy No 7.
     M.G. Officer.   Copy No 8.

116th Brigade
39th Division.

11th BATTALION

ROYAL SUSSEX REGIMENT

AUGUST 1 9 1 6

Vol 6.

A.M. 6.E.
15 sheets

Confidential

War Diary

of

the 11th Battalion Royal Sussex Regiment

From 1st August 1916 to 31st August 1916 (inclusive)

(Volume VI)

WAR DIARY or INTELLIGENCE SUMMARY

Army Form C. 2118

(Erase heading not required.)

Instructions regarding War Diaries and Intelligence Summaries are contained in F.S. Regs., Part II. and the Staff Manual respectively. Title Pages will be prepared in manuscript.

Place	Date Aug	Hour	Summary of Events and Information	Remarks and references to Appendices
BETHUNE	1st		Cleaning up Billets, Inspection of Clothing & equipment. Weather hot & fine	
"	2		Parade Inspections by Coy Commanders, Weather fine	
"	3		Usual Inspections by Coy Commanders, Physical Exercise & training. Route march 8 miles. Weather fine	
"	4	5 pm	Inspection of Coys by C.O.	
"	5	7 am	Inspection by Brig General. Weather fine	
		3.30 pm	Bn Paraded under C.O.	
"	6	7 am	Practice Scheme for Intercommunication between reconnoitring aeroplanes & Infantry	
		10 am	Reconnaissance of line to be taken over next day. Weather hot	
		3.45 pm	Inspection by G.O.C. 39th Div.	
			Ceremonial Church Parade in Great Square to commemorate 2nd Anniversary of War.	
"	6	6.30 pm	Bn marched to GIVENCHY right sector & relieved 17th Notts & Derbys in the trenches Relief Complete. 1 O.R. wounded (APPENDIX 3)	
		11.15 pm	Enemy quiet	
GIVENCHY Rt Subsector	7		Weather fine & very hot. Enemy very active throughout day with his Artillery & Heavy Trench Mortars. He destroyed our sap to RED DRAGON CRATER. Many grenades also fell in our lines. We retaliated & all the 1. O.R. killed	
		9.30 pm	Onwards very quiet.	
do	8		Weather very fine & warm. Enemy again shelled our Subsector. We retaliated on his front line	
		9.30 AM	Our Very Heavy T.M's fired on Enemy front line & did considerable damage to his works	
		2.30 pm	Our Artillery cut Enemy wire. Enemy retaliating with H.E. Shrapnel	
		11.20	During night his M.G's were very active	

WAR DIARY or INTELLIGENCE SUMMARY

Army Form C. 2118

Place	Date 1916 Aug	Hour	Summary of Events and Information	Remarks and references to Appendices
GIVENCHY - Subsector	9	5.15 AM	Enemy showed himself in many places along our front, tall whisper overhead with own men.	
		2.30 PM	Two direct hits from Enemy art on "C" Coy Billets at Village Row. 2 O.R. wounded	
		9.30 PM	Enemy M.Gs very active throughout night	
		11.30 PM	2nd Lt REDWAY had a fighting patrol out to engage Enemy working party but were unsuccessful in encountering him. 1 O.R. Killed, 2 O.R. wounded	
do	10	5.30 AM	A fire operation was carried out opp "D" Coy front. Artillery, H.T.M, L.T.M, T.M.B. Co-operated. This retaliation was weak there no damage	
		4.0 PM	One H.T.M fired on Enemy front line trenchwork — he retaliated with "Minnie" but did no damage. His M.Gs throughout night were active.	
do	11		Battn was relieved by 18th King's LIVERPOOLS they then marched to bivouac at FERME DE ROI Completed about noon thence having dinner tea, after which march on to Billets at AUCHELL arriving at 8.30 P.M (APPENDICES 4 & 5)	
AUCHEL	12		Battn rested at Billets all day Weather still hot	
"	13	6 am	Marched from Billets to bivouac at BOIS DE LIME rested then till 5.30 pm then marched on to Billets at MONCHY BRETON arriving at 8.30 pm	
MONCHY BRETON	14	8.30	Bn paraded & marched on to the 3rd Army Div Training area where special training was carried out & returned to Billets at 8.30 P.M.	

WAR DIARY
or
INTELLIGENCE SUMMARY

(Erase heading not required.)

Army Form C. 2118

Place	Date 1916	Hour	Summary of Events and Information	Remarks and references to Appendices
MONCHY BRETON	15		Showery - Special training. Coy + Bn Drill carried out on Training area	JH 23p
do	16		as above	JH
do	17		Officers + N.C.O. instructed in quick wiring. Usual training carried out.	JH 23p various
do	18	9.30PM	Night operation, consolidating supposed Hun Captured trenches. (APPENDIX 6) German trench returned to Billets 12.30 A.M.	JH
do	19		Usual training during morning. In afternoon a Tactical Exercise was carried out by the Battn. 1 Officer + 1 NCO per Coy detailed to reconnoitre new front line.	JH
do	19		Digging dummy trenches to represent German system opposite our new front.	JH Hadow
do	20		Lecture by Maj. Campbell on Bayonet fighting. Sunday. Weather fine. Lecture on the "FLAMMENWERFER", the Battn rested during afternoon	JH MG JH
do	21		Practising the attack over the dummy trenches	JH
do	22		do	JH
do	23		Preserval scheme carried out. In Conjunction with above	JH
do	24	8.00pm	Battn marched to entraining point. Entrained for LIGNY-ST-FLOCHEL then marched to billets at LA SOUICH arriving about 2.30 pm (APPENDIX 7)	JH

Army Form C. 2118

WAR DIARY
or
INTELLIGENCE SUMMARY
(Erase heading not required.)

Instructions regarding War Diaries and Intelligence Summaries are contained in F. S. Regs., Part II. and the Staff Manual respectively. Title Pages will be prepared in manuscript.

Place	Date 1916	Hour	Summary of Events and Information	Remarks and references to Appendices
LA SOUICH	25	7.40 AM	Battn. leave Billets, march to Bois DE WARNIMONT arriving at 2.00 p.m. (APPENDIX 8)	JH
BOIS DE WARNIMONT	26		Physical training, bayonet fighting. A party of Officers & N.C.O.s reconnoitred our new front. Weather showery	JH
do	27.		Front line again reconnoitred by Officers & N.C.O.s Battn. marched off to new Bivouacs at P.18.b and d. (MAILLY WOOD) (APPENDIX 9) Weather still showery	JH JH
MAILLY Wood	28	6.30 pm	Battn. rested	JH
" "	29		The Battalion equipped for the coming attack. Billets shelled at intervals during day.	JH
" "	30		Showery weather. Programme for attack postponed for 24 hours, Billets again shelled.	JH
" "	31		" " Programme again postponed for 24 hours, and again	JH

G.K. Hannan Lt Col.
Comm'g 11th R. Sussex Regt.

SECRET.

OPERATION ORDER No 24.   Copy No

RELIEF.   1. The 11th Bn. R. Sussex Regt will be relieved by the
               5/6th Cheshires on the afternoon of today August 1st,
               and on the relief will proceed to Billets at BETHUNE.

ADVANCE   2. One Officer per Coy and one N.C.O. per platoon to
PARTIES.   report to 2nd Lieut Lintott at L'ECOLE DE JEUNE FILLES
               BETHUNE at 3 p.m. This party will leave Headquarters
               at 2 p.m.

DRESS.   3. Full Marching Order; water bottles full.

ROUTE.   4. RUE DU BOIS. Companies will move by Platoons at
               100 yds distance till clear of ESSARS, (W.30.b.10.0).
               From here the Battalions will march in together.

ORDER.   5.   C. Company
                         B. Company
                         A. Company
                         D. Company
                         Headquarters.

KIT.   6. All Company Stores, Officers' Kits, etc must be
               ready outside billets for the transport at 2.45 p.m.
               to be conveyed to new billets in BETHUNE.

BILLETS.   7. The usual Certificates will be obtained.

LEWIS GUN   8. Coy Lewis Gun Teams will join their Coys on arrival
TEAMS.   at BETHUNE in accordance with Bn Order No 646.

                              (Signed)   R. M. Lupton,
                                          Lt. & A.Adjutant,
               1.8.16.   11th R. Sussex Regt.

               Copy No 1 issued to O.C. A.Coy
                    " 2   "   " O.C. B.Coy
                    " 3   "   " O.C. C.Coy
                    " 4   "   " O.C. D.Coy
                    " 5   "   " Officer Commanding.
                    " 6   "   " Quartermaster.
                    " 7   "   " Transport Officer.
                    " 8   "   " Machine Gun Officer.
                    " 9 retained for Office use.

Appendix 3.

SECRET.

OPERATION ORDER NO 23.

Copy No ....

Relief. 1. The Battalion will take over Trenches from the 17th Notts. & Derby Regt. in the GIVENCHY Right Sub-Section, on the night of Sunday, August 6th. Companies will take over in the following order, B. Coy. on Left, A. Coy. in Centre, D. Coy. on Right, C. Coy. in Reserve.

Advanced Parties. 2. The C.O., O.C. Companies and 1 N.C.O. per Platoon to take over Trench Stores etc., will proceed at 2 p.m. August 6th. They will not return to BETHUNE but will await the arrival of the Battalion in the Trenches. Specialists will proceed with this party and take over by Daylight.

Main Body. 3. The Main Body will move off from Billets at 6.30 p.m. in the following order:-
   Battalion Headquarters.
   B. Company.
   A. Company.
   D. Company.
   C. Company.

Route. 4. CANAL BANK. All movement will be by Platoons at 200 yards interval to GORRE and thence by Sections with 100 yards interval.

Dress. 5. Full Marching Order. Water Bottles will be filled.

Guides. 6. Guides will meet Battalion at VAUXHALL BRIDGE at 9 p.m.

Transport. 7. All Kit for removal by Transport must be stacked on the Barrack Square by 6 p.m.

Reports. 8. Reports of "Relief Complete" to Battalion Headquarters in Trenches. Trench Store Lists will be sent to Battalion Headquarters as soon after as possible after relief.

(Signed) R.M.LUPTON.
Lt. A/Adjutant.

Issued at 6 p.m.
5/8/16.

Copies to:-

  No. 1 to O.C. 17th Notts & Derby Regt.
   2 to O.C. A. Company.
   3 to O.C. B. Company.
   4 to O.C. C. Company.
   5 to O.C. D. Company.
   6 to Q.M. & T.O.
   7 to Lewis Gun Officer.
   8 to Signals.
   9 to Commanding Officer.
   10 to Medical Officer.
  11 & 12 to War Diary.

OPERATION ORDER NO. 26. SECRET.

(APPENDIX 4) Copy No 9.

Relief. 1. The Battalion will hand over Trenches to the 18th King's Liverpool Regiment on the morning of 11/8/16 and will proceed to Bivouac near FERME DU ROI (E.6.c.7.3.).

Guides. 2. 1 Guide per Platoon and 1 from H.Q. will be at VAUXHALL BRIDGE at 6 a.m.

Order of Relief. 3. Companies will be relieved in the following order B.Coy. D.Coy. A.Coy. C.Coy. Companies will move as far as GORRE by sections at 200 yards intervals and from GORRE by Platoons at 100 yards intervals.

Routes. 4. B.Coy. WOLFE RD - VAUXHALL BRIDGE ROAD.
A.Coy. FINCHLEY RD - OXFORD TERRACE - ORCHARD RD - VAUXHALL BRIDGE ROAD.
D.Coy. CHEYNE WALK - VAUXHALL BRIDGE ROAD.
C.Coy. VAUXHALL BRIDGE ROAD.
Bn. H.Q. VAUXHALL BRIDGE ROAD.

Specialists. 5. Snipers, Observers and Lewis Gun Detachments will be relieved on the morning of 10/8/16. They will send guides to CANAL HOUSE at 7 a.m. on that day to conduct the incoming parties to the Trenches. On 11/8/16 they will start early being clear of Communication Trenches by 6 a.m. and proceed independantly as far as GORRE.

Dress. 6. Full Marching Order with packs slung as these will be taken on from GORRE by Lorries.

Transport. 7. All Officers' Kits, Company Stores etc. not carried by hand to be at Bn.H.Q. by 9 p.m. tomorrow, 10th inst. These will include Grenade Rifles, Sniperscopes, Lewis Guns, but not Periscopes and Very Pistols which must be carried by hand. The minimum quantity of Camp Kettles etc. necessary for breakfasts only to be retained. These will be put on the Lorries at GORRE. Officers' Chargers to be at WESTMINSTER BRIDGE at 7 a.m. 11/8/16.

Rations. 8. Only Breakfast rations will be issued on 10/8/16 for consumption the next day. Other rations at FERME DU ROI. Dinners and Teas at FERME DU ROI. The Quartermaster will arrange to have all camp kettles etc. with water at FERME DU ROI so that the troops may have an extra issue of tea during the march to their Billets.

Handing Over Lists. 9. Companies will be responsible for preparing the necessary lists for handing over stores to the incoming Unit. Receipts for Stores handed over will be sent to BN.H.Q. as soon as possible after handing over.

Reports. 10. "Relief Complete" by runner to Battalion H.Q. "Company in Bivouac" on arrival at FERME DU ROI.

(Signed) R.H.LUPTON.
Issued at 10 p.m. 9/8/16.   Lieut. & A/Adjutant.

Copy No.1 O.C. 18th Liverpool's.
2. A.Coy.
3. B.Coy.
4. C.Coy.
5. D.Coy.
6. L.G.O
7. Q.M.

Copy No. 8. Transport Officer
9. C.O.
10. 2nd i/c
11. Adjutant
12. Officer Records
13. War Diary
14. do.

SECRET.

AMENDMENT TO OPERATION ORDERS NO.26.

Copy. No.....

Reference to para 2. 1 Guide per Platoon and 1 from H.Q. will be at VAUXHALL BRIDGE at 7.a.m. and not 6 a.m. as stated.

                                      (Signed) R.H.LUPTON.
                                           Lieut. A/Adjutant.
19th August 1916.   11th Bn. Royal Sussex Regiment.

(APPENDIX 5)

SECRET. Operation Order No 27.   Copy No. 8

1. The Battalion will parade ready to march on markers at 5.40 pm. and will march to AUCHEL where it will be billeted for the night.

HQ + Sigs
B Coy
C Coy
D Coy
A Coy
pd June T.

2. Order of march as per margin. Route:- BETHUNE – CHOCQUES – PONT DU REVEILLON – ALLOUAGNE – LOZINGHEM – AUCHEL.

3. Tea will be issued on the march at the 2nd halt about 7.50 pm.

Transport 4. Transport will be drawn up on main LOCON-BETHUNE road with its head on the CANAL BRIDGE and will join the Battalion as it passes this point.

Bombers 5. Bombers will rejoin their Companies for this march.

Lewis Guns 6. H.Q. L.G. Section will march in rear of the Bn with their limbers. Coy Sections in rear of their Companies.

Pack mules 7. Pack mules will march in rear of their companies.

Baggage 8. The Transport Officer will ensure that no kits of any sort which should be carried on the men are put on the Transport wagons.

Any men not actually employed as brakesmen or for any other purpose connected with the wagons will be marched in 4's in rear of transport under a responsible NCO and strict march discipline will be maintained.

Halts 9. The usual halts will be observed.

(sd) R.H. Lupton,
Lt. & a/Adjt.

11/8/16

Copies to.
OC's Coys. Nos 1 - 4
Qr. & TO. 5 - 6
CO 7
War Diary 8 - 9.

APPENDIX 6.

NIGHT EXERCISE 17th August 1916.

A successful assault on the German 3rd Line System on the morning of the 17th August, has resulted in the occupation of the enemy's trenches between points U.10.a.9.9. and U.10.a.5.7. by the 11th Royal Sussex Regt. AREA "B" Training Area.

It is the intention to consolidate this position during the night 17/18th August.

The length of front held by the 11th Royal Sussex Regt. includes a portion of Trench between the Track and the Wood the other portion being in the Wood itself.

That portion of Trench outside the Wood will be consolidated by A & B Coys. that portion inside the Wood by C & D Coys.

While the consolidation of the main trench and the Wood which represents a Strong Point is in progress the front of each Company will be covered by an Outpost line placed in accordance with the ground some 300 yards in advance of the Main Trench. These Outpost groups will likewise dig in with the object of a new line of trenches being finally constructed and communication trenches from these outposts will be started back to the main Trench.

The outpost groups posted in front of each Coy, will consist of at least 1 Platoon per Coy.

GENERAL INSTRUCTIONS.

The Wood will be considered a Strong Point in our Main Line and will be put in a state of defence. The front will be wired and trenches constructed. If tools are insufficient entrenching tools will be used. Outposts will use entrenching tools until they are dug in deep enough to obtain cover for using a shovel.

Constant communication between all parts of the Battalion will be maintained by Runner and constant verbal and written messages sent back to Battalion Headquarters.

Battalion Headquarters will be at CROSS ROADS U.3.d.6.3.

O.C.s. Coys. will meet the C.O. at the present bivouack at 11.30 a.m.

17/8/16.

(Signed) G.H. HARRISON.
Major, Commanding.
11th Bn. Royal Sussex Regiment.

APPENDIX 7

SECRET.

OPERATION ORDER NO 22.

Copy No. ....

Move.	1.	The 11th Bn. Royal Sussex Regiment will leave MONCHY-BRETON on the morning of 24/8/16 and proceed by train to Billets at IVERGNY.
Stations.	2.	The Battalion will entrain at LIGNY ST FLOCHEL and detrain at BOUQUE MAISON.
Advance Party.	3.	1 N.C.O. per Coy. will parade under 2/Lt.J.C. Keliher at 8 a.m. outside B.Coys. Headquarters and will proceed to LIGNY ST FLOCHEL STATION where they will meet the Battalion on arrival.
Main Body.	4.	The Battalion will fall in in Column of Route with the Head of the Column outside A.Coys. Billets at 9 a.m. Order of March - Bn. H.Q. A.Coy. B.Coy. C.Coy. D.Coy Coy. Lewis Gun Teams in rear of their Coys. H.Q. Lewis Gun Teams in rear of Battalion. Dress - Full Marching Order.
Route.	5.	CHELERS ROAD to CROSS ROADS U.8.b.4½.½. - BAILLUEL-AUX-CORNAILLES - to main ST POL ROAD U.25.c.8.10. - to LIGNY ST FLOCHEL STATION T.23.d.6.0.
Transport.	6.	Camp Kettles" Officers Kits, Company Mess Boxes, etc., will be conveyed by lorry to Station and must be outside Billets by 8 a.m. Lewis Gun Handcarts, dixies etc., will travel in the brake van.
Billets.	7.	All Billets will be inspected before marching off and Companies are responsible that Billets are left in a thoroughly clean and sanitary condition.
Discipline.	8.	No man will enter the train or on arrival at BOUQUE MAISON leave the train without direct orders from an Officer.
	9.	2/Lt. J.C.Keliher will report to an Officer of the 117th Brigade Staff at 10 a.m. on the platform at LIGNY ST FLOCHEL STATION.

(Signed) R.H.LUPTON.
Lt. A/Adjutant.
Issued at 7.30 p.m. 23/8/16.   11th Bn. Royal Sussex Regiment.

Copies to:-
Nos. 1 to 4. O.C.s.Coys.
5. C.O.
6. 2nd in Command.
7. Adjutant.
8 & 9. War Diary.
10. Office Records.

APPENDIX 8

SECRET.

OPERATION ORDER NO. 30.

Copy No. ...10...

March	1.	The Battalion will march tomorrow 25/6/16 to bivouac at BOIS DU WARNIMONT.
Starting Point.	2.	Road Junction T.15.b.5.6. The Battalion will pass the Starting Point at 7.45 a.m.
Route.	3.	LUCHEUX - HALLOY - THIEVRES.
Hour of Parade.	4.	Reveille 4 a.m. Breakfast 4.45 a.m. Parade at 6.30 a.m. in Column of Route. Head of Column will be outside D.Coys Headquarters Order of March as per margin.

Bn. H.Q.
B. Company.
C. Company.
D. Company.
A. Company.
1st Line Transport.
(Less Baggage Waggons(

Dress.	5.	Full Marching Order - Water Bottles full. Haversack ration will be carried.
Baggage.	6.	Officers Kits, Stores etc. must be stacked outside Battalion Headquarters by 5.45 a.m.
Transport.	7.	Baggage Wagons will march behind NO.2 Coy. Divisional Train and will pass the Starting Point T.15.b. 5.6. at 8.17 a.m.

(Signed) R.H.LUPTON.
Lt. A/Adjutant.
11th Bn. Royal Sussex Regt.

Issued at 8.30 p.m. 24/6/16.

Copies to Nos. 1 to 4. O.C.s Coys.
          5. C.O.
          6. 2nd in Command.
          7. Adjutant.
       8 & 9. War Diary.
         10. Office Records.
         11. Transport Officer.
         12. Quartermaster.

Refce map
Sheet 57ᴅ

APPENDIX 9

SECRET.

OPERATION ORDER NO 31.

Copy No. ....

March.	1.	The Battalion will move to Quarters in WOOD P.18.b.&.d. on the afternoon of 27/8/16.
Starting Point.	2.	S.E. Corner of WARNIMONT WOOD I.19.c.9.7. The Battalion will pass the Starting Point at 5.49 p.m.
Route.	3.	Via BERTRANCOURT.
Order of March.	4.	Order of March as per margin:-

Bn. H.Q.
C. Company.
D. Company.
A. Company.
B. Company.
1st Line Transport
(Less Baggage Wagons)

Rate of march 2½ miles per hour, including halts.
There will be an interval of 3 minutes between Companies and 3 minutes between last Company and First Line Transport.

Dress.	5.	Full Marching Order. Water Bottles full.
Transport.	6.	Baggage Wagons will pass the Starting Point at 8.35 p.m. All baggage for Transport to be at the entrance of the Wood by 5 p.m.

(Signed) R.H.LUPTON.
Lt.A/Adjutant.

Issued at 3.30 p.m. 26/8/16.   11th Bn. Royal Sussex Regiment.

Copies to:-

    Nos. 1 to 4. O.C.s. Companies.
         5. C.O.
         6. 2nd in Command.
         7. Adjutant.
         8. Quartermaster.
         9. Transport Officer.
   10 & 11. War Diary.
        12. Office Records.

SECRET. Provisional.

OPERATION ORDER No.39.

Relief.	1.	The 11th R.Suss.R. will relieve the 1st Herts and 4/5th Black Watch in the Line tomorrow 7/10/16.
Front.	2.	The 11th R.Suss.R. will hold the Line from the ANCRE to PICADILLY (both inclusive).
		C.Coy. will be on the left PICCADILLY to LONG SAP.
		B.Coy. will be in the Centre LONG SAP to ROYAL AV.
		D.Coy. will be on the ~~Left~~ Right ROYAL AVENUE to THE MILL.
		A.Coy. in Reserve.
Advanced Party.	3.	D.Coy. will send 16 men under 2nd. Lt. Naylor to take over the MILL. A guide will meet them at JACOBS LADDER in MESNIL at 3 a.m.
Main Body.	4.	Reveille will be at 3-30 a.m. Breakfasts at 4-30 a.m. The Battalion will move off at 5-30 a.m.
HdQrs.		Order of march as per margin.
C.Coy.		All movement will be by Platoons at 100 yards distance with 200 yards between Companies.
B.Coy.		
D.Coy.		Route. via MARTINSART to MESNIL.
A.Coy.		
Guides.	5.	Platoon guides and 1 per Lewis Gun will meet the Battalion at the PUMP MESNIL. at 6-15 a.m.
Transport	6.	All Coy. Stores, Office Boxes etc for Transport Lines will be stacked ready for loading on the road at 5-15 a.m.
		All Officers Mess stores, Stores etc for Trenches will be stacked on the road in a separate pile ready for loading at 5-15 a.m.
		The Transport Officer will arrange for the necessary transport for the above.
		Each Company will leave 6 men to act as a Carrying Party to go with the Transport. These will wait at MESNIL till their respective Companies send guides to conduct them on.
		The M.O's stores will be carried from MESNIL by the M.O's Staff and H.Q. Stretcher Bearers who will move off with Bn. H.Q. and wait at MESNIL for the transport.
Rations.	7.	Each man will carry the day's rations with him.
Dixies.	8.	Platoons will carry their own dixies.
Dress.	9.	Full marching order. Water bottles full.
Reports.	10.	Relief Complete will be sent by wire or runner to Battalion H.Q. immediately on relief. Code word "Stumps Drawn".
Bn. H.Q.	11.	Battalion Headquarters will be in POTTAGE.

(Signed) R.H.LUPTON,
Lieut & A/Adjutant.
11th. R. Sussex Regiment.

6/10/16.

Issued at 10-45 p.m.

Copies 1 to 4. O.Cs Coys.   5. C.O.
           6. 2nd. i/c.   7. Adjutant.
           8. Trans. Off.   9.& 10 War Diary.

OPERATION ORDER NO 40.

SECRET.

Copy No........

Reference Map. Sheet 57. D. S.E. 1/20,000.

The 118th Infantry Brigade is to capture the remainder of the SCHWABEN REDOUBT, and establish a chain of Observation Posts in front at ZERO hour on "Z" day.

"Z" day will be 13th October and Zero hour will be 3.17. p.m.

The 116th Infantry Brigade will co-operate by a Smoke Discharge and by Vickers Maxim Gun, Lewis Gun and Rifle Fire as follows:-

(a) Lewis Guns will fire on Points North of the line Q.24.d.8,7. to R.19,Central. to R.19.b,9.3.
(b) Rifle Fire on same points.
(c) Smoke will be discharged by each Smoke Party as follows:-

At ZERO	=3.17.p.m.	4 Smoke Bombs distributed over its 25 yards front
At ZERO plus 4, = 3.21.p.m.	6 Smoke Candles	" " " " " "
At ZERO " 6. = 3.23.p.m.	6 "	" " " " " "
At ZERO " 8. = 3.25.p.m.	6 "	" " " " " "
AT ZERO " 10. = 3.27.p.m.	6 "	" " " " " "
At ZERO " 12. = 3.29.p.m.	4 "P" Smoke Bombs	" " " " " "
At ZERO " 16. = 3.33.p.m.	6 Smoke Candles.	" " " " " "

and so on; 4. "P" Smoke Bombs being thrown by each paryy at ZERO plus 24 minutes, 36 minutes, and 46 minutes, and Smoke Candles at the same intermediate intervals as above.

(d) Time keepers will be responsible that Smoke Bombs and Candles are thrown at the correct time and intervals.

The front on which the smoke is to be discharged will be divided into lengths of 25 yards, in each of which a party of:-

1. N.C.O. (Timekeeper)
2. Throwers. (Bombers).
1. Carrier.

will form the Smoke Party.

All Smoke discharge will cease at ZERO plus 52 minutes = 4.9. p.m

Synchronisation of watches will be at 9.a.m. and 12 noon by phone.

(Signed) R.H. LUPTON, Lt.,
A/Adjt., 11th Royal Sussex Regt.

12.10.16.

Issued at 11.45.p.m.

Copy No.1. to O.C. "A" Company.
" " 2. " " "B" "
" " 3. " " "C" "
" " 4. " " "D" "

SECRET.   Provisional.

OPERATION ORDER NO. 41.

Copy N° 5.

RELIEF.   1. The 11th. Bn. Royal Sussex Regt. will be relieved by the HOOD Bn. Royal Naval Division on a day and at a time to be notified later.

DISPOSITIONS   2. All Companies will hand over their present dispositions exactly to the incoming Unit and render them all assistance in their power.

ROUTES.   3. The incoming Unit will come in and the 11th R. Sussex Regt. go out by the following routes. Companies will move off as soon as relieved.

                    HEADQUARTERS. MESNIL, JACOBS LADDER, POTTAGE.
                    LEFT COMPANY. via MESNIL, KNIGHTSBRIDGE, GABION AVENUE.
                    CENTRE COMPANY. via MESNIL, JACOBS LADDER, ROYAL AVENUE.
                    RIGHT COMPANY. via MESNIL, JACOBS LADDER, POTTAGE TRENCH, DEVIAL AVENUE.
                    RESERVE COMPANY. Two platoons will accompany the Left Company as far as KNIGHTSBRIDGE. Two platoons will accompany the Right Company as far as HAMEL.

            The order of Companies of the incoming Unit will be as above.

ADVANCE PARTIES.   4. A small Advance Party composed of C.S.M.'s, Signallers and other specialists will arrive before the Main Body and take over.

GUIDES.   5. "A", "B" and "C" Companies will send one guide per platoon to MESNIL (end of JACOBS LADDER) at a time to be notified later. These guides are personally responsible that they get hold of their correct platoons. Each guide will be provided by O.C., Company with a written slip shewing his platoon and Company (Right, Centre and Left etc.) e.g. Reserve platoon of Centre Company.
          "D" Company will supply one guide per post to be at MESNIL (JACOBS LADDER) at a time to be notified later. These guides are under the same responsibilities and will adopt the same precautions as the above. Headquarters will similarly supply one guide.

HANDING OVER LISTS.   6. Handing over lists must be prepared and Trench Stores ready to be called in and handed over. The usual receipts will be obtained on relief. Special attention to be paid to handing over of Gum Boots.

RELIEF COMPLETE.   7. This will be notified to Bn. H.Q. by wire by the Code message "WIRE REPORT LATER".

TRANSPORT.   8. All Officers kits and baggage for Transport must be packed up and stacked as under at a time to be notified later.
"B", "C" and ½ "A" at KNIGHTSBRIDGE.
H.Q. ½ "A" and "D" at MESNIL.

                                                                                             P.T.O.

LEWIS GUNS. 9. Lewis Gun Teams will proceed with their Companies and O.C., Companies are responsible that they are shewn their correct positions.

of Relief
N.B. The <u>probable</u> hour/will be at 8.30. a.m.
If this is the correct hour O.C. Companies must arrange to have their kits etc. at KNIGHTSBRIDGE AND MESNIL at that hour.
The <u>actual</u> time will notified as soon as received.

(Signed) R.H. LUPTON, Lieut.,
Adjutant, 11th R. Sussex Regt.

15.10.16.

Issued at 6.30.p.m.

Copy No. 1 to 4. to O.C. Coys.
          5   to 2nd i/c.
          6   to CO.
          7   Transport Officer.
          8   Adjutant.
          9   War Diary.
         10   Ditto.
         11. Relieving Bn.

N.B. All guides must be at MESNIL by 8. a.m. and all kits etc., stacked ready for Transport at the places mentioned at that hour.

(Signed) R.H. LUPTON, Lieut.,
Adjutant, 11th R. Sussex Regt.

SECRET.
Copy No.........

OPERATION ORDER NO. 41.

RELIEF. 1. The 11th Battalion, Royal Sussex Regiment will relieve the 12th Battalion, Royal Sussex Regiment in REDOUBTS SECTOR to-morrow 19th October 1916. The relief will be complete by 11.0. a.m.

ADVANCE PARTY. 2. 1 Officer and 4 N.C.O.'s from "D" Company and 1 N.C.O. from "B" and "C" Companies will proceed to take over trenches leaving Battalion Headquarters at 7. a.m.

MAIN BODY. 3. The main body will leave Camp as per order in margin, starting at 8. a.m.
Headquarters.
"D" Company.
"B" Company.
"C" Company.

DRESS. 4. Fighting Order No. 2. with waterproof sheet.
Assaulting Companies will go equipped as arranged for forthcoming attack.

TRAFFIC. 5. All movement will be by Sections at 50 yards distance.

DUMPS. 6. O.C.'s Companies will take care that all dumps etc. prepared for the forthcoming operation will be left intact. O.C. "D" Company will at once set a guard over the forward dump of the 12th Battalion, Royal Sussex Regt., situate in BAINBRIDGE TRENCH.

TRANSPORT. 7. All packs, Officers Kits etc. for removal by transport to be stacked at R.E. DUMP WOOD POST by 6.30. a.m. 19th October 1916.

RELIEF COMPLETE. 8. This will be notified to Battalion Headquarters by Code Signal "MY SOCKS HAVE BEEN MENDED".

GUIDES. 9. The O.C., 12th. Battalion Royal Sussex Regt., will send guides to meet Companies at SCHWABEN REDOUBT Trench.

RATIONS. 10. Each man will carry 2 days rations in addition to his emergency rations. ALL WATER BOTTLES WILL BE FILLED, and no water will be drunk without permission of an Officer.

(Signed) R.E. LEECH, Lieut.,
Adjutant, 11th R. Sussex Regt.

18.10.16.

SECRET.

Copy No....6....

OPERATION ORDER NO. 47.

INTENTION.	1	The 11th Bn. Royal Sussex Regt. will parade to-night for digging a Reserve Line NORTH of THIEPVAL. Companies will parade <u>as strong as possible</u>. The Battalion will be required to do 4 hours actual digging and Intensive Digging should be practised.
DRESS.	2.	Slung Rifles and 20 rounds of ammunition, in pockets, will be carried.
ORDER OF MARCH.	3.	Companies will move off as under:-

        "A" Company.   5.30. p.m.
        "B" Company.   5.45. p.m.
        ~~"C" Company.~~
        Headquarters.   6. 0. p.m.
        "C" Company.   6.15. p.m.
        "D" Company.   6.30. p.m.

ROUTE.	4.	THIEPVAL AVENUE.
GUIDES.	5.	Guides will be arranged by R.E. and will meet Companies at R.25c.8.0. "A" Company will be at R.25.c.8.0. by 6.0. p.m.
TOOLS.	6.	mTools will be provided under arrangements to be made by the G.R.E.

                          (Signed) R.H. LUPTON, Lieut.,
                      Adjutant, 11th R. Sussex Regt.

Issued at 3.30 p.m.

28.10.16.

Copy No. 6 to. Adjutant.

VERY SECRET.

OPERATION ORDER NO. 41.

Copy No. 8

Reference Map. 1/5,000 St. Pierre Divion.
" " 1/5,000 Trench Map.
" " 1/6,000 Grandcourt.
" " 1/20,000 K.17. to M. 31.

1. (a) The enemy are holding STUFF TRENCH and REGINA TRENCH.

   (b) Our Troops are holding SCHWABEN REDOUBT, HORNBY TRENCH, STUFF REDOUBT, HESSIAN TRENCH.

INTENTION. 2. On the 18th October at an hour to be notified later the 116th Infantry Brigade will attack and capture the hostile trench between Points R.20.b.2.8. exclusive and R.20.d.9.8.

FRONTAGE. 3. The frontage allotted to the 11th Bn. Royal Sussex Regt. is from R.20.b.2.3. to R.20.a.5.1. exclusive. The 14th Bn. Hampshire Regt will be on our left and the 13th. Bn. Royal Sussex Regt. on our right.

ATTACK. 4. The battalion will attack as under:-
"B" and "C" Companies will be the assaulting Companies. "B" on the right and "C" on the left.
These Companies will assault in three waves, 2 platoons of each Company forming the first waves, 1 platoon of each Company the second wave and 1 platoon of each Company the third wave. The distance between the first and second wave of each Company will be 25 yards and between the second and third waves 50 yards.
"A" Company will be in support holding the present front line (HORNBY TRENCH) "D" Company in Support holding the left portion of SCHWABEN TRENCH.
Companies will assemble move to their assembly formations under orders that will be issued verbally to O.C. Coys. Company frontages for assaulting Companies will be issued as soon as decided upon.

ARTILLERY. 5. The assault will be preceded by 10 minutes intense bombardment, during which the assaulting waves will crawl up as close as possible towards the enemy trenches vide attached Time Table.

CONSOLIDATION. 6. On reaching the objective consolidation will be started immediately and a strong point will be constructed by "B" Company at Point R.20.a.5.1.

FLARES. 7. Each man in the assaulting Companies will carry two Flare Lights, these will be lighted as a signal to Aeroplanes at Zero plus 1 hour and Zero plus 2 hours.

COMMUNICATIONS 8. Up to HORNBY TRENCH existing communications or the open will be used, between HORNBY TRENCH and the objective communication trenches will be dug from about Point R.20.d.9.9. to R.20.d.7½.7. and from R.20.c.2.7. to R.20.a.5.1, and will be used when completed.

DUMPS. 9. The Field Works Officer will arrange to establish a battalion forward Dump in some convenient position in HORNBY TRENCH about Point R.20.d.9.5. This dump will contain S.A.A., Bombs, R.E. Material and Water.

BOMBS. 10. The Battalion Bombing Officer will arrange to draw sufficient bombs to provide each man of the assaulting Companies with four bombs and will generally supervise

RATIONS.	11.	Each man in the Battalion will carry two days rations in addition to his Iron Rations. ALL WATER BOTTLES WILL BE FILLED before leaving WOOD POST and no water will be drunk without permission from an Officer.
TOOLS.	12.	In the first wave one man in four will carry a tool. In the second wave one man in three will carry a tool. In the third wave every man will carry a tool. More shovels than picks will be carried.
EQUIPMENT.	13.	Fighting Order No.2. with waterproof Sheet strapped on belt, Each man will carry two extra bandoliers and four bombs. Each man will carry two sandbags worn under the shoulder strap. Men should be reminded that these Bombs are <u>not</u> to be thrown indiscriminately but are to be considered as a reserve and dumped immediately on arrival in the hostile trench, where they will be collected by the Company Bombers.
MESSAGES.	14.	Constant messages will be sent back by runner to Battalion Headquarters reporting the situation, each Officer will have two runners detailed for this purpose and each Company Commander will have six runners. Messages will invariably be written <u>not</u> verbal.
LEWIS GUNS.	15.	Lewis Guns will be at the disposal of Company Commanders.
ZERO.	16.	Zero hour will be notified later.
MOPPING UP PARTIES.	17.	Company Commanders are responsible that adequate mopping up and clearing parties are detailed for clearing dug-outs in the captured trenches. O.C. "C" Company will be responsible for clearing and consolidating, communication trench on his left.
SYNCHRONISATION OF WATCHES.	18.	Watches will be synchronised under arrangements to be made by Battalion Commander.
BN. H.Q.	19.	Battalion Headquarters will be at 13th Bn. Royal Sussex Regt. Headquarters in ZOLLERN TRENCH.

(Signed) G.H. HARRISON, Lieut-Col.,
Comdg., 11th R. Sussex Regt.

10.10.16.

Copy No. 1. to C/O.
" " 2. " O.C., "A" Company.
" " 3. " O.C., "B" "
" " 4. " O.C., "C" "
" " 5. " O.C., "D" "
" " 6. " Bombing Officer.
" " 7. " Field Works Officer.
" " 8. " Adjutant.
" " 9. " R.S.M.
" " 10. " Records.
" " 11. " War Diary.
" " 12. " " "

"A" Form.
MESSAGES AND SIGNALS.
Army Form C. 2121.

Prefix....Code....m.	Words / Charge	This message is on a/o of:	Recd. at....m.
Office of Origin and Service Instructions.	Sent	Service.	Date
	At....m.		From
	To		By
	By	(Signature of "Franking Officer.")	

TO { RN

Sender's Number.	Day of Month.	In reply to Number.	A A A
* OK 14	23/10		

Casualties for 21st October AAA
Killed T/2Lt C W DOOGAN AAA
T/2Lt E.H.H. IVENS AAA T/Lt F H SALTER
AAA OR 11 AAA Wounded
T/2Lt V H B D'IVERNOIS AAA T/2Lt P J HAYES
AAA OR 118 missing OR
134

From R1
Place
Time

116th Brigade.
39th Division.
9----------

11th BATTALION

THE ROYAL SUSSEX REGIMENT

SEPTEMBER 1 9 1 6

116/3911. R Sussex
Vol 7

L. Abraham
7. E
11thets

Confidential

War Diary

from 1st to 30th September 1916.
(inclusive)

Volume VII

11th & 13th Royal Sussex Regiment

Army Form C. 2118

WAR DIARY
or
INTELLIGENCE SUMMARY
(Erase heading not required.)

Place	Date Sept	Hour	Summary of Events and Information	Remarks and references to Appendices
MAILLY WOOD	1		The Battalion rested and were equipped for coming action. The Billets were shelled at intervals during day & night. Weather showery.	ih.
"	2	6.30pm	Preparation made for going into action. Battalion march off to trenches & relieved the Cheshires Regt. The relief was complete by 11.30 p.m. and all Companies established in their assembly positions.	ih.
BEAUMONT HAMEL	3	5.10am	Operations commence. Artillery barrage opens. The Companies left assembly trenches and reassembled in No-Mans-Land. First wave succeeded in entering Enemys front line but owing to Enemys barrage across No-Mans-Land the 2nd & 3rd waves suffered many casualties especially amongst the Officers. T/Capt. Michell witnesses of the Reserve Coy. now that some disorganisation would occur to these waves, without leaders, quickly went forward & rallied them & took them forward. 2nd Lt. Cassels greatly assisted in this work. Some of the party succeeded in entering the German 2nd line lead by T/Capt. NORTHCOTE + remained there throughout the day in spite of the great odds. Capt MICHELL took up a position between Enemy wire & Front-line parapet & consolidated a line of shell holes there. They had many casualties from shrapnel bombs but hung on till ordered to withdraw by the C.O. Capt NORTHCOTE hung on in his precarious position all day & withdrew at 6.30 p.m. but was killed in leading his party across No-Mans-Land. One only survived of this party. The war wounded. Casualties were as follows:- Officers killed NIL. Officers wounded 3 Officers missing 8. Other Ranks killed 5 wounded 160 missing 123	ih.
		5.30pm	The Battalion was relieved by the Cheshire Rgt. and went into billets at ENGLEBELMER	ih.

APPENDIX

J.H.Hammond

WAR DIARY
or
INTELLIGENCE SUMMARY
(Erase heading not required.)

Army Form C. 2118

Place	Date April	Hour	Summary of Events and Information	Remarks and references to Appendices
BEAUMONT HAMEL ENGLEBELMER	4		Battalion rested. Rolls called casualties estimated. The following Officers were reported missing :- T/Capt Northcote, Capt Tuttiett (3rd R Sussex R attached 11th R Sussex Regt.) Capt Pennefather, Rt Groves, 2nd Rt VonEsy, 2nd Rt Mole, 2nd Rt French, 2nd Rt Fish. 2nd Rt J Keller + 2nd Rt Redway wounded + 2nd Rt Rogan wounded + at duty.	K.
"	5		Battalion rested. Owing to the Heavy casualties the Battn was made into two Coys. A + D making N°1 Coy + B + C making N°2 Coy. T/Capt Michell commanding N°1 Coy and 2nd Rt Cavash commanding N°2 Coy. Billets shelled at intervals throughout day + night - no damage done. Showery all day.	K. K.
"	6		Fine day. Battalion moved to billets in BEAUSSART. Draft of 1430.R.s arrive from 1st, 6th, 7th, 8th, Bedfords + 2/4th + 2/5th Norfolks.	K. K.
BEAUSSART	7		Battalion carried out programme of Training, Physical Training, Bayonet fighting etc. Courses of instruction were commenced in Bombing, Sniping, Signalling, Lewis Gunnery, & draft of 94 O.Rs arrived from 11/4th + 1/5th Suffolks + N°15 Staff.	K. K.
"	8		Programme of Training continued. Fine day.	K. K.
"	9		A new draft of 80 O.Rs arrived from 2/1st Herts. Carried on with training programme + courses of instruction.	K. K.
"	10		A draft of 94 O.Rs arrived from E Anglian Coy Cyclists + Reserves. Coy equipment inspection. Usual training carried out. Coys nightly advantages made up. The day was fine.	K. K.
"	11		A draft of 40 O.Rs arrived from 14th Sussex. 1 Officer taken on the strength 2nd Rt Irens posted to "B" Coy. The Brigade go into the line, the 11th Bn R Sussex Regt being in reserve remain at BEAUSSART. Usual training carried out. Working parties supplied to R.E.s. A draft of 30 other Ranks arrive from 2nd + 12th R Sussex Regt.	K. K.

[signature]

WAR DIARY
or
INTELLIGENCE SUMMARY
(Erase heading not required.)

Army Form C. 2118

Place	Date Sept	Hour	Summary of Events and Information	Remarks and references to Appendices
BEAUSSART	12.		Company Commanders reconnoitre the new line at Lt subsection BEAUMONT. Batten carry on with training. The day was fine	JK
"	13.		Programme of training carried out - the usual courses of instruction under specialist officers + N.C.O.s Officers, N.C.O.s reconnoitre the new line + routes thereto.	JK
"	14.	9.30am	Battalion move into the trenches at BEAUMONT relieve the 12th R Sussex Regt, relief complete 12.30 pm with no casualties. The line was fairly quiet throughout day + night.	JK
BEAUMONT Lt Subsection	15.		Enemy artillery very active on front + support lines also on back areas by his H.T.M. Here also very active but did no damage. Much work to be done in line + all available men on working parties. "A" + "B" hold front line "C" Coy in supp at "D" Coy in Reserve at AUCHONVILLERS. Enemy Artillery + H.T.M.s very active at AUCHONVILLERS. Patrols were sent out to find out state of enemy wire — this was found to be very thick, no less than 5 distinct belts comprising his system. General maintenance, repairs to trenches +parapet was carried on 1 O.R. killed 4. O.Rs wounded	JK JK
"	16.			JK
"	17.		Enemy H.T.M.s active, otherwise fairly quiet throughout the day, until evening when he put up a barrage across No-Mans-Land, evidently suspicious of a raid from us. Patrols were sent out by the 12. R.S.R. opposite our Rt Coy front (C) to examine Enemy wire which our artillery had been cutting, it was found however to be uncut + the intended raid postponed in consequence. (Appendix 10) 1.O.R wounded and at duty. 2nd Lt Sellen reported to the Battn. & was posted to "B" Coy.	JK JK

J H Hammond Lt Col

Army Form C. 2118

WAR DIARY
or
INTELLIGENCE SUMMARY
(Erase heading not required.)

Place	Date Sept	Hour	Summary of Events and Information	Remarks and references to Appendices
BEAUMONT LEFT SUB SECTION	18		Weather Wet. Morning very quiet, very little activity either by our Artillery or Inf. During afternoon Enemy Artillery & H.T.Ms very active on our front line. Our Artillery retaliated. During the night the Enemy T.Ms shelled our wire, salvos of Aerial Torpedoes were also sent over at intervals. 2.O.R.s wounded (shell shock) & 1 accidentally wounded. 4.O.R. rejoined the Battn from the Base. The following Officers reported to the Battn were posted to Coys. 2nd Lt Scott "B" Coy. 2nd Lt Drew to "A" Coy 2nd Lt Hay to "C" Coy & 2nd Lt Naylor to "D" Coy	
"	19		Rained again during night & day causing much damage to trenches. Enemy shelled our front line & C.T. to AUCHONVILLERS also shelled. Working parties working day & night on trench repairs. Lt Burgess rejoined the Bn. 2nd Lt Mee reported & was taken on strength posted to "C" Coy	H
"	20		Still very wet. During the morning Enemy shelled our observation post without success, but made several direct hits on a M.T.M emplacement remarked in one of our dugouts. It again opened up a heavy bombardment on our front line & supports during the evening. He did much damage breaching our parapet in several places. He also blew in our Mine shaft at the junction of Marlboro' & Hunter Trenches. Our Artillery retaliated with heavy howitzers on their Supports with apparent good results. 3. O.R.s killed 6 O.R.s wounded.	H
"	21		Weather fine. Enemy apparently less active throughout day though much air reconnaissance was carried on by our aircraft during the Aft/N. Repair work was carried out in all Fire Trenches & C.T. Much progress accomplished. 1 O.R. accidently wounded. Much activity well on our right in direction of THIEPVAL. A draft of 125 O.R.s arrived, these remained at MAILLY-MAILLET when they were equipped for the trenches.	H

J.W. Hammond Lt Col

WAR DIARY
or
INTELLIGENCE SUMMARY
(Erase heading not required.)

Army Form C. 2118

Instructions regarding War Diaries and Intelligence Summaries are contained in F.S. Regs., Part II. and the Staff Manual respectively. Title Pages will be prepared in manuscript.

Place	Date Sept.	Hour	Summary of Events and Information	Remarks and references to Appendices
BEAUMONT at Subsector	22		Weather fine. During the day Enemy fairly quiet, at intervals he shelled the village of AUCHONVILLERS. In the Evening he was more active shelling our front line & C.T. Very little damage was done. Our Artillery was very quiet. Our Lewis guns dispersed an Enemy working party.	J.H.
"	23	2.30 p.m.	Enemy shelled Battn H.Qrs with Gas Shells. The Gas was chiefly lachrymatory but Gas Helmets were worn for about half an hour. Our Artillery retaliated. The new draft came into the trenches & went to their various Coys. During the early part of the night the Enemy heavily shelled our front line and close supports with "Crumps" heavy Minenwerfer & slight damage was done to our trenches. Casualties. 2 O.Rs killed. 5 wounded.	J.H.
"	24		Weather fine. Enemy fairly quiet during day. His usual T.M activity on our R Coy Front during night. Our Artillery retaliated.	J.H.
"	25		Weather fine. Enemy more active on this day, Front & Supports & Back Areas. Our retaliation was not brisk. 1 O.R. wounded. Fine Weather. Operation for co-operation with Corps on our Right in their attack	J.H.
"	26	12.44 P.M	ON THEIPVAL. Dummies were used & put up over parapet to represent troops going over. A Smoke barage was also put up, it had the desired effect of distracting the Enemy's fire & he shrapnelled our front line & supports; he also put up a shrapnel barage across NO-MAN'S-LAND. No casualties resulted. Usual maintenance work was carried out Improvements were made including a new dugout. (Appendix "").	J.H.

(Appendix W) J.W. Hornwell Lt

WAR DIARY or INTELLIGENCE SUMMARY

Army Form C. 2118

(Erase heading not required.)

Place	Date	Hour	Summary of Events and Information	Remarks and references to Appendices
BEAUMONT Rt Subsection	27		This day was wet. The Left of our Reft. Coy was again heavily shelled by Enemy T.Ms. Our Artillery retaliated. His Rifle Grenades were also very active on our Reft. Coy front.	
"	28		Weather damp, Drizzly. Enemy fairly quiet but his usual T.Ms busy on our Reft. Coy front. 2.ORs wounded	
"	29		Fine Weather. Enemy again quiet owing to our aircraft activity. AUCHONVILLERS heavily shelled at intervals during day.	
"	30		Weather Fine. "C" Coy were relieved by "A" Coy in the Left Coy front. Casualties in AUCHONVILLERS on the way up to relief. Enemy very active with his aerial torpedoes causing some damage to Chevaulx 2.ORs Killed and 7 ORs Wounded.	

Appendix 10

Reference Map N.R. S.E.   SECRET.

OPERATION ORDER   No   Copy No. _____

Intention. The 116th Infantry Brigade will cooperate in operations
to be carried out on 16.9.16 by Reserve Army.
In accordance with the above order the 11th R. Sussex R.
will carry out the following fire and/or operation.

1. (a) The 116th Infantry Brigade is making a raid on the
    hostile Front Line Trenches between C.17.b.6.5. and
    C.17.b.5.4. at 5.45 a.m. on 16.9.16

2. (a) Lewis Gun and Rifle Fire will be opened at 5.45 a.m.
    on enemy's Trenches on our immediate front and will
    continue until 6 a.m.

3. (b) Each Front Line Company will divide its front into
    lengths of 25 yards for the purpose of delivering a
    smoke barrage. In each length of 25 yards 1 N.C.O.
    (timekeeper) and 2 throwers (bombers) and 1 carrier will
    form a Smoke Party for throwing Smoke Bombs. These
    Party will be under the supervision of 2/Lt Munden and
    2 N.C.O.'s who will assist the Brigade Bombing Officer,
    who will be in charge of all arrangements.

    TIME TABLE FOR SMOKE BARRAGE.
    (a) 5.45 a.m. Each party will throw 4 "P" Bombs to its
    immediate front.
    (b) 5.50 a.m. Starting at 5.50 a.m. Each party will
    throw 6 Smoke Candles every 2 minutes to its immediate
    Front until 6.00 a.m. at which moment all Smoke dis-
    charges will cease.
    (c) 6. - a.m. Lewis Gunners and Rifle Fire etc. cease.

    N.B. N.C.O.'s and throwers selected should if possible
    be experienced men.

                            (Signed)   R.R. LUPTON,
                                       Lieut & A/Adjt.,

14.9.16.

SECRET.
Copy No......

Appendix 11

OPERATION ORDER NO 37.

INFORMATION. 1. (a) Certain Corps of the Reserve Army are making an attack on the Enemy South of this Battalion at Zero hour on "Z" Day.
(b) Zero hour and "Z" Day will be notified you later.
(c) The 11th Royal Sussex Regt. will deliver a feint attack on the front Q.10.d.6.7. to Q.4.d.8½.3. at Zero minus 10 minutes on "Z" Day and iss assisting the main operations with Artillery.
(d) The fient attack is to include a discharge of smoke by the 11th Royal Sussex Regt.
(e) No. 2 Special Company R.E. is assisting with 4 guns near BROADWAY, 2 guns in SEAFORTH TRENCH and 2 guns in BRIDGE END.

SMOKE 2. Smoke will be discharged on the front held by the 11th Royal Sussex Regt. from Zero minus 11 to Zero on "Z" day in accordance with the attached programme (Appendix "A") and instructions (Appendix "B")
Smoke will not be used unless directed by Battalion H.Q.
Code word for discharge of Smoke Bombs and Candles will be "GASPERS"

INFANTRY. 3. (a) The Companies in the line will be thinned out as far as possible from Zero minus 30 minutes onwards and kept under cover.
(b) Every effort must be made to provide sentries with protected look-out posts. O's C. Coys. will report immediately what has been done in this respect.
(c) On conclusion of the smoke, the smoke parties will be withdrawn to dug-outs.
(d) At Zero minus 10 minutes dummies will be hoisted over the parapet to represent troops going over (Appendix "B")
(e) At Zero minus 05, 7 Red Very Lights will be fired by the Battalion at uncertain intervals and places.

OBSERVATION 4. (a)
POSTS. An O.P. on both Company fronts will be manned from Zero hour onwards and will keep an especially close observation on the Valley of the River Ancre and the ground to the South of the River under the direction of the Brigade Intelligence Officer.

SYNCHRONIZATION An Officer will call at each Company H.Q. with a
OF WATCHES. 5. synchronized watch and all watches will be carefully synchronized from this. The Officer must not be delayed.

RUNNERS. 6. A system of runners will be arranged between sentry groups and Company H.Q. and any information gained by sentries will immediately be reported.

(Signed) R.H. LUPTON
Lt. A/Adjt.
11th Royal Sussex Regt.

Issued at ,........

Copy No. 1 to O.C. "A" Coy.
" " 2 " " "B" "
" " 3 " " "C" "
" " 4 " " "D" "

PROGRAMME.
APPENDIX "A"

TIMES.

Zero minus 11   Smoke commences along the whole of the Battalion Front.

Zero minus 10   Dummy figures raised over parapet along whole of Front.

Zero minus 5   Battalion will fire 7 red Very Lights at uncertain intervals and places.

Zero 0   Smoke discharge ceases and smoke parties retire to Dug-outs.

INSTRUCTIONS FOR SMOKE BARRAGE.
APPENDIX "B"

1. No smoke will be discharged unless the wind is between South and West.
    2/Lt Blunden will be held responsible for this.

2. 2/Lt. Blunden and 2 N.C.O's will assist the Brigade Bombing Officer who will be in charge of the smoke arrangements.

3. (a) The Battalion front will be divided into lengths of 25 yards in each of which a party of:-

            1 N.C.O.   (Timekeeper)
            2 Throwers (Bombers)
            1 Carrier.

    will form the smoke party.

    (b) Each smoke party will throw "P" Smoke bombs and Smoke Candles as follows:-

    At Zero minus 11 minutes 4 "P" Bombs distributed over its 25 yards front
    "   "   "   7   "   6 Smoke Candles "   "   "   "   "   "   "
    "   "   "   5   "   "   "   "   "   "   "   "   "   "   "
    "   "   "   3   "   "   "   "   "   "   "   "   "   "   "
    "   "   "   1   "   "   "   "   "   "   "   "   "   "   "

    All smoke discharges will cease at Zero.

    (c) The timekeeper will be responsible that smoke bombs and Candles are thrown at the correct times and intervals.

    (d) The carriers will bring up smoke bombs and candles from the Reserve store of each party which will be formed in the Front Line under Battalion arrangements.

4. During the discharge each smoke party will hoist dummy figures over the parapet after the "P" Bombs have been thrown.

116th Brigade.
39th Division.

11th BATTALION

THE ROYAL SUSSEX REGIMENT

OCTOBER 1 9 1 6

Confidential 116/39

S. Ephrat

War Diary
of
11th Bn Royal Sussex R
for the month
of
Oct 1916

Army Form C. 2118

WAR DIARY
or
INTELLIGENCE SUMMARY
(Erase heading not required.)

Place	Date	Hour	Summary of Events and Information	Remarks and references to Appendices
BEAUMONT 1st Sub section	1st		Weather wet, schemes for proposed raids submitted by Coys. Usual maintenance work carried out in trenches & new work accomplished. Enemy were active with aerial Torpedoes & H.T.Ms on left Coy's front. Trenches damaged. 2nd Lt Cragg rejoins Battn from 116 Bde & took over command of "C" Coy. 2nd Lt Clark joins Battn & is posted to "A" Coy.	
"	2nd		Weather still unsettled. Enemy activity quiet, our Artillery shelled their new works throughout day & night. They retaliated on AUCHONVILLERS and MAILLEY-MAILLET. His H.T.Ms were also active on Right Coy front. 1 O.R. wounded	
"	3rd		Weather improving. Quiet all day & night.	
"	4th		Weather showery. Situation quiet during morning, supposed relief by Enemy was denied by H.T.M.s on our Right and 12th R SUSSEX Rd on our left. During afternoon the Battn Enemy shelled C. 7 D support line during relief, also AUCHONVILLERS. 1 O.R. killed 1 O.R. wounded. Battn marched from trenches & bivouaced in wood at ENGLEBELMER.	
ENGLEBELMER WOOD	5th		2/Lt CASSELS started Military Class. Coys at disposal of Coy Comdrs during morning cleaning equipment rifles etc. C.O. inspected Lewis & equipment in afternoon also visited to HUB Posts with the Battalion marched to MARTINSART WOOD to HUB Posts with the CHESHIRES and came under command of the 117th Bde. 2nd Lt Kelly joins the Battn & posted to "D" Coy.	
MARTINSART WOOD	6th		Weather fine. Battn clean up & Battn. The Officers & N.C.O.s reconnoitre the new line at THIEPVAL.	
		7oc	Battn march to command of 116th Bde. C.O. reconnoitre the new line at HAMEL	

WAR DIARY or INTELLIGENCE SUMMARY

Army Form C. 2118

Place	Date	Hour	Summary of Events and Information	Remarks and references to Appendices
MARTINSART WOOD.	7th		Weather fine. Battalion moved to trenches at HAMEL and relieved the 1st HERTS and 4/5 BLACK WATCH on the line from the ANCRE to RONSSOY. Relief completed by 12 noon. Enemy quiet throughout day/night.	JK
HAMEL.	8th		Weather fine. Scheme for raid submitted by Coys. Enemy artillery active on front line and close supports. Some damage done to trenches. 3 O.Rs wounded. 2 O.Rs on Lewis gun course killed whilst on fatigue duty.	JK
"	9th		Weather fine. Enemy artillery active. Also their H.T.Ms on our right doing damage from C.T.6. Major the Hon. Ryston attached to E.H.Q. to supervise his duties at Bde M.G. Bn. 1 O.R. wounded.	JK
"	10th		Weather fine. Enemy artillery. Our artillery & T.Ms carried out an operation along whole of enemy front, doing much damage to their trenches & wire. They retaliated weakly. 2 O.Rs wounded.	JK
"	11th		Weather fine but cold. Maintenance parties carry on their work on repair to trenches & reserve defences. Our wire strengthened. Enemy active on our left. 6 O.Rs wounded. Major C. MILWARD left Battn to proceed to Battn Course.	JK
"	12th		Weather fine. Special training in England carried out and an operation in co-operation with R.A. attacking SCHWABEN REDOUBT. Quick charge of troops was put up to divert enemy fire which we most successful. Our M.Gs opened fire on numerous targets, many of the enemy were distinctly seen in this way. Capt. MICHELL fell while going to F.A.	JK

WAR DIARY or INTELLIGENCE SUMMARY

Army Form C. 2118

Place	Date Oct 1916	Hour	Summary of Events and Information	Remarks and references to Appendices
HAMEL	13th		Weather fine - Enemy fairly quiet although showed some activity on our Left Coy front, slight damage to our Trenches. Our Artillery active on Enemy's near work.	JL
"	14th		Enemy very quiet. Every man in front line fired a rifle grenade at 9 P.M.2.5. Bomb No.23. slight retaliation by Enemy.	JL
"	15th		Fine Weather. Enemy fairly active throughout the day. His artillery damaged our C To Support line + 5 O.Rs wounded. Our Artillery retaliated on his front line doing much damage to his defences.	JL
"	16th	8.30 a.m.	The Battalion is relieved in the line by the "HOOD" Batn Rl Naval Div. and marched to huts at MARTINSART WOOD arriving at 12 noon. Troops had dinner	JL
"		2 p.m.	Battn march to Reserve line at AUTHUILLE WOOD — 1 Coy v HQ at WOOD Post Y 3 Coys in old German trenches at LEIPZIG SALIENT.	JL
AUTHUILLE WOOD	17th		Weather fine - General clean up of equipment rifles. Remainder of day Troops rested. Enemy shelled the wood throughout night.	JL
"	18th		Weather wet - Carrying & Working parties supplied. Enquiry & arrangements made for the coming operations. 2 O.Rs wounded	JL
"	19th		Still Raining. Carrying & working parties. Final arrangements made for Operations.	JL

Army Form C. 2118

WAR DIARY
or
INTELLIGENCE SUMMARY
(Erase heading not required.)

Instructions regarding War Diaries and Intelligence Summaries are contained in F.S. Regs., Part II. and the Staff Manual respectively. Title Pages will be prepared in manuscript.

Place	Date Oct-1916	Hour	Summary of Events and Information	Remarks and references to Appendices
REDOUBT SECTOR	20th		Battn. relieved the 13th Sussex Regt. in the REDOUBT SECTOR (Rt. Subsection) Advance party left at 7am Mainbody at 9am. Guards march to billets at AVELUY.	JK
"	21st		The Battn. employed in carrying Rations etc to Front line. The Battn. capture German Front line (STUFFTRENCH) "B" + "C" Coys assaulted "A" + "D" Coys reinforced them in the new line. Heavy Casualties were inflicted on the Enemy many prisoners taken. 2nd Lieuts. Lunn, Salter + Doggan killed, 2nd Lieut. K.H.B. D'Amores + 2nd Lt. P.J. Hayes wounded — 11 ORs killed, 186 ORs wounded and 77 OR missing.	JK
AVELUY WOOD	22nd		The Battn. was relieved + marched to South side of AVELUY WOOD where they bivouaced under shelter Tents.	JK
"	23rd		Weather wet. — Party (stretcher bearers) went up to trench captured position to collect wounded, many brought in to F.A. 10 OR wounded 2 Lt. ST JOHN rejoins Battn. reported to — Coy. Rest of Battn. rested.	JK JK
"	24th		Weather still unsettled — showers 7/c M.O. carried out Foot + Clothes inspection. Feet All mens feet treated to prevent TRENCH FEET. General cleaning up of equipment replacing deficiencies.	JK
RIVER SECTOR THIEPVAL	25th	9.30am	Weather Wet — Advance party consisting of 1/2 B + C Coy. marches off under Lieuts. MOTTS + DERBY & MILLS POST. The rest of Battn. struck Camp at 12.20 pm march to THIEPVAL WOOD + occupied dugouts in RIVER SECTOR, Enemy quiet during relief. During evening shells [illegible] — later [illegible] fire.	JK

1875 Wt. W593/826 1,000,000 4/15 J.B.C. & A. A.D.S.S./Forms/C. 2118.

WAR DIARY or INTELLIGENCE SUMMARY

Army Form C. 2118

Place	Date	Hour	Summary of Events and Information	Remarks and references to Appendices
RIVER SECTOR THIEPVAL	Oct 1916 26th	5.6 am	Enemy artillery very active on front line. Our artillery retaliated vigorously. During day situation quiet. Slight hostile shelling during night	JK
		10 pm	Mine Operation No.1 ANCRE which our artillery Co-operated. 1 O.R. wounded. 2 Lt G. SALTER slightly wounded but remains at duty.	JK JK
SOUTH BLUFF	27th		Battn is relieved by 16th RIFLE BDE & moved to SOUTH BLUFF and occupied Dugouts. 1 O.R. killed	JK
	28th		Battn rested & re-equipped.	JK
	29th	9.20 am	Weather wet - every available officer & O.R. (13 Officers 390 O.Rs) marches to THIEPVAL WOOD to dig Reserve Trench under R.Es. Strenuous digging was carried out. Much progress made. 1 O.R. wounded. Orders received for move to SCHWABEN REDOUBT. Lt F Caswels reports to Battalion with 10 O.Rs.	JK
	30th	7.26 pm	Battn marches and relieves 13th R Sussex Rt in SCHWABEN REDOUBT. Heavy rain during afternoon & night. All casuals sent to Transport line	JK JK
	31st		43 O.Rs (reinforcements) arrive from H/5 Sussex Rt & go through Rt to remain at Transport lines over night. Weather much improved	JK

WAR DIARY or INTELLIGENCE SUMMARY

Army Form C. 2118

Place	Date	Hour	Summary of Events and Information	Remarks and references to Appendices
SCHWABEN REDOUBT	30 OCT.		Lieut. T.S. Perry was severely wounded during the relief. The Battalion relieved the 1/1st HERTS. in SCHWABEN REDOUBT. The enemy observed the relief and the left company had much difficulty in getting to their posts. The guides were his and both Battalions suffered several casualties in the confusion. However by 2.45 p.m. all coys were in position. The rest of the day was comparatively quiet, but torrential rain turned the trenches into mud and caused the greatest discomfort. Wind was fresh and in our favour.	E.B.
	31	6.15 am	After an ordinary night, when our artillery carried out their usual programme in enemy's back areas, a sudden bombardment broke out on our left at 6.15 a.m. This was short-lived and our immediate front was not shelled. Shrapnel was put over MARTIN'S LANE intermittently throughout the day.	
		4 p.m.	At 4 p.m. a barrage was put on the right of SPLUTTER Rd. and extended almost at once along our whole front line: nothing was sent behind until 4.15, when after a moment's pause the enemy guns lifted to our Support line and repeated the practice. Our field guns and 4.5 howitzers made a good reply. This strafe ended up with casual shelling of Front & Support line and Bn H.Q. No infantry action at all was reported. The enemy's range was poor and we escaped casualties. One white light and several red were thrown from STRASSBURG LINE during this bombardment. The night was fairly quiet, but at no period did the enemy guns remain silent for long.	E.B.
	1 Nov.	8.45 am	The Battalion was relieved by the 6TH CHESHIRES, whose front coys. were guided into their positions without loss; but as our men (sic) moving down they were noticed and heavy shelling (5.95 and 102 mm) began at once. Eventually the Bn got clear with very few casualties, but those of the CHESHIRES on the front line were considerable. In view of the terrible state of the trenches and exhaustion of the men, as well as the direct enemy observation of all movements and immediate shelling, this relief was carried out skilfully: it began at 8.45 a.m. and was reported complete at 1.20 p.m. After relief the Battalion returned to Billets at SOUTH and CENTRE BLUFF.	E.B.

J.H. Mawson Lt Col.

"A" Company
11th Royal Sussex Reg't

To
Adjutant

Please find enclosed
"Missing" Roll with all
information obtainable
thereon.

From
A/C.S.M
C.S.M.

12/10/1916

O.C. a Coy.   E.J.M 15

With reference to the undermentioned roll of men reported Missing 3-9-16 will you please make enquiries and insert against each name any information that can be obtained e.g. "Believed Killed," "Believed Prisoner of War" etc, & whether known to be wounded as well as missing.

Please return the roll as soon as possible as this information is urgently required by DAG Base for the purposes of reporting Home.

(Sd) R H Lupton Lt-a/Adjt

Reg.No.	Rank & Name	Remarks
2	Sgt Barham J	Killed. (Confirmed from several sources)
25	Pte Braiden J	
35	" Bray F	
41	" Barnard J.	Believed Prisoner of War. (Last seen alive in 2nd line)
57	" Freeland E.J.	
65	" Beal H.E.	Killed. (Confirmed from several sources)
72	" Haggar J	
75	" Hoskins A.A.	
82	L/Cpl Lambert E.	
90	Pte Nicholls H.C.	Believed Prisoner of War. (Last seen alive in 2nd line)
112	L/Cpl Sutton H.G.	
127	" Watson C.A.	
131	Sgt Welshman P.S.	Wounded (By German wire. Several sources)
148	Pte Burchett W.	
17	" Coleman E.E.	Wounded. (Believed Prisoner of War)
159	" Cheal E.R.	Killed. (Confirmed several sources)

Reg.No.	Rk & Name	Remarks
170	Pte Duke W.H.	Wounded. (German 2nd Line)
203	L/Cpl Lander F.	
208	Pte Martin J.	
231	" Stevens W.J.	Wounded. (German 1st Line)
389	" Bromley A.S.	
391	Cpl Booth M.F.	
429	Sgt Hoad F.A.	Believed Killed. (confirmed several sources)
484	Pte West J.H.	
927	" Farrant W.	Wounded. Believed Prisoner of War.
262	" Blackford P.R.	
3891	" Hambrook A.G.	Wounded. (confirmed several sources)
3835	" Wadey C.J.O.	
3848	" West P.	Believed Killed.
3875	" Donington A.	Wounded
3876	" Dunning J.	Killed. (confirmed several sources)
3895	" Coward W.	
3906	" Hudson G.	Wounded. (German 1st Line)
3910	" Best P.W.	
4835	" Reed F.S.E.	
4863	" George A.J.	
4872	" Smith H.	
5055	" Elliott E.	
4816	Sgt	Smithers

URGENT.   EJM 15/2

O.C. B Coy.

With reference to the undermentioned roll of NCOs & men reported missing 3-9-16 will you please make enquiries and insert against each name any information that can be obtained e.g. "Believed killed", "Believed Pris. of War", or whether known to be wounded as well as missing, etc.

Please return the roll as soon as possible as this information is urgently required by D.A.G. Base for the purposes of reporting home.

(Sd) R A Lupton Lt a/Adjt

Reg No	Rank	Name	Remarks
209	L/Cpl	Martin S.P.	
270	Sgt	Budd R	wd & Believed Prisoner of War
273	Sgt	Howell S.	Believed Wounded & Missing
274	L/Sgt	Atkins E.W.	Known to be Pris. of War
284	Pte	Barton A.J.	
294	Pte	Binyon J.C.	Believed Wounded & Missing
300	Cpl	Corbett F	
321	Pte	Henty J.R.	
305	"	James W.R.	
323	"	Jocelyn H.	
348	Cpl	Roberts R.C.	
364	Pte	Stanford J.	
433	"	James H.B.	Believed Killed
448	Cpl	Minns G.	Believed seriously wounded & missing
699	Pte	Kewsett S	— Wounded & Missing
728	"	Roach W.	
978	"	Williams C.H.	Killed

1002	Pte	Bailey W	
1018		Clark J.	
1028		Duvall F.	Believed seriously Wounded & missing
1048		Hauman A	
1052		Hook A H.	
1053		Hook W	
1095		Sharpe J.	Believed Killed
1111		Willett A.	
3662		Plummer T	Believed Killed
5746		Jains C.	
640	CSM	Stevens E.	Believed seriously Wounded, reported by 2 men of Black Watch Killed

No clear information can be obtained about Ranks left blank.

CSM

NOMINAL ROLL OF CASUALTIES.

OFFICERS.

KILLED.
2/Lt. G.K. Doogan.
2/Lt. F.H. Salter.
2/Lt. F.H.H. Ivens.

WOUNDED.
2/Lt. V.H.B. D'Ivernois.
2/Lt. E.P. Hayes.

OTHER RANKS.
KILLED.

5638.	Pte	Boswell W.	"A" Coy.
G.15395.	"	Snelling R.G.	"
334.	Sgt.	Seamer A.G.	"B" Coy.
435.	Pte.	Holmwood O.	"
G.15134.	"	Allcock. T.	"C" Coy.
804.	"	Brown T.	"D" Coy.
G.15767.	"	Keates. W.	"
831	"	Prior H.J.	"
2991.	"	Perham R.	"
2418.	"	Rice A.	"
G.15080.	"	Wood S.	"

WOUNDED.

572.	Pte.	Winser F.	"A" Coy.
	"	Chatfield A.W.	"
G.15124.	"	Clarke J.	"
G.15790.	"	Gates P.C.	"
5339.	"	Minns F.H.	"
5634.	"	Stone A.J.	"
4135.	"	Weaver W.	"
1042	Sgt.	Gower H.U.	"B" Coy.
G.15761.	Cpl.	Verral H.	"
301.	L/Cpl.	Cosstick. R.	"
G.15267.	"	Gathercole A.	"
385.	"	Knight. H.	"
G.15885.	"	Budd W.	"
1032.	"	Fairman. P.G.	"
G.15791.	"	Geary. A.	"
G.15252.	Pte.	Aldus. J.W.	"
G.15038.	"	Bloxam. H.	"
G.15036.	"	Bailey A.	"
G.15033.	"	Brown J.H.	"
G.15037.	"	Bishop A.C.	"
G.15034.	"	Bottomley C.W.	"
G.15884.	"	Blunden T.A.	"
G.15237.	"	Duffield. W.	"
G.15225.	"	Dwight. S.G.	"
314.	"	Hopkins. H.	"
G.15732.	"	Hayner. A.	"
G.15395.	"	Hallett. C.	"
G.15237.	"	Hunt S.	"

No.	Rank.	Name	Coy.
G. 15532.	Pte.	Jeffs. A.A.	"B" Coy.
5507.	"	James A.G.	"
617.	"	Matthews J.	"
3745.	"	Marsh F.	"
3513.	"	Manktelow J.	"
G. 15851.	"	Mitchell R.B.	"
557.	"	Osman A.E.	"
G. 15257.	"	Oakley W.	"
G. 15289.	"	Parker A.R.	"
G. 15857.	"	Parsons W.H.	"
468.	"	Rogers. F.	"
G. 15299.	"	Reynolds R.	"
G. 15056.	"	Rolleston W.	"
8800	"	Smith S.	"
G. 15258.	"	Saunders. E.W.	"
G. 15010.	"	Starling. T.W.	"
G. 15563.	"	Ward C.N.	"
G. 15892.	"	Goody C.	"
G. 15856.	"	Parsons. E.J.	"
498.	C.S.M.	Lee. E.	"C" Coy.
513	A/Sgt.	Feest F.J.	"
3006.	"	Saxby. F.	"
1085.	L/Sgt.	Phillips. R.L.	"
G. 15742.	Cpl.	Hunt. G.	"
692.	"	Holt. T.	"
1598.	A/Cpl.	Loveland E.	"
8933.	L/Cpl.	Hudson J.	"
G. 15546.	"	Crane C.B.	"
G. 15147.	"	Brooks. F.	"
	"		"
4831.	"	Crisford. E.	"
4890.	"	Edmonds E.	"
G. 15113.	"	Bloor. E.	"
G. 5164.	Pte.	Allen H.	"
G. 15110.	"	Armitage J.	"
650.	"	Allfrey L.F.	"
5746.	"	Ansell. C.	"
4197.	"	Ashford. R.	"
G. 15616.	"	Belshaw T.W.	"
G. 15494.	"	Biggs. C.	"
G. 15155.	"	Barlow R.W.	"
G. 15157.	"	Belton J.	"
5110.	"	Boxall. C.	"
G. 15165.	"	Bastard H.	"
G. 15143	"	Burton L.	"
G. 15137	"	Burks H.	"
394	"	Brown S.	"
582	"	Cutler. A.	"
G. 15567.	"	Clibbow. H.J.	"
G. 15705.	"	Clark. A.E.	"
G. 15115	"	Churchill. D.	"
G. 15803	"	Carver. W.A.	"
G. 15711	"	Daniels H.J.	"
665	"	Denman C.	"
G. 15214	"	Fuller J.	"
G. 15225	"	Felts S.A.	"
G. 15163	"	Fitt. E.	"
G. 15118	"	Greatbatch. B.	"
G. 15724	"	Groves H.E.	"
G. 15215	"	Goodyer D.	"
G. 15407	"	Hobbs H.	"
G. 15735	"	Horner G.B.	"
G. 15820	"	Harrison F.	"
G. 15830	"	Hoad G.	"
G. 15744	"	Johnson J.C.	"
605	"	Jarvis B.	"
5854	"	James W.	"
442	"	Kennard.	

No.	Rank.	Name.	Coy.
4819.	Pte.	Larkin F.	C.
G. 15120.	"	Mangan T.	C.
G. 15172.	"	Pickering A.	C.
G. 15174.	"	Preston J.	C.
G. 15176.	"	Richardson F.	C.
G. 15565.	"	Rolls E.	C.
G. 15562.	"	Sutterby W.F.	C.
4814.	"	Sherwood J.	C.
G. 15179.	"	Smith A.	C.
G. 15769.	"	Topham A.T.	C.
5848.	"	Smith G.	C.
G. 15755.	"	Taylor H.S.	C.
582.	"	Williams T.	C.
G. 15221.	"	Weston W.J.	C.
3611.	"	Woodgate G.	C.
752.	"	Winchester C.	C.
G. 15506	"	*THURLEY H.S*	C
887	Pte.	Bateup S.	D.
5925	"	Burch T.	D.
895	"	Bagg G.	D.
5846	"	Button A.	D.
G. 15792.	"	Barton F.C.	D.
3952	"	Copping J.	D.
405	"	Clancy W.	D.
911	"	Deadman A.	D.
G. 15812	"	Elphick J.H.	D.
G. 15817	"	French C.	D.
G. 15282	"	Grief W.A.	D.
G. 15727	"	Guest D.T.	D.
G. 15730	"	Herring H.	D.
941	"	Harris W.	D.
G. 15824	"	Harrison C.	D.
G. 15168	"	Moates W.	D.
G. 16166	"	Moore W.E.	D.
783	"	Newcombe A.	D.
893	"	Marshall J.	D.
G. 15846	"	Mabbett G.	D.
3970	"	Maryon A.	D.
G. 15604	"	Parker C.G.	D.
G. 15050	"	Pickering A.	D.
G. 15053	"	Powdrill S.	D.
G. 15228	"	Reeves E.R.	D.
G. 15196	"	Taylor F.H.	D.
G. 15015	"	Taylor C.A.	D.
G. 15023	"	Warden P.R.	D.
~~825~~	"	~~Yeates A.~~	~~D.~~

MISSING.

No.	Rank.	Name.	Coy.
155.	L/Cpl.	Carter H.	A.
5355	Pte.	Cribb H.J.	A.
5795	"	Coley L.	A.
G.15129	"	Hammond F.	A.
G.15250	"	Kett W.	A.
G.15860	"	Richards L.	A.
G.15780.	"	Spencer T.	A
874.	A/C.S.M.	Green. E.J.	B
G.15244.	L/Cpl.	Smith. E.E.	B
1038.	"	Gannon. R.G.	B
G.15491.	"	Gentle. W.	B
G.15012.	"	Sullivan C.	B
G.15750.	"	Pagett A.	B
5882.	Pte.	Bower H.	B
G.15515.	"	Barton W.	B
G.15794.	"	Birchman W.	B
G.15883.	"	Brown E.	B
406.	"	Cook. J.	B
298.	"	Clark. W.	B
G.15937.	"	Curry H.	B
G.15708.	"	Cook. A.	B
G.15044.	"	Dodds. S.F.	B.
G.10955.	"	Day. A.	B
G.15811	"	Emmett. T.	B
G.15280.	"	Finn. G.	B
G.15717.	"	Fredman. A.	B.
4864.	"	Green W.	B.
G.15551.	"	Groom F.R.	B.
G.15725.	"	Gosling. F.	B.
5159.	"	Hobday G.H.	B.
G.15743.	"	Jay. A.	B.
G.11063.	"	Jones E.	B.
G.15252.	"	Larter G.	B
G.15746.	"	Lawrence G.E.	B.
5963.	"	Lagatt. A.	B.
G.15841.	"	Lambert R.C.A.	B.
329.	"	Miller A.	B.
G.15748.	"	Millican G.D.	B.
G.15848.	"	Messer. T.F,	B.
G.15242.	"	Rush J.,	B.
G.15053.	"	Rackley A.	B.
G.15055.	"	Robey A.	B. ~~Since reported Wnded~~
~~254~~	"	~~Myers. N.W.~~	~~B.~~ Since reported Wounded
~~G.15778~~	"	~~Sade B.~~	
G.15/110.	"		
3780.	"	Stoner J.	B.
G.15057.	"	Thorpe. J.	B.
G.15243.	"	Watts W.	B.
G.15298.	"	Wright R.	B.
G.15027.	"	Warner S.H.	B.
G.15021.	"	Wright. C.	B.
G.15025.	"	Whisker. R.	B.
G.15733.	Sgt.	Hiscock A.	C.
2931.	"	Habgood W.R"	C.
G.15550.	"	Grimley. H.	C.
G.15231.	Cpl.	Pierce S.	C.
G.15265	L/Cpl.	Eke. F.	C.
G.15784.	"	Tyler. C.T.	C.
G.15158.	"	Bunn A.	C.
G.15724.	"	Green F.J.	C.
5872.	Pte.	Arnold T.H.	C.
G.15160.	"	Barber H.	C.
5777.	"	Bowers G.	C.
G.15154.	"	Bradbury S.	C.
G.15146.	"	Burnett A.	C.
G.15207.	"	Burch L"A.	C.
G.15148.	"	Burgess W.	C.
G.15141.		Bilby G.	

MISSING. Cont'd.

No.	Rank.	Name.	Coy.
5662.	Pte.	Butcher. L.G.	C.
G.15789.	"	Bailey. C.	C.
G.15787.	"	Cawley. J.	C.
684.	"	Dean W.	C.
G.15946.	"	Folkard F.	C.
5411.	"	Gallop. A.	C.
G.16886.	"	Hobday. H.	C.
G.15834.	"	Jarrett. J.	C.
1075.	"	Merricks. B.W.	C.
2343.	"	Mansell L.	C.
G.16169.	"	Milton. E.P.	C.
1136.	"	Mitchell.	C.
5870.	"	Mattin. A.	C.
5847.	"	Meekings. J.H.	C.
G.15501.	"	Nottage. A.W.	C.
G.15775.	"	Potter A.W.	C.
G.15859.	"	Pullen W.	C.
G.15858.	"	Pilbeam F.	C.
3666.	"	Relf. W.	C.
5537.	"	Reed. J.	C.
G752.	"	Ross. F.	C.
G.15127.	"	Shaw. J.	C.
3024.	"	Sumner A.	C.
G.15864.	"	Scaterfield. J.	C.
744.	"	Taylor. A.F.E.	C.
G.15529.	"	Woods F.	C.
G.15782.	"	White W.G.	C.
852.	Sgt.	Stenning A.	D.
491.	Cpl.	Walker. W.	D.
	L/Cpl.	Fisher. L.	D.
400.	Pte.	Bishop J.	D.
G.15117.	"	Dean P.	D.
G.15046.	"	Fisher R.H.	D.
G.15023.	"	Harmer H.	D.
G.150754.	"	Rodgers. C.E.	D.
G.15184.	"	Stanforth G.	D.
G.15537.	"	Streets R.	D.
856.	"	Stace H.	D.
G.15510.	"	Warren R.W.	D.
G.15584.	"	Wilkins. P.	D.

Roll of Nurses — H.L. Nurses

No.	Rank	Name	Date Struck	CCS	3rd W	4th W
843	S	Mathews J	24/9/16	CCS	W	√
15392	"	Jeffs AM	"	"	W	√
403	"	Slaney W	"	"	W	√
1032	Hope	Harman S.G.	"	"	W	√
3052	S	Copping J	"	"	W	√
587	Hope	Pilchup S	"	"	W	√
1516	"	Barton W	"	"	W	√
1530	"	Winchester C	"	"	W	√
15740	CRS	Hunt G	"	"	W	√
15838	S	Saunders EW	"	"	W	√
404	"	Kennard H	"	"	W	√
15463	"	Gurin L	"	"	W	√
15303	"	Clarke AE	"	"	W	√
15759	"	Taylor HS	"	"	W	√
15120	"	Margaret T	"	"	W	√
815	Hope	Hughes H	"	"	W	√
15834	S	Stone W	"	"	W	√
15797	"	Stiles L	"	"	W	√
15857	"	Sommers ST	"	"	W	√

Roll of Wounded
J. L. Parker

No.	Rank	Name	Date	Place to	Sent	Remarks
15163	Pvt	Bastard H	3/15/10	CCS	"	W
15244	"	Fells JA	"	"	"	W
15165	"	Hill E	"	"	"	W
915803	"	Gane AW	"	"	"	W
1298	Cpl	Ireland ET	"	"	"	W
1547	Sgt	Hurt D	"	"	"	W
15015	"	Hodges D	"	"	"	W
5199	"	Hatfield Cnr	"	"	"	W
15144	"	Dombey Cnr	"	"	"	W
605	"	Jones LR	"	"	"	W
572	"	Williams T	"	"	"	W
15387	CSM	Elkton MQ	"	"	"	W
498	Pte	Ic E	"	"	"	W
5146	"	Arrell C	"	"	"	W
15444	"	Kipp C	"	"	"	W
3811	Mpe	Snodgato Q	"	"	"	W
15546	"	Evans C	"	"	"	W
15198	Pte	Taylor FH	"	"	"	W
15166	"	Moore JOS	"	"	"	W

Roll of Howard — W S Howard

No	Rank	Name	Sale 21.12.10	Joined To CCS	Joined To So W
15631	Pte	Mitchell LW	"	"	✓
15792	"	Bashs HC	"	"	✓
15880	"	Blinkhorn TA	"	"	✓
5144	"	Allen R	"	"	✓
15296	"	Andrews H	"	"	✓
15292	"	Reynolds AD	"	"	✓
1042	Sgt	Jones WC	"	"	✓
5861	Pte	Jones W	"	"	✓
15146	"	Jones WE	"	"	✓
15892	"	Brown JD	"	"	✓
15790	"	Yates EA	"	"	✓
665	"	Bowman C	"	"	✓
15113	A/Cpl	Bloor E	"	"	✓
15155	Pte	Bacon RN	"	"	✓
15174	"	Preston J	"	"	✓
15357	"	Dudley V	"	"	✓
15670	"	Galway R	"	"	✓
357	"	Snow GE	"	"	✓
513	Sgt	Scott T	"	"	✓
15144	Pte	Johnson JC	"	"	✓
15115	"	Taylor EA	"	"	✓
15780	"	Bish L	"	"	✓
1534	"	Stone AT	"	"	✓

List of Wounded 1st R Munster Fus

No	Rank	Name	Date	Place	How
15985	Sgt	Judd W	9/9/16	693	W
15757	Lcpl	Bryant J	"	"	W
6245	"	Deacon A	"	"	W
5110	"	Dorall C	"	"	W
15786	"	Herring MJ	"	"	W

[Signature]
for O.C. 1st R. Munster Fus.

[Stamp: 22 OCT 1916]

Killed
Boswell. W   5628.
Snelling. R.S.   15295   (2)

Wounded
15720   Patr   E a   Wounded.
5634   Pte   Stone. A. J.   Do   (3)
4125   "   Weaver. W.

Missing
155.   Cpl   Carter. H
5355   Pte   Cribb. H. J
5199   "   Chatfield. AW
15114 "   Clarke J/L   (12)
5195   "   Coley. L
15580 "   Cox. F.
15729 "   Hammond. Fa
15250 "   Lett W
5239   "   Mann F H
15860 "   Richards L
15780 "   Spencer. F.
15299 "   Watkins H

Nominal Roll of Evacuation/Transfer 1st Surge

No	Rank	Name	Date	Evac to Surgery	Airfield
15169	Pte	Mills T P	C. Cy 31-10-46	—	S	39 BTS
15172	"	Pickering A	at D.	—	S	—
L15692	"	Battersby C	at D.	22	—	—
155	Sgt	Carter R	at A	—	—	—
15853	"	Pomerée E. D.	Powbrik	23?	—	C.G.l.
852	Sgt	Fleming G.	t D.	—	S	—
15026	Pte	Freeman J	a?	24	—	—
15809	"	Amy R.		—	"	—
15176	"	Scade J		—	"	—
15561	"	Secceiss?		—	"	MRS
1123	L/Cpl	Rich S		—	"	A/trans. Lieut R.A.M.C

[Stamp: 134th FIELD AMBULANCE 25 OCT 1946]

to O.C. 134th FIELD AMBULANCE

To 11 Hussars (39D).

The undermentioned of the Unit under your command been disposed of as follows :-

No	Rank and Name	Unit	Coy	To Duty	Trans to D.A.S.	Evac to 4 C.C.S.
15787	Pte Sharp T.H.	11 Hussars	D			20/10/16 Injured

Date 21/10/16

A. [signature]
Lt Col R.A.M.C.
O.C., 76th Field Ambulance

132ND Field Ambulance

To O.C. 11TH Royal Sussex. 39TH Div.

Roll of Men Evacuated. (Wounded & Sick)

COY	REG No	RK & NAME	DATE EVACUATED	TO WHERE EVACUATED	SICK OR WOUNDED
D ✓	15504	Pte Parker C. G.	21-10-16	C.C.S.	Wounded
✓	15830	" Hoad G.	"	"	"
D ✓	895	" Bagg G.	"	"	"
✓	2923	4/Cpl Hudson J.	"	"	"
✓	468	Pte Rogers F.	"	"	"
✓	15118	" Greatbatch B.	"	"	"
✓	G/15829	" Harrison F.	"	"	"
C ✓	15491	" Hopps H.	"	"	"
✓	G/15510	" Warren R.	"	"	"
✓	15267	4/Cpl Gathercole H.	"	"	"
✓ C	G/15176	Pte Richardson L.	"	"	"
✓	15710	" Armitage J.	"	"	"
✓	650	" Allrey L. J.	"	"	"
✓ C	4813	4/Cpl Cresford E. V.	"	"	"
✓ B	4864	Pte Green W.	"	"	"
✓ D	G/15812	" Elphick J. H.	"	"	"
✓ F	15147	4/Cpl Brookes R.	"	"	"
✓	G/15168	Pte Moates W.	"	"	"
✓ C	15211	" Daniels S. G.	"	"	"
✓ C	15115	" Churchill D.	"	"	"
✓ B	614	" Matthews J.	"	"	"
✓ D	15846	" Mabbett E.	"	"	"
✓ B	G/15921	4/Cpl Geary H. E.	"	"	"
✓	G/15732	Pte Heymes H.	"	"	"
✓	G/15563	" Ward F. W.	"	"	"
✓	4197	" Ashford R.	"	"	"
✓ B	2745	" Marsh F.	"	"	"
✓	3513	" Manktelow J.	"	"	"
✓	10384	4/Cpl Gammon R. G.	"	"	"
D ✓	911	Pte Dedman A.	"	"	"
✓	3008	Sgt Saeby S. J.	"	"	"
✓	15214	Pte Fuller J.	"	"	"

Cont.

Roll of Men Evacuated (Wounded & Sick)

COY.	REG. NO.	RK	NAME	DATE EVACUATED	WHERE EVACUATED	SICK OR WOUNDED
✓	3/5761	Cpl	Verrall H.C.	21-10-16	C.C.S.	Wounded
C. ✓	3/15221	Pte	Weston W.J.	"	"	"
✓	3/15827	"	Hunt S.J.	"	"	"
✓	15562	"	Sutterby W.H.	"	"	"
✓	4819	"	Larkin H.	"	"	"
✓	15010	"	Starling D.W.	"	"	"
✓	5050	"	Thurley H.	"	"	? "
✓	15228	"	Reeves E.	"	"	"
D ✓	15817	"	French C.	"	"	"
✓	15856	"	Parsons E.G.	"	"	"
✓	4814	"	Sherwood L.	"	"	"
✓	4890	L/Cpl	Edmonds A.J.	"	"	"
✓	15633	Pte	Rolls E.	"	"	"
✓	15036	"	Bailly A.	"	"	"
✓	2970	"	Maryan H.	"	"	"
✓ D	15023	"	Warden J.H.	"	"	"
✓	394	"	Brown G.J.	"	"	"
✓ P.	587	"	Cutler H.	"	"	"
✓ P.	3/15824	"	Harrison C.	"	"	"
✓ C.	5848	"	Smith G.R.	"	"	"
D.	872	Drum	Yeates H.C.	"	D.R.S.	Sick
C.	15132	L/Cpl	Barnett	"	"	"
✓	5719	Pte	Harbridge R.C.	18/10/16	CCS	Wounded
	15770	Sgt	Orton J.C.	"	"	Sick
	704	L/Cpl	Lavington J.J.	"	"	"
✓	15152	Pte	Barber M.	"	"	Wounded
✓	15855	"	Payne M.	"	"	"
	15249	"	Howard C.	"	DRS	Sick
✓	15822	"	Boddy G.J.	"	"	Wounded
	931	"	Gardiner A.S.	"	"	Sick
	15830	"	Laker C.	"	"	"
	9592	"	Holden A.S.	"	"	"

132nd Field Ambulance

To O.C. 11th Royal Sussex   39th Div.

Roll of Men Evacuated (Wounded or Sick)

COY	REG NO.	RK.	NAME	DATE EVACUATED	WHERE EVACUATED	WOUNDED OR SICK
B. ✓	15793	Pte	Bryant H	21-10-16	C.C.S.	Wounded
✓	15729	"	Hammond A.	"	"	"
✓	771	"	Allen R.V.	"	"	Sick
✓	5863	"	Butcher L.G.	"	"	Wounded
✓	15146	"	Barrett A.	"	"	"
✓	15794	"	Burchmore W.	"	"	"
✓	941	"	Harris W.	"	"	"
✓	15435	"	Horner G.Y.	"	"	"
✓	15289	"	Parker A.R.	"	"	"
✓	400	"	Bishop J.	"	"	"
✓	15184	"	Stanforth G.	"	"	"
✓	15508	"	Teale A.V.	18/10/16	DRS	" ?

A Martin Capt. R.A.M.C.
for O.C. 132nd FIELD AMBULANCE.

To O.C. 11 Rhodes

The undermentioned of the Unit under your command been disposed of as follows:—

No.	Rank and Name	Unit	Coy	To Duty	Trans to D.S.	Evac to C.C.S.
491	Cpl Walker W.J. Reported Missing					22/10/16

A. Kinnes
Lt.Col.
R.A.M.C.
O.C., /6 th Field Ambulance

Date 25/10/16

Roll of Wounded

No.	Rank	Name	Date Wounded	Date Admitted to CCS	Sent to
8506	Cpl	Smith S			Sgt
572	Pte	Stewart F. S			W
15058	"	Sommerill S			W
5846	"	Ayrton A			W
5325	L/Cpl	Bencell F			W
15760	Pte	Topham A			W
5225	"	Shorter J.G			W
15638	"	Nicolsons M			W
15037	"	Aislop C.			W
301	L/Cpl	Townsend Rd			W
314	Pte	Hopkins H			W
5447	"	Leonard H			W
5507	"	James A. G			W
15325	Cpl	Hallett Cyril H			W
692	Pte	Lott T			W
15114	"	Glanks J			W
15239	"	Munro F.H.			W
16179	"	Smith A			W
73	"	Newcomb A			W

23 OCT 1916
134th FIELD AMBULANCE

for O.C. 134th FIELD AMBULANCE.
R.A.M.C.

Of 11 Royal Sussex. 39 D.

The undermentioned of the Unit under your command been disposed of as follows:—

No	Rank and Name	Unit	Coy	To Duty	Trans to D.A.S.	Evac to C.C.S.
1085	Pte Phillips A.O.			—		21/10/16.
15237	Pte Duffels A.H		R			21/10/16.

Date. 22/10/16.

[signature] R.A.M.C.
O.C. 76th Field Ambulance

[stamp: 76th FIELD AMBULANCE R.A.M.C.]

"C" Form (Duplicate).
MESSAGES AND SIGNALS.

Army Form C. 2123.
(In books of 50's in duplicate.)
No. of Message ....

Service Instructions.

Charges to Pay. £ s. d.

Office Stamp.

Handed in at .... Office .... m. Received .... m.

TO   R1

Sender's Number	Day of Month	In reply to Number	
0310	22/10		A A A

No. 35632 Pte Cooper was wounded yesterday aaa This man was attending the bombing school

FROM

PLACE & TIME

A. Coy   11th R.S.F.   Oct 23rd

Amended Casualty List

Killed
15295   Pte. Snelling. R.G.
 5628   "   Bredwell. W.

Wounded.
15720   "   Pater. E.A.
 5634   "   Stone. A.J.
 4125   "   Heaver. H.

Missing
  155   L/Sgt. Carter. R.C.
 5355   Pte. Cribb. H.
                Clayton R.W.
15114   "   Clarke. J.
 5795   "   Coley. L.
15520   "   Cox. F.
15729   "   Hammond. F.A.
15250   "   Kett. N.
 5239   "   Minns. F.H.
15860   "   Richards. L.
15780   "   Spencer. F.
15276   "   Beveridge. P.S.
15853   L/Cpl. Powell. J. (sick in Carloy)

J.H. Chuzet.

The undermentioned of the Unit under your command been disposed of as follows:-

No.	Rank and Name	Unit	Coy	On Duty	Trans to	Evac to C.C.S.
15695	Pte Blackwell E.		B		51 F Amb 22/10/16	—

Date 23/10/16

76TH FIELD AMBULANCE.
No................
Date................

O.C. 76th Field Ambulance
A.A.M.C.

Roll of Mourners: 11th Sussex

No.	Rank	Name	Date	Disposal	
15183	Cpl	Steele W.	B'ly	23-10-16 W.	C.O.S
94	L-Cpl	Page N	"	"	"
15199	Pte	Hutchinson B	" D.	"	"
15052	"	Pilgrim ?	" B	"	"
15170	"	Noto ?	" C	"	"
5626	"	Richardson C.	" B	"	"
237	"	Lingo ? W.	" B	"	"
815	L-Cpl	Keay ? F.	" A	"	"	Jury Missing
15877	Pte	Dean ?	" B	"	"
15293	"	Simpson G.W.	" B	"	"
812	Sgt	Stanning A.	" D	"	"	Essop Missing
15276	Pte	Beveridge P.S.	" A	"	"
15150	"	Barton H	" C	"	"

O.C. 134th FIELD AMBULANCE R.A.M.C.

134th FIELD AMBULANCE
24 OCT 1916

"A" Form.
MESSAGES AND SIGNALS.

Army Form C. 2121.

TO {	RV		

Sender's Number	Day of Month	In reply to Number	
OR 14	23/10		AAA

Casualties for 21st October AAA Killed T/2/Lt. G W DOOGAN AAA T/2/Lt. F. H. H. IVENS AAA T/2nd Lt. F H G SALTER AAA OR 11 AAA Wounded T 2/Lt V. H. B D'IVERNOIS AAA T/2/Lt P J HAYES AAA OR 118 AAA Missing OR 134

From
Place R 1
Time

Nominal Roll of Evacuations & Transfers
for Week Ending Oct. 26. 1916   1/4th R. Sussex

Reg. No	Rank	Name	Date	Sick or Wounded	Where sent
15194	Pte	Yelley H. ✓	24-10-16	S.	? R.S. Maritype
15698	L/Cpl	Bunford B. ✓	"	"	"
15770	Pte	Jennings J.P. ✓	"	"	39
972	"	Savage W.T. ✓	"	"	"
15531	"	Richardson E.A. ✓	"	"	"
c.15262	Cpl	Adams A.J. ✓	"	"	"
3894	L/Cpl	Tyler J.H. ✓			
80	L/Cpl	Lightfoot A.S. ✓			

[Stamp: 133rd FIELD AMBULANCE 25 OCT 1916]

R. Pyemonte Lieut Col
O.C. 134th FIELD AMBULANCE

Nominal Roll of Evacuations & Transfers
for Week Ending Oct 16 1916

Regt No	Rank	Name	Where sent.
562	Pte	Williams J	11th R Sussex
15724	"	Ernest R	
3952	"	Bopping J	These N.C.O. & 9 Men
887	L/Cpl	Batchelor S	were sent to 39 D.R.S
5199	Pte	Hatfield. W	instead of 66.3 as
692	L/Cpl	Hall. Y.	previously advised
15276	Pte	Beveridge P.	
763	"	Newcomb. A	
852	Sgt	Stenning a	
15183	Cpl	Steele W	
94	L/Cpl	Page H	
15199	Pte	Wilkinson A	
15052	"	Pilgrim J	
15877	"	Dean J	
15561	"	Sullivan J	
15914	"	Lilley H	

R.P. Macmillan R.A.M.C.
O.C. 134th FIELD AMBULANCE.

134th FIELD AMB
25 OCT 1916

"A" Form.
MESSAGES AND SIGNALS.
Army Form C. 2121.

TO: O C A Company.

Sender's Number.	Day of Month.	In reply to Number.		AAA
GH 4	30/10/16			
Your	message	just	received	AAA
Let	me	know	when	you
are	in	touch	with	right
and	left	AAA	Presume	the
rockets	you	brought	up	with
you	are	good	AAA	what
does	Caldwell	wish	done	about
his	Lewis	guns	do	you
want	2	more	teams	sent
up	AAA	Report	to	me
fully	when	you	can.	

From: O.C.
Time: 2.15 pm

"A" Form.
Army Form C. 2121
MESSAGES AND SIGNALS.

Prefix ...... Code ...... m.	Words	Charge	This message is on a/c of:	Recd. at ...... m.
Office of Origin and Service Instructions.	Sent		.... Service.	Date ......
	At ...... m.			From ......
	To			
	By		(Signature of "Franking Officer.")	By ......

TO { O. C. D. Coy.

Sender's Number.	Day of Month.	In reply to Number.		A A A
*GH 5	30/10/16			

Are	you	all	right	now
and	are	you	in	touch
with	the	Coy	on	my
left	and	right	AAA.	Let
me	know	your	dispositions	
as	soon	as	possible	AAA
How	about	you	SOS	rockets.

From: O.C.
Place:
Time: 3.15 pm.

"A" Form.
Army Form C. 2121.
MESSAGES AND SIGNALS.

Prefix	Code	m.	Words	Charge	This message is on a/c of:	Recd. at	m.
Office of Origin and Service Instructions.		Sent			Service.	Date	
		At	m.			From	
		To				By	
		By		(Signature of "Franking Officer.")			

TO { O C B Coy.

| Sender's Number. | Day of Month. | In reply to Number. | |
| GH 6 | 30/10/16 | — | A A A |

Send up 1 Lewis gun and team to report to A Company. This guide will show you the way.

From   O C
Place
Time   3.15 pm

(Z)   R Harris

"A" Form.
MESSAGES AND SIGNALS.
Army Form C. 2121

Prefix .... Code .... m.	Words	Charge	This message is on a/c of:	Recd. at .... m.
Office of Origin and Service Instructions.	Sent		.... Service.	Date ....
	At .... m.			From ....
	To			
	By		(Signature of "Franking Officer.")	By ....

TO — O.C. A. Coy:—

Sender's Number.	Day of Month.	In reply to Number.	
* G4 of	30/10/16		AAA

Message received AAA. I know you have had a real hard time of it and the men too AAA very sorry to hear of your casualties especially Shirley AAA You need not send down to me tonight unless you have anything to report AAA. Have sent up to you rations for tomorrow and shall not send up more at present as they always get spilt and spoilt AAA. I shall try to put a light outside HQrs tonight to guide runners to you then AAA. Do not forget listening posts they are most essential if

From — you can manage it AAA. Are
Place — you in touch with the V.M. Gs.
Time —

"A" Form.
MESSAGES AND SIGNALS.

Army Form C. 2121

If you have you should get the Lewis touch and cooperate. AAA I have sent up a gun & team from B Coy to relieve the Herts gun and in place of the team you had knocked out AAA. Be sure you get your Lewis guns safe and bring them away with you. AAA Also we must not leave any wounded in the line. so help me if you in trouble in this respect AAA. What read have you in the line if urgently required I can send you up 6 boxes.

From **C.O.**
Time **4.30 PM**

"A" Form.
MESSAGES AND SIGNALS.
Army Form C. 2121.

Prefix .... Code .... m.	Words	Charge	This message is on a/c of:	Recd. at .... m.
Office of Origin and Service Instructions.				Date ....
	Sent		.... Service.	From ....
	At .... m.			
	To			
	By	(Signature of "Franking Officer.")	By ....

TO: O C D Coy

| Sender's Number. | Day of Month. | In reply to Number. | AAA |
| G H 8 | 30/10/16 | | |

Message received. AAA Many thanks know you have had a hard time of it and the men too. AAA If possible put out listening posts they are most essential AAA What s[trength] ca[n] have you in the line AAA What casualties have you had. AAA Tell Caldwell that before I received his note I sent up 1 Lewis gun and team this should be sufficient to replace his casualties. AAA You now have rations for tomorrow & I shall not send up more at present. AAA You need not send me the 2 hourly report tonight unless you have anything to report the mud is too bad :—

From
Place
Time C O. 4.45 pm

The above may be forwarded as now corrected. (Z)

Censor.   Signature of Addressor or person authorised to telegraph in his name.
* This line should be erased if not required.

"A" Form.
Army Form C. 2121.
MESSAGES AND SIGNALS.

TO **Lieut Caldwell.**

On receipt of a message saying that 2 L.G. Teams had been knocked out I sent up 1 Reserve team from B Coy. This may not be quite what you wanted but you can get your men from this team to replace casualties AAA Tonight hope to mark Bn HQ with a camp fire mirror.

From C.O.
Time 4.45 pm

"A" Form.
Army Form C. 2121

MESSAGES AND SIGNALS.

TO: RV.

Sender's Number: GA 9
Day of Month: 30/10/16
AAA

Situation now quieter AAA heavy shelling about 2pm on our front & support lines. AAA Our artillery active.

From: R.1
Time: 4.50 pm.

"A" Form.
Army Form C. 2121.
MESSAGES AND SIGNALS.

TO R.V.

Sender's Number: GH 10.
Day of Month: 30/10/16.
AAA

Dispositions - 2 Companies and 4
Lewis guns between points 19 and
99. front line (Schwaben), forming
block at point 19. AAA. 1 Company
in support RANSOME TRENCH. AAA
1 Company in Reserve in THIEPVAL AAA
Head Quarters R.25.C.7.2. AAA
Further details with Sketch will
follow later.

From: R.1.
Place:
Time: 8.45 p.m.

"A" Form.
MESSAGES AND SIGNALS.

Army Form C. 2121.

TO: O.C. D. Coy

Sender's Number.	Day of Month.	In reply to Number.		AAA
* GH 3	30/10/16	—		
Your	message	received	AAA	Let
me	know	how	you	get
on	and	do	not	let
HERTS	go	till	your	relief
is	complete	AAA	the	missing
platoon	may	have	been	taken
up	by	some	other	route
owing	to	shelling	or	may
be	sheltering	in	some	dug
out	AAA	let	me	know
what	S.a.a	you	have	in
the	front	line.		

From: CO
Place / Time: 12.25 pm

Signature: G H Ansell

"A" Form — MESSAGES AND SIGNALS.
Army Form C. 2121.

TO: RV

GH 9   30/10/16.

Situation report AAA There is no telephone communication with front line and it is pitch dark runners keep on losing the way AAA The 2 front line Companies and 4 Lewis guns are in position (2.45 pm) and are in touch with Coys on right and left AAA Weather conditions have been very bad AAA Relief was spotted by the Boch artillery and much delayed and some confusion AAA The Boch artillery shelled heavily for over an hour casualties at present reported roughly 1 Officer wounded severely 3 men killed and some 12 wounded AAA 1 Officer carried away sick AAA Head Quarters have been well shelled.

From: CO R1.

Time: 8.40 pm (Z)

"A" Form.
MESSAGES AND SIGNALS.

Army Form C. 2121.

Prefix .... Code .... m.	Words	Charge	This message is on a/c of:	Recd. at .... m.
Office of Origin and Service Instructions.				Date ....
	Sent		.... Service.	From ....
	At .... m.			
	To			
	By		(Signature of "Franking Officer.")	By ....

TO O.C. A Coy.

Sender's Number.	Day of Month.	In reply to Number.	AAA
GH 11	30/10/16		

Don't worry about sending runners every 2 hours and pass on to D Coy. AAA Also try and get enclosed messages delivered 4 pm each. AAA Am very glad you put out listening posts. Hope D Coy have done the same AAA. Thanks for next clear message. AAA. Don't worry if runners do not return AAA I have a light on my Head QS to guide runners. AAA Will send up water first thing tomorrow morning. AAA Cpl Loft & Sgt Howlett are here and will guide up water in the morning.

From O.C.
Place
Time 9.5 pm.

"A" Form.
MESSAGES AND SIGNALS.
Army Form C. 2121

TO — D

Sender's Number: G¹¹ 812 Day of Month: 30/10/16   AAA

Arrangements have been made to send up coolies first thing in the morning and two of your men who have been detained here will increase the party up AAA I sent some messages up to you via A Coy 2 hrs ago AAA I also sent up 3 jars rum to both front line Coys to OC A Coy it is all available other jars lost AAA Am sure you are doing all you can to improve matters sorry you are having such a bad time AAA You need not send runners in one every 2 hrs only when you have any urgent message to report AAA Let me have your disposition in detail when you can in the morning.

From: disposition
Place: in the morning
Time:

O.C. 10.55 p.m.

"A" Form.
MESSAGES AND SIGNALS.

Army Form C. 2121.

TO: O.C. A & C Companies

Sender's Number: G K 14 Day of Month: 31/10/16

AAA

Am sending up rolies to O.C. C Coy must send for them aaa The rations you have must last you till you are relieved about midday tomorrow aaa He go back to the same place he came from aaa Pay special attention to the men's feet and have them rubbed without fail and prevent trench feet at all costs aaa Have the 12 "B" got a bombing post in FIENNES STREET that is just S of Point 19 your left post aaa Let me know what ammunition you have in your line

Urgent

From: C.O.
Time: 8.15 am

"A" Form — MESSAGES AND SIGNALS.
Army Form C. 2121

TO: O.C. H.C. Coys.

Sender's Number: GH 14 **Day of Month:** 31/10/16

AAA

Am sending up lorries to Coy HQ to meet need for this aan. AAA The patrols you have must last you till you are relieved about midday tomorrow AAA we go back to the same place we came from AAA. Pay special attention to the mens feet and have them rubbed without fail and prevent trench feet at all costs AAA Have the 12th Bn got a bombing post in PIERRES STREET that is just South of Pont 19 your left post AAA let me know what ammunition you have in your line. urgent.

From: C.O.
Place:
Time: 8.15 a.m.

"A" Form.
MESSAGES AND SIGNALS.

Army Form C. 2121.
No. of Message ....

Prefix ...... Code ...... m.	Words	Charge	This message is on a/c of:	Recd. at .... m.
Office of Origin and Service Instructions.	Sent		.... Service.	Date ....
	At ...... m.			From ....
	To			
	By		(Signature of "Franking Officer.")	By ....

TO { O-C A B C D Coys.

Sender's Number.	Day of Month.	In reply to Number.	
*G H 15	31/10/16		A A A

Orders just received from the Division that every occupied dug out is to be kept in good repair mud cleared from entrance and steps and every effort made to reclaim and make every possible dug out please get on with this without delay AAA. With regard to the relief tomorrow detail officers juniors so to thoroughly reconnoitre the best way for bringing up the relief and the best way of carrying it out. Take every possible trouble to prevent casualties. OC Coys will be responsible that the juniors know the way AAA being fine juniors will also be required AAA Relief will take place same time as yesterday AAA Men signed of to see that relieving unit has taken over good position.

From ....
Place C O
Time 10.10 A.M.

The above may be forwarded as now corrected. (Z)
Censor. Signature of Addressee or person authorised to telegraph in his name.
* This line should be erased if not required.
225,000 W 14042—M 44. H. W. & V., Ld. 12/15.

"A" Form.
MESSAGES AND SIGNALS.

Army Form C. 2121

TO: ~~O.C.~~ ~~And Coy~~ R.V.

Sender's Number: Q.4.18
Day of Month: 31/10/16

AAA

Situation normal until 4 pm except for constant shelling of C.T. ATTR 4pm enemy opened heavy barrage on entire front line and also 4.15 pm heavy barrage on support line and C.T. ATTR enemy put up 2 white rockets and after some interval 2 red rockets or lights ATTR our guns light and heavy replying ATTR situation still obscure but no sign of infantry movement up to date.

From Place: R1
Time: 4.55 pm

"A" Form.
MESSAGES AND SIGNALS.

Army Form C. 2121.

Sender's Number.	Day of Month.	In reply to Number.	AAA
* GH 16	31	96/M	

| Receipt | for | maps | given | to |
| bearer | on | 29th | | |

From R1

Signature of Addressee: E. C. Blunden

116th Brigade.

39th Division.

―――――――

11th BATTALION

THE ROYAL SUSSEX REGIMENT

NOVEMBER 1 9 1 6

9.E.
Orhick

Vol 9

War Diary
of
1st B. Royal Sussex Regt

Nov 1st 1916 to 30 Nov 1916

VOL IX

WAR DIARY or INTELLIGENCE SUMMARY

Army Form C. 2118

Place	Date	Hour	Summary of Events and Information	Remarks and references to Appendices
SCHWABEN REDOUBT	Nov. 1		Battalion relieved by 1/6TH CHESHIRES whose front coys. was guided into their positions without loss; but as our men were moving down they were noticed and heavy shelling (5.9's and 102 mm) began at once. Eventually the Bn. got clear with very few casualties, but those of the CHESHIRES in the front line were considerable. In view of the terrible state of the trenches and exhaustion of the men this relief was carried out splendidly. It began at 8.45 a.m. and was reported complete at 1.20 p.m. After notifying the Bn. returned to Dugouts in S. and CENTRE BUFF. Afternoon spent in foot-rubbing and rest. Our total casualties during this tour in SCHWABEN REDOUBT 2ND LT. PERRY Wounded (afterwards died): 3 OR's killed, 23 Wounded, and 5 Missing.	
CENTRE BLUFFS	2		Rest and re-equipment. Lewis Crew + Stretcher Bearer Classes. A wet morning but fair afternoon.	
SENLIS	3		Battalion marched back to SENLIS arriving about 12 noon. Fine weather prevailed. In the evening all the old originals and some others went to 18 DIVISIONAL FOLLIES ~~Pantomime party~~.	
	4		5 Officers and 250 O.R. paraded at 5.30 a.m. for Working Party, but after considerable delay received orders to stand by. They eventually proceeded in the afternoon. Weather good.	
RIVER LEFT	5		Battalion relieved 16TH NOTTS & DERBY in RIVER LEFT SECTION, less No 6 Platoon (B Coy) isolated for Diphtheria and left at Transport Lines. Battalion was thus disposed: C Coy in FRONT LINE RIGHT, B Coy in MILLS POST (LEFT): remainder in Support in PAISLEY AV. 2/Lt. J.S CASSELS took out a patrol to capture a prisoner if possible but the Bosche was lying very low.	
	6		At 12.30 p.m. the Bn. was relieved by the 16TH NOTTS & DERBY and marched to former billets at SENLIS. All in billets by 4 p.m. Zeppelins over at 11 p.m.	
SENLIS	7		Every available man employed for Working Party at AVELUY and NAB VALLEY. Parade was at 7.30 a.m. Heavy rain throughout the day. The tasks given could have been done better by about 120 more and reports were sent in to 116 Bde. by CAPT. COPLING and 2/LT. BLUNDEN. A few shells from a high velocity gun fell in SENLIS (on BOUZINCOURT RD).	
		10 p.m	2/LT. LEWIS joined the Bn. from the H.A.C. CAPT. A.P. FORD went to Field Ambulance suffering from Trench fever and was replaced by CAPT. MILNE. 8 casualties rejoined the Battalion.	

WAR DIARY
or
INTELLIGENCE SUMMARY

(Erase heading not required.)

Army Form C. 2118

Place	Date	Hour	Summary of Events and Information	Remarks and references to Appendices
SENLIS	Nov. 8		Troops rested. Church Service in afternoon. 7 Casualties rejoined Bn. Heather bad.	E.B.
	9		Heather better. Brigadier-General HORNBY inspected boots, and the C.O. inspected Billets. Orders received to take over SCHWABEN REDOUBT next day.	E.B.
	10		Battalion relieved the 1/1st CAMBS. in SCHWABEN REDOUBT, and went fortunate in having no casualties on the relief. B & C Companies were in the front-line, D being in Support and A in Reserve in THIEPVAL. Sergeant ASHFORD contrived to put Bt.H.Q. in communication not only with the Reserve and Support Coys but also with both front-line Coys. The Battalion looked very hard at clearing out dugouts. A Coy. carried Rations etc. to the front-line. 1.O.R. was killed while carrying S.A.A. and 3 wounded. B Coy. continued work on three T-saps in front of SPUTTER WAY. A number of dead were buried by parties detailed only for this work.	
SCHWABEN REDOUBT	11		Dull and heavy. Organised bombardment of enemy line in the Early morning drew only moderate retaliation. Work carried on; in the evening a Bombing Raid under Serjeant Stickland attempted to rush the German Block R 19 a 91 but found it very thickly wired and could not force an entry. They bombed it and managed to catch two prisoners; and waited outside the wire for further orders. These were that they were to withdraw. Prisoners were of the 95th Regt.	E.B.
	12		Dull but no rain. Another morning bombardment was carried out by our gunners and the enemy retaliated with 10 minutes' Shrapnel and whizzbang fire followed by methodical "Krumps" on our front and support lines. During the day four fresh dugouts were cleared in THIEPVAL. The front line companies were relieved after midnight by the assaulting troops due to attack on the 13th; but the sentry posts in RIDDELL TRENCH were retained until the attack had been made when they too withdrew to THIEPVAL. (1. O.R. killed).	E.B.
	13		Battalion in THIEPVAL. At 4 p.m. orders came through for 300 men and a proportion of officers under Capt. COOLING to carry coils of wire and wire pickets to point R 19 c 01, and a patrol of 1 officer and 1 runner were immediately sent up to find out the best way. They had a lively	E.B.

WAR DIARY or INTELLIGENCE SUMMARY

(Erase heading not required.)

Army Form C. 2118

Place	Date	Hour	Summary of Events and Information	Remarks and references to Appendices
THIEPVAL	13		Journey and onwards their mark, almost reaching GRANDCOURT. Eventually returning via HANSA LINE, SERB WAY, ST PIERRE DIVION, MILL ROAD & THIEPVAL WOOD, they reported a heavy barrage behind SCHWABEN and a worse on the HANSA LINE. The orders were then modified and the party carried the wire up to the SCHWABEN REDOUBT, point 86. The Battalion went back to huts in PIONEER RD.	E.B.
PIONEER RD	14		Battalion moved at 1.30 p.m. to WARLOY. A German plane bombed this place and fired with a maxim on the roads the same night.	E.B.
WARLOY	15		Battalion marched from WARLOY to DOULLENS (about 13 miles). Though in many cases tired feet gave much trouble, all ranks did well and came in with a swing to DOULLENS to the regimental songs. Motor lorries assisted in moving transport.	E.B.
DOULLENS	16		Battalion in rest.	E.B.
DOULLENS	17		2/Lts AMON, WRIGHT and CHESTER joined the Battalion. Battalion made preparations for entrainment and left DOULLENS for the North at about 2.30 p.m. They detrained at POPERINGHE and marched to M CAMP which they reached between 4 and 5 in the morning of the 18th. The weather was bitterly cold.	E.B.
M CAMP	18		Battalion in rest.	E.B.
	19		Cleaning up and inspections by Company Commanders.	E.B.
	20		Inspections. Games Committee begun. Battalion Orders arranged by 2/Lt. J.S CASSELS in the evening	E.B.
	21		A fine clear day. C.O. inspected the Battalion in marching order in the forenoon.	E.B.
	22		Training begun. Specialist courses for LEWIS GUNNERS, BOMBERS, WIRERS and SNIPERS. Squad and Platoon Drill under Coy. arrangements. Bayonet fighting and Physical Training. Weather fine.	E.B.
	23		Inspection of Bn. including Transport, Kitchens, etc. by Corps Commander.	E.B.
	24		Fine. Routine work carried on.	E.B.
	25.		Rain all day. Training and lectures inside huts. 2 Coys to BATHS at COUTHOVE	E.B.
	26.		Colder. Baths for rest of Bn. Divine Services.	E.B.

WAR DIARY or INTELLIGENCE SUMMARY

Army Form C. 2118

Place	Date	Hour	Summary of Events and Information	Remarks and references to Appendices
M Camp	27/11/16		Battalion Route March with First Line Transport, via HATOU, about 8½ miles.	E.B.
	28		C.O's Inspection. Routine training.	E.B.
	29		Regimental Exercise without troops for Coy Commanders & L.G.B.	E.B.
	30		C.O's Inspection. Battalion Drill. Baths for a part of the Bn. Night alarm assembly practised.	E.B.
			ADDENDUM	
			MILITARY CROSS awarded to 2/Lt. C.A. ALLEN, 2/Lt. G. SALTER, CAPT. C.L. MICHELL	
			MILITARY MEDAL awarded to SERGT. COX, SERGT. HOPKINS, SERGT. PATRICK, SERGT. BALL, SERGT. ALLCHORN, SERGT. DAVEY, SERGT. HUKINSON, PTE. BISHOP, PTE. HORTON, PTE. TAYLOR, PTE. VINTER, PTE. RICH, PTE. SHIRLEY, PTE. BAILEY, CPL. DYBELL, PTE. BAILEY	E.B.
			CAPT. J.H. COOLING granted Temporary Rank of MAJOR whilst 2/C in command. 2/Lt. F. CASSELS, 2/Lt. C.A. ALLEN, 2/Lt. G. SALTER, 2/Lt. R.F. DREW appointed T/Captains while commanding Coys.	

Signed /Lt. Col.
Commanding XI TH R. Sussex R.

SECRET.

Copy No. ....

OPERATION ORDER NO. 50.

RELIEF. 1. The 11th Bn. Royal Sussex Regiment will relieve the 16th Notts and Derby Regt. in the RIVER LEFT SECTION to-morrow 5.11.16.

ADVANCE PARTY. 2. 1 Officer per Company and 1 N.C.O. per platoon will will proceed to take over the trenches.

DISPOSITIONS. 3.
    1. Front Line Right.   "C" Company
    2. MILL POST)
      (1 Officer & 35.O.R.) "B" Company
    3. Supports.) "A" Company, "D" Company
      PAISLEY AVENUE) and remainder of "B" Coy.

GUIDES. 4. The Battalion will be met by guides 800 yards beyond LANCASHIRE DUMP where the tram line leaves the road, at the following hours:-
    Advance Party.   11.0. a.m.
    Main Body.   12.0. noon

ROUTE. 5. BOUZINCOURT - MARTINSART WOOD - AVELUY WOOD - LANCASHIRE DUMP.

MOVEMENT. 6. The Battalion will move off in the following order:-
    1. MILL POST party, under 2/Lt Lapworth and one Lewis Gun.
    2. "C" Company plus 1 Lewis Gun, KOYLI WEST.
    3. Bombing Post of 1 N.C.O. and 8 men
    4. Remainder of Company for No 3 Tunnell plus two Lewis Guns.
    5. Headquarters.
    6. "A" Company.
    7. "D" Company.
    8. Remainder of "B" Company.
The main body will move off at 9.0. a.m. Movement will be by platoons at 200 yards distance. After entering AVELUY WOOD all movement will be by sections at 50 yards distance.

DRESS. 7. Fighting Order No 2. Overcoats and waterproof worn rolled on the back. Jerkins will be worn. WATERBOTTLES FULL.

TRANSPORT. 8. All Company packs, Officers valises etc., to be returned to the transport will be stacked outside Companies in a Central position by 8.0. a.m.
Officers Trench Kits, Stores etc., for the trenches will will be stacked separately outside Companies by 8.0. a.m.

REPORTS. 9. Company Commanders will give relieved Company Commanders a written acknowledgement as to the positions taken over. Copies of these acknowledgements together with a report of dispositions with rough sketch will be sent to Battalion H.Q. by 5.0. p.m.

LEWIS GUNS. 10. Dispositions
    1 Lewis Gun in MILL POST. "B" Company.
    1 Lewis Gun in KOYLI WEST. "B" Company.
    2 Lewis Guns in No. 3 TUNNEL "C" Company.

    Lewis Guns will proceed with their Companies.
    Listening Posts will be put out by Comapnies in the
    Front Line. The position of these will be shewn on the
    sketch of dispositions to be sent to Battalion H.Q.
    by 5.0. p.m.

RELIEF COMPLATE.
    11. Relief Compalte will be notified to Battalion H.Q.
    in PAISLEY EVENUE.

                                 (Signed) R.H. LUPTON, Lieut.,
                                   Adjutant, 11th R. Sussex Regt.

4.11.16.

Copy No. 1 to C.O.

SECRET.

OPERATION ORDER NO. 51.   Copy No. 2....

RELIEF.   1. The 11th Bn. Royal Sussex Regt. will be relieved to-day
                    the 6th instant, in the River Left Section by the 18th.
                    Notts and Derby R.R.

GUIDES.   2. Guides will not be required. Leading Platoon of 18th.
                    Notts and Derby will pass LANCASHIRE DUMP at 12 noon.

BILLETS.   3. The Battalion will be billeted in SENLIS.

ADVANCE
PARTIES.   4. 6 N.C.O.'s from "A" Company, 6 from "B" Company, and
                    4 from "D" Company will proceed under an Officer to take
                    over all Billets, leaving Battalion H.Q. at 8.0. a.m.

ROUTE.   5. The Battalion will move by sections as far as the AVELUY
                    end of AVELUY WOOD, thence by platoons at 100 yards interval
                    via PIONEER ROAD, MARTINSART WOOD, NORTHUMBERLAND AVENUE,
                    BOUZINCOURT and SENLIS.

HANDING OVER.   6. Company Commanders will hand over on relief:-
                    (1) All plans and sketches of their dispositions.
                    (2) All reserves of S.A.A. and Mills Grenades.
                    (3) All other Trench Stores.
                    (4) All details of incomplete work and all possible
                         information.
                    They will obtain an acknowledgement from the relieving
                    Company Commanders, which they will leave at Battalion
                    H.Q. on their way down. This applies also to O.C. MILL
                    POST.

CASUALTIES.   7. All casualties must be brought down before the Battalion
                    leaves the trenches.

OFFICERS
KITS.   8. Trench Kits and Mess Boxes will be at the trolley line
                    by 10.00. a.m. Companies will provide any extra pushing
                    parties required.

DISCIPLINE.   9. March discipline will be most carefully attended to during
                    the move. Officers and N.C.O.'s will move up and down their
                    platoons frequently to ensure this.

ALL IN
BILLETS.   10. Company Commanders will lose no time in reporting this to
                    Battalion H.Q. in SENLIS.

RELIEF
COMPLETE.   11. Company Commanders will personally report this to the C.O.
                    on their way down. Also O.C. MILL POST.

                                    (Signed) E.C. BLUNDEN, 2/Lt.,
                                    Asst. Adjutant, 11th R. Sussex Regt.

6.11.16.

Issued at 10.0. a.m.

Copy No. 2 to Adjutant

File   SECRET.

OPERATION ORDER NO. 52.   Copy No........

RELIEF. 1. The 11th Bn. Royal Sussex Regt. will relieve the 16th. Notts and Derby Regt., in the RIVER LEFT SECTION to-morrow morning 7.11.16.

DISPOSITIONS. 2. The following will be the dispositions:-
"D" Company will hold MILL POST, (2/Lt Nayler and 35 other ranks and 1 Lewis Gun)
"A" Company will be Right Front Company plus 3 Lewis Guns.
Headquarters   )
"B" Company.   )
"C" Company   )   PAISLEY DUMP.
Remainder of "D"   )
   Company.   )

LISTENING POSTS. 3. Listening Posts will be put out each night by both MILL POST and RIGHT FRONT COMPANY (at KOYLI WEST)

MAIN BODY. 4. The Main Body will move off at 9.0. a.m. as under:-
Headquarters.
Mill Post Party.
Remainder of "D" Company.
"A" Company.
"B" Company.
"C" Company.

GUIDES. 5. There will be no guides provided. Companies will find their own way to their positions. There will be no ADVANCE PARTIES.

TRAFFIC. 6. Movement will be by platoons at 200 yards distance as far as AVELUY WOOD. Thence by sections at 50 yards distance.

DRESS. 7. Fighting Order No. 2. with waterproof sheets and Great-Coats rolled. WATERBOTTLES FULL.

TRANSPORT. 8. All packs, Officers Kits, Company stores etc., for removal to Transport Lines will be stacked outside Companies at 8.0. a.m.
Trench Stores, Officers Kits etc., will be stacked in a separate pile outside Companies at 8.0. a.m., Officers are warned to take as little as possible as there is grave danger of losing what they have.

DISCIPLINE. 9. No man will consume any portion of his Iron Ration or drink from his waterbottle without permission from an Officer.

BILLETS. 10. Billets must be left scrupulously clean and tidy. O.C.'s Companies will inspect their billets before leaving. A cleaning party will be left behind of 1 N.C.O. and 2 men per platoon. These will assemble at SENLIS CHURCH when their work has been done, and will be marched to the trenches by the senior N.C.O. present.

RELIEF COMPLETE. 11. Reports of Relief Complete will be rendered to Bn. H.Q. as soon as possible after relief.

(Signed) R.H. LUPTON, Capt.,
Adjutant, 11th Royal Sussex Regt.

6.11.16.
Issued at 7.15. p.m.

Copy No.   to

SECRET.

OPERATION ORDER No. ..   Army No. ....

READIEF. 1. The 11th Br. Royal Sussex Regt., will relieve the
             1/4th Queens Regt., in the River Right Section
             (Riverbank Redoubt) to-morrow ....

DISPOSITIONS. 2. The dispositions of the Battalion in the line will be as
                 follows:-
                 "A" Company.   Left Front Company.
                 "B" Company.   Right Front Company.
                 "C" Company.   Support Company.
                 "D" Company.   Reserve Company.

GUIDES. 3. Guides will be provided by the 1/1st Queens. In addition
           Companies which have been in the Front line before will
           supply guides for the present Front Line Companies and
           Reserve Companies for the present Reserve Companies, as
           arranged this morning.

RESERVE
COMPANIES. 4. Guides will meet "D" and "C" Companies at the top of
              TRAFALGAR AVENUE (Point ??) at ?. ?.?.
              These Companies will therefore move off at 11. ?.?.
              "D" Company leading.

ADVANCE
PARTY. 5. Support and Reserve Companies will send an advance
          party.
          "C" Company. ? O.C. Company and 1 N.C.O. per platoon.
          "D" Company. ? O.C. Company and 1 N.C.O. per platoon.
          This party will start at ??.??. a.m. and will be met
          by guides at Point ?? at ..... a.m.

MAIN BODY. 6. The Main Body will start as under:-
              Headquarters, "A" Company, "B" Company.
              Guides will meet these at ??.??. a.m. at Point ??.

ROUTE. 7. BUSHYCOURT - CARTHENARY WOOD - FITCHER ROAD - BLACK
          HORSE BRIDGE - AVENELLE - POINT ?.??.

TRAFFIC. 8. All movement as far as AVENELLE WOOD will be by platoons
            about ?? yards distance. Thence by sections at ?? yards.

DRESS. 9. Fighting Order No. ?. Greatcoats and Waterproof sheets
          rolled on back. WATERBOTTLES FULL.

BOMBS AND
RATIONS. 10. Extra bombs at the rate of ?? of each will be carried.
             Rations for the following 24 hours will also be carried.
             These will be distributed to the men in ??????? village.

DISCIPLINE. 11. All men must be fully impressed upon them that their
                rations are to last them 24 hours and that no more will
                be forthcoming. Water must be used as sparingly as
                possible as supply of it is difficult.

TRANSPORT. 12. All Company stores, Officers Mess, kits etc., for removal
               to Transport Lines will be stacked outside Companies at
               ?.?.?.
               All Trench Stores, Officers Trench kits, etc., will be
               stacked in separate piles outside Companies at ?? a.m.

COOKS. 13. Company Cooks will be accompanied by the Reserve Cooking
           and all the ava..., will be made there and conveyed to
           the Front Line by Ration Limbers.

                                 (Signed) R.H. LEVER, Capt.
                                 Adjutant, 11th Royal Sussex Regt.

116th Brigade.
39th Division.

11th BATTALION

THE ROYAL SUSSEX REGIMENT

DECEMBER 1 9 1 6

10.E
Hotchkis

Confidential Vol 10

War Diary
of
1st Br Royal Sussex Regt
for
the month of December 1916

Vol 10

Army Form C. 2118.

WAR DIARY
or
INTELLIGENCE SUMMARY.
(Erase heading not required.)

Instructions regarding War Diaries and Intelligence Summaries are contained in F. S. Regs., Part II. and the Staff Manual respectively. Title pages will be prepared in manuscript.

Place	Date	Hour	Summary of Events and Information	Remarks and references to Appendices
M CAMP	DEC. 1		Daily training and inspections by Commanders. Issues of new Box Respirators.	S.B.
	2		Gas tests with P.H.G. and Box Respirators in the morning for specialists under C.O. Capt. A.G.L.OWEN joined the Bn.	S.B.
	3		Divine Service taken by C.O. and Y.M.C.A. Hut. Capt. J.H. COLLINS rejoined from Leave.	S.B.
	4		Inspection by C.O. Games in afternoon.	S.B.
	5		Battalion marched to POPERINGHE and entrained. Entrained at ST OMER and marched to ZELCEM via MOULLE. Gas &.C.M.	S.B.
MOULLE	6		G.H. HARRISON went on leave to England. Capt. OWEN took command. 2nd Lt. VIALER, BARLOW and WHITLEY joined the Bn.	S.B.
	7		Battalion rested. Cleaned up billets + kits. Gas tests and repeated daily until the 14th Aug. Returned to billets 4.30 p.m.	S.B.
			Battalion marched out about 2 miles from MOULLE to construct rifle ranges under R.E. Returned to billets 4.30 p.m.	
			Extract from GAZETTE :- T/Lieut F.CASSELS to be T/Captain & been seconded for Service from Sept. 4th 1918	S.B.
			T/A/Lt. E.BARTON to be T/Lieut. into seconding from Sept 4th 1918	
	8		Battalion digging rifle ranges until 3 pm.	S.B.
	9		Battalion digging rifle ranges in morning. Games in afternoon.	S.B.
	10		Digging a.m. Football p.m.	S.B.
	11		Heavy rain, consequently no digging took place. Lectures in billets upon gas, rifle, discipline etc.	S.B.
	12		Digging resumed. Training for Lewis Gunners began.	S.B.
	13		Digging. Games in afternoon.	S.B.
	14		Digging. 1 Coy. to Baths in afternoon. Capt. COLLING to G.H.Q.	S.B.
	15		Battalion left MOULLE and entrained at ST MOMELIN via CHEESE MARKET POPERINGHE to ASYLUM ST YPRES. Relief am.	S.B.
YPRES N. (CANAL BANK)	16		Marched N. of YPRES to dugouts in CANAL BANK casualty 1/1st HERTS. Relief Quick, completed by 8.30 p.m.	S.B.
(HILL TOP LEFT)	17		Patrolling, gas tests, and hut inspections in morning. After dark the Bn. successfully relieved XIII G.R.S.R. in front line (CHANGED LIAKE)	S.B.
	18		Slight enemy shelling at LA BELLE ALLIANCE + FOCH FM. Patrols - strong as usual	S.B.
	19		Slight enemy shelling at FOCH FM and LA BELLE ALLIANCE do. 2nd Lieut. M.C. OSBORN joined Bn.	S.B.
(CANAL BANK)	20		Quick.	S.B.
			Battalion relieved in front-line by XIth R.S.R. and returned to dugouts in CANAL BANK	S.B.

Army Form C. 2118.

WAR DIARY
or
INTELLIGENCE SUMMARY.
(Erase heading not required.)

Instructions regarding War Diaries and Intelligence Summaries are contained in F. S. Regs., Part II. and the Staff Manual respectively. Title pages will be prepared in manuscript.

Place	Date Dec.	Hour	Summary of Events and Information	Remarks and references to Appendices
CANAL BANK	21		Battalion in reserve. Parades and inspections under Coy. arrangements. Working parties provided for Front Line. 1st Reconnoitring Party sent off to sector life of that part held by us. Visiting party provided.	E.B.
	22		As 21st. 2nd Reconnoitring Party.	E.B.
	23		Battalion employed as above in morning, but in evening quietly relieved by 1/1st HERTS. & returned to E. CAMP	E.B.
E. CAMP	24		General cleaning up and company inspections. Lt.-Col. G.H. HARRISON returned to the Battalion. Christmas services held by C.O. Xmas Christmas dinner visited by C.O., 2nd in command and Adjutants.	E.B.
	25		Boxing Day. Rest and celebration combined	E.B.
	26			E.B.
	27		Training started. Inspection and Rifle Drill in Full Marching Order (C.O.'s parade).	E.B.
	28		Route March & Specialist Courses. C.O. & 1st Party reconnoitre front line at BOESINGHE.	E.B.
	29		Training under Coy. arrangements. 2nd Party reconnoitred BOESINGHE Line.	E.B.
	30		Bn. marched from E. Camp to relieve 10th SOUTH WALES BORDERS in BOESINGHE front line. Quite relief, complete 8 p.m. Patrols of one & No Man's Land to in front of Stephens Line. Same night. Have been clearing dirt.	E.B.
	31		Bill working and nothing doing. Brigadier-General Commanding inspected trenches through day.	E.B.

ADDENDUM

DISTINCTIONS
Lieut. Col. G.H. HARRISON awarded D.S.O.
136 Sergt. H.A. ASHFORD   "   MILITARY MEDAL
1171 Cpl. G.A. SARGENT   "   "
1084 L/Cpl. J.C. PERRY   "   "
373 Pte. P. WHITTON   "   "
307 Pte. H.E. FISHER Bedf.   "   "

G.H. Harrison
Lt Col
1/1st Royal Beds Regt
1/1/17

11 E
h sheet

Vol XI

Calcutta

1st Bn Royal Sussex Regt

War Diary

4 mnths of January 1918

Vol XI

Army Form C. 2118.

WAR DIARY
or
INTELLIGENCE SUMMARY.
(Erase heading not required.)

Instructions regarding War Diaries and Intelligence Summaries are contained in F. S. Regs., Part II. and the Staff Manual respectively. Title pages will be prepared in manuscript.

Place	Date	Hour	Summary of Events and Information	Remarks and references to Appendices
BOESINGHE	Jan. 1st		Battalion in trenches. Minenwerfers busy especially on Belgian front.	E/3
	2nd		Minenwerfers again busy, and M.G. General in front line trenches.	E/3
	3rd		Are relieved without casualties by 14th HANTS and marches to relieve billets at ROUSEL FARM, ELVERDINGHE. Capt. R.H. Lupton goes to Corps H.Q.	E/3
ROUSEL FM.	4th		Rest and cleaning. Brigade working parties supplied in evening. Camp maintenance and improvements begun.	E/3
	5th		Working parties continued. Capt. E.H. Moore R.S.O. takes over duties as M.O. vice Capt. Milne (to R.A.C.)	E/3
	6th		Working parties.	E/3
	7th		Divine Service under Capt. Thorn M.C. Inspections.	E/3
	8th		Working parties	E/3
	9th		2nd Lieut. J. Cubitt takes over duties as Officebrink. Bown employed in Railway Construction all day.	E/3
	10th		Railway Construction. Reconnoitring party sent to the RAILWAY WOOD SECTOR of the Ypres Salient.	E/3
	11th		The same	E/3
	12th		The same.	E/3
	13th		Heather dismal. Railway construction impossible. Inspections in billets	E/3
	14th		Sunday. No working parties required.	E/3
YPRES	15th		Battalion marches after dark into YPRES and rests on the outskirts of that CONVENT and Rooms near the STATION	E/3
POTIJZE	16th		Battalion marches up by night to relieve 2/5th KINGS LIVERPOOL/IRISH in RAILWAY WOOD Last. H.Q. in POTIJZE CHAT. grounds. Relief successfully carried out + reported Complete 9.20 p.m.	E/3
	17th		Heavy snow. Last day Quiet. Father Ross joins Bn. vice Father BAMFORD (transferred to C.O.S.) Officers patrols sent out	E/3
	18th		More snow. Bocke again quiet. Bn. again sharp up well as airport patrols	E/3
	19th		Quiet. 1 man wounded by sniper. Hows do good work take over V-System trenches. Patrols continued.	E/3
	20th		Day Quiet. Bn. the evening Bn. relieved by 14th HANTS and returns to its billets in CONVENT S. near STATION, YPRES	E/3
YPRES	21st		2.Lt. CASSY joins the Bn. Working parties supplied for trains on CAMBRIDGE TRENCH and wiring in front of X LINE	E/3

M/Maj. M. Berthoff/Major
for Lt. Col.
Comdg. 11th Royal Sussex Regt.

Army Form C. 2118.

WAR DIARY
or
INTELLIGENCE SUMMARY.
(Erase heading not required.)

Place	Date	Hour	Summary of Events and Information	Remarks and references to Appendices
YPRES	22nd 23rd 24th		Working parties on as for 21st and also on new dugouts in the X LINE N. of its junction with PICCADILLY. Working parties continued. Wire defences hampered by shelling. Enemy aircraft very busy and 2 planes of ours driven down. Heavy shelling of BUHS all day. Hostile Batteries supported to R.E. and Town Major. Battalion successfully relieved the 11th HANTS at POTIJZE. Specialists before daylight remainder in the evening. Enemy snipers patrolled by us	S.S. S/3. S/3
POTIJZE	25th		Early in the morning Boche put on a violent barrage and bombing. Boche huts on a violent current and intervening barrage round our extreme right and raised our night Bombing Post in strength. Our casualties MISSING 3 KILLED & DIED OF WOUNDS 5; also several slighter wounds. Enemy left three dead behind, one being the Officer in charge. Quiet day follows. Our planes bring down 2 enemy planes between 3 & 4 p.m. In the evening a false gas alarm raised an artillery strafe. 30 cobs of wire put out on our front. Enemy registers our left and supports. Third anomal activity. False S.O.S. at 6 p.m. brings our guns into action. Major R.C. MILLWARD returns to Bn. as 2nd in Command	E/3. E/3.
	26th			
	27th		Bitter, bitterly cold. Guns and planes all the morning. Few operation order Refer L.G. & Bombs at Ypres by Regtl Coy, which Boche continue to reply to. Patrols on both Coy fronts heavily through the night.	E/3. E/3.
YPRES	28th 29th 30th 31st		Some artillery during the day. Coy continues Prophylactic dose the same. Bath relieved by 14th HANTS. 2 Platoons remain in DRAGOON Bn. Bath in German billets. Inspection. Pay parade. Working parties. Gas & a little snow. Working parties during the night. More snow — working parties B Coy take over dugouts on HALF MOON TR. & HUSSAR FM.	E/3. S/3. E/3. E/3. E/3.

(signature)
for Lieut. Col.
Comdg XIth Royal Sussex Regt.

Confidential

War Diary Vol 12

1st to 15th February 1914
1st Bn Royal Sussex Reg

Vol XII

12E
5 sheets

WAR DIARY or INTELLIGENCE SUMMARY

Army Form C. 2118.

1st Bn ROYAL SUSSEX REGT

Place	Date 1917 July	Hour	Summary of Events and Information	Remarks and references to Appendices
YPRES	1		Bn. marches to relieve 1st Hants at POTIJZE. Quiet night follows. Usual patrols + wiring.	a/per
	2		Enemy Guns active. B.H.Q. during bombs + 4.2's at 4.5 p.m. Otherwise day quiet. 1 O.R. wounded. 3 Batts to made.	a/per
	3		Day quiet. Cold intense + WOR almost impassable. A+C coys relieved by 16th R.B. marching to YPRES + DRAGOON FARM. B+D + 2 platoons Q. Coy remain in support line.	a/per
	4		A+C + H.Q. coys bivouac nr YPRES, detrain BRANDHOEK + march to A Camp. B+D + ½ C. Coy remain in Trenches.	a/per
A. Camp.	5		Inspection parade + reconnaissance parties. Lt N.S. Lewis + 2/Lt J.C. Newman join Bn.	a/per
	6		Training of specialists under new scheme begins. Reconnaissance continued.	a/per
	7		Specialists paraded, fatigue party for unloading Corps Ammn Dump. Sgt Shackland + 2 bombers wounded at Bombing practice.	a/per
	8		Training of specialists cont'd. Party detailed to assist R.B. in preparing for raid. Rifle + musketry practice on Range.	a/per
	9		Bn lecture 16st Officers attend lecture at POPERINGHE. Party again lent to R.B. for practising Raid.	a/per
	10		Route March. Bn lecture + Lt Col Hammers returns from Army School.	a/per
	11		Divine Service 11.45 a.m. M.D.S. inspection. Baths for A.C.	a/per
	12		Training. B+D Coys in YPRES.	a/per
	13		Training B+D Coys in out post to R.B's raid. RAILWAY WOOD SECTOR.	a/per
	14		B+D Coys relieved. march to Brass B/A Camps where training continued	a/per
	15		A.O. have baths + M.O. inspection. C.O.S. Musical service	a/per
	16		Bn marches to CHEESE MARKET station & entrains for BOLLEZEEL arriving 7pm.	a/per
BOLLEZEEL	17		Bn. resting. Cleaning. Reorganization commenced	a/per
	18		Training of specialists + reorganization. 2/Lt Milling appointed Bn Concert	a/per
	19		Specialist training. Baths. and the Coy. Reorganised	a/per

Army Form C. 2118.

WAR DIARY
or
INTELLIGENCE SUMMARY.
(Erase heading not required.)

Instructions regarding War Diaries and Intelligence Summaries are contained in F.S. Regs., Part II. and the Staff Manual respectively. Title pages will be prepared in manuscript.

Place	Date 1919	Hour	Summary of Events and Information	Remarks and references to Appendices
BOLLEZEEL	20th		Specialist & Company training under Coy. arrangements	
	21.		Sunday. Officers Reunion in H.Q. mess in Evening	
	22.		Divisional General inspected billets and compliments Bn. Band inspected owing to bad weather.	
	23.		Training of units 2nd day a/w 11 A.M. Gruffs Concert in evening.	
WINNIPEG CAMP	24.		Bn. leaves BOLLEZEEL for WINNIPEG CAMP, OUDERDOM, marching from POPERINGHE.	
	25.		Bn. in Wpg. Camp. GAS + FEET inspection. At 4.30 pm marched to billets in + around YPRES.	
YPRES	26.		Bn. in billets. A+C Coys duspatch in ZILLEBEKE BUND. B+D in YPRES. Officers carry out reconnaissance of OBSERVATORY RIDGE. 2/Lt. R.W.	
	27.		Reconnaissance continued by officers of units. occupied (-) 14th HANTS. 2/Lt. Olive to hospital with measles	
	28.		Bn in front line, left Sub-sector OBSERVATORY RIDGE, relieving 14 Hants. A+D front line, B Coy in Support. C+C companies	
		10 pm	Encounter with hostile bombing patrols on our right. Units to S.O.S. signals from Enemy + own + right Bn. Our front line severely strafed with Minenw, Rifle Grenades + artillery. Our artillery gave hostile retaliation + L.G's fired from battle positions. Our casualties 2 officers wounded (2/Lt. Hollis) & B. Welch M.D.R. wounded. Bn. under command Major Milward during Col. Harrison absence on leave. B.H.Q. came under hostile shelling. R.S.M Arnold being mortally wounded. All quiet at 11pm except of rifle.	

Confidential

Vol 13

War Diary
of
1st Bn Royal Sussex Reg.
for
March 1914.

a.d. 13 E
6 sheets

MARCH.

WAR DIARY
or
INTELLIGENCE SUMMARY.

11TH ROYAL SUSSEX REGT. Army Form C. 2118.

(Erase heading not required.)

Instructions regarding War Diaries and Intelligence Summaries are contained in F. S. Regs., Part II. and the Staff Manual respectively. Title pages will be prepared in manuscript.

Place	Date	Hour	Summary of Events and Information	Remarks and references to Appendices
OBSERVATORY RIDGE	1/3/17		Battn in front line LEFT SUB-SECTION – RIGHT SECTION Quiet day. own mine + bombardment during night on left 1 Casualty. Lt. H.S. LEWIS takes over 2nd I/C vice MAJOR W.C. MILLWARD who took command of Battn vice Lt. Col. G. H. HARRISON D.S.O. returned to England.	11/6/6
"	2		Front Line Compys subjected to activity from Minnewerfers in morning. Communication duckboards shelled. Casualties Capt Dr MOORE wounded slightly, carried on. 1 man killed in listening Post. Night quiet	
	3		Battn relieved from OBSERVATORY RIDGE SECTOR by 1st/1st CAMBRIDGESHIRES. Entrained at YPRES ASYLUM at 2AM arrived BRANDHOEK 5.30 AM WINNEPEG CAMP at 4AM	
WINNIPEG CAMP	4		Cleaning up. Rifles equipment etc. baths at WINNIPEG CAMP.	
"	5		Bath Parade. C.O's Inspections. Inter Coy Football in afternoon. 2nd LT.G. SALTER. M.C. to be 2/Capt dates 26/12/16	
"	6		Company Drill & Training. Surprise visit by CORPS COMMANDER who complimented C.O. on appearance of Battn.	
"	7th		Capt A.G. LOWEN returns to duty takes over 2nd I/C	
"	8th		Company Drill Training of all Specialists under Specialist Officers. Football in the Afternoon	
"	9th		" D° " Reconnaissance by Companies of G.H.Q. Line – RIDGE WOOD SECTOR (DICKEBUSCH). EMERGENCY LINE. Football v Regimental Canteen in the evening	
			Cleaning up Camp. Medical Gas Helmet Ammunition Inspections etc. Marches off 5.30 PM. Entrained at BRANDHOEK 7.0PM. Detrained YPRES ASYLUM. 7.20 PM. Held up 20 mins owing to Bombardment over YPRES. BATTN relieves 6th CHESHIRE REGT in ZILLEBEKE BUND. (BRIGADE RESERVE).	
ZILLEBEKE BUND	10th		Quiet day. bad visibility. Trench maintenance works. Night carrying returning parties under Brigade orders.	
	11th		Artillery fairly quiet both sides. Aerial activity over YPRES during morning. 2 own 'planes brought down. Supply of Night wiring & carrying parties.	
	12th		Raining very much. Inspections Trench water & especially drainage owing to Rain Ports. Night wiring & carrying parties. 2nd LT J.D.LEWIS left on operat leave to ENGLAND. 2nd LT LIMBERY B.S.E returned to duty. 12 men returned from Divisional School. 2nd LT. H. AMON returned from Bombing course.	

WAR DIARY
or
INTELLIGENCE SUMMARY.
(Erase heading not required.)

Army Form C. 2118.

Instructions regarding War Diaries and Intelligence Summaries are contained in F. S. Regs., Part II. and the Staff Manual respectively. Title pages will be prepared in manuscript.

Place	Date	Hour	Summary of Events and Information	Remarks and references to Appendices
ZILLEBEKE BUND	13/3/17		CAPT A.G.L. OWEN returned to Hospital. LT H.S. LEWIS takes over 2/C vice CAPT OWEN. Quiet day. Artillery actively counter battery work. NW of BUND RAINING in AFTERNOON relieved 14th HANTS REGT in the front line OBSERVATORY RIDGE RIGHT SECTOR - Left sub sector relief complete 10.20 PM. 11 OPM heavy bombardment thrown extreme right. 2ND LT A.G. GYDER evacuated to hospital.	A.G.R.
OBSERVATORY RIDGE RIGHT SECTOR	14/3/17		Raining hard during morning. Usual desultory shelling. Hostile relief completed. Guns turned on 10.15 PM slow bombardment 3 hrs. YPRES bombarded 7 PM. BRIGADIER paid line visit in morning.	A.G.R.
	15/3/17		Raining cleared up later. Hostile intermittent shelling of our communications. "SILENT PERIOD" test by CORPS SIGNALS. 9 AM to 3.0 PM. 1 Sniper killed. Enemy observation balloon signalling over HILL 60. Late + all round signalling. Report of signalling taken - forwarded with morning Intelligence.	A.G.R.
	16/3/17		Very quiet slight shelling. BHQ. hit no casualties. Returns up late owing to rearrangement + congestion of traffic. 2 Hostile planes brought down our own lines. Bad visibility.	A.G.R.
	17/3/17		Artillery - aircraft active. Rear lines shelled. Between 11 - 12 noon air fight over front line 1 hostile machine brought down in flames behind his own lines + 1 other hit but in our control. A 30 PM several enemy planes over but was driven off. BATTN relieved by 14th HANTS returned to billets in KRUISSTRAAT. YPRES to THE BUND (DIVISIONAL RESERVE) all in billets 10-30 PM.	A.G.R.
KRUISSTRAAT (Bivouacks Reserve)	18/3/17		Quiet night and day. Men cleaning up inspections of kit etc. Night working parties under Brigade arrangement 2 B.A.G. VIOLER returned for duty.	A.G.R.
	19/3/17		Bright morning - Lake gale with rain. Quiet. Night working parties as before.	"
	20/3/17		Quiet night. Rain snow sleet very windy. Night working parties as before. New draft arrived of 14 ORs.	"
	21/3/17		Bright day. The BUND N end shelled heavily in afternoon. Battalion relieved by 1/1st Herts Regt 11 PM. marched to Billets at WINNIPEG CAMP. arrived all in billets 1.30 AM next morning.	"
WINNIPEG CAMP	22/3/17		Cleaning up inspections by Company Officers. 7 Kit. Deficiencies etc. Working parties under R.E. in afternoon. C.O.'s Inspections. Company Training. Training of Specialists under programme in "Orders" morning. Baths in afternoon. Exchange of Clothing for Fumigation. Inoculation commenced. Inspection of Previous Draft. New Draft arrived 12 ORs Artillery active during night.	

Army Form C. 2118.

WAR DIARY
or
INTELLIGENCE SUMMARY.
(Erase heading not required.)

Instructions regarding War Diaries and Intelligence Summaries are contained in F. S. Regs., Part II. and the Staff Manual respectively. Title pages will be prepared in manuscript.

Place	Date	Hour	Summary of Events and Information	Remarks and references to Appendices
WINNIPEG CAMP	24/3/17		Company Specialist Training as before. Football in the afternoon. Baths - Inoculations continued. Major W.C. MILLWARD proceeded to Acting Rank of Lt Colonel whilst commanding Battalion. Capt F. CASSELS rejoins for duty. Artillery very active. Considerable shelling of VLAMERTINGHE. Working Parties out all day.	NGR
	25/3/17		Voluntary Church Parade. Inoculations continued. Capt F. CASSELS took over as 2I/C. Lt H.S. LEWIS posted to take over Command of 'A' Day.	NGR
	26/3/17		Heavy rain in morning precludes parades. Working parties all day as usual. Inoculations complete. Football in afternoon.	NGR
	27/3/17		Very cold with rain, cleaning up camp. Preparations for moving into line. Lt H.S. LEWIS takes over duties of Adjutant vice 2Lt LINTOTT evacuated to Hospital. also 2Lt A.G. VINER evacuated to Hospital. Battalion entrained at BRANDHOEK for YPRES. 8.55 pm Arrived at YPRES. Relief held up owing to heavy shelling. Relieved 1/1st Herts OBSERVATORY RIDGE SECTOR RIGHT BRIGADE left our sector. 2.10 am next morning.	NGR
OBSERVATORY RIDGE SECTOR	28/3/17		Quiet night. Heavy except for hostile shelling of Back areas. Night wiring parties, improvement of trenches.	NGR
	29/3/17		Wet day - dull. Considerable artillery activity in back areas. Heavy shelling for about 15 mins in morning & afternoon of B.H.Q. hostile support line.	NGR
	30/3/17		Quiet day - bright weather. Occasional shelling of Communication trenches. 2ND Lt L. CLARK proceeds on special leave to England.	NGR
	31/3/17		Considerable shelling of back areas Communications by Enemy, especially B.H.Q. VALLEY COTTAGES necessitating evacuation of Same & seeking temporary billets in ZILLEBEKE. Relieved by 14th HANTS at 11.30 pm. returned to Brigade Reserve billets in SOUTH BUND, ZILLEBEKE.	NGR

W Gray Millward Lt Col
O.C. 11th Bn Royal Sussex Regt

Confidential

Y.K. 14

War Diary
of
11th B.R. Sussex Regt.
for
April 1917

L.B.
1H.E.
5 sheets

Army Form C. 2118.

WAR DIARY
or
INTELLIGENCE SUMMARY.
(Erase heading not required.)

APRIL 1917. 11th ROYAL SUSSEX REGT.

Instructions regarding War Diaries and Intelligence Summaries are contained in F. S. Regs., Part II. and the Staff Manual respectively. Title pages will be prepared in manuscript.

Place	Date	Hour	Summary of Events and Information	Remarks and references to Appendices
S. of THE BUND ZILLEBEKE	1.4.17		Quiet day but considerable shelling of back areas. Night working parties under Brigade arrangement.	
"	2.4.17		Quiet day but considerable aerial activity on both sides. Hostile sounding battery under Brigade worked on. N. end of BOND heavily shelled. 2nd Lts CHESTER and OLIVE returned to duty. 2nd Lt BOND GRICE G. joined from England reported for duty.	
"	3.4.17		Heavy thunderstorm during night. Following morning dense fog. artillery quiet, night working parties as before.	
"	4.4.17		Quiet day. Relieved 11th HANTS REGT in L/F sub-section OBSERVATORY RIDGE at 11.50 p.m. CAPT E.M. MOORE DSO RAMC evacuated sick. CAPT J. GATCHELL vice CAPT MOORE attd. for duty. A/CAPT SALTER G. left for England on leave.	
OBSERVATORY RIDGE Left Sector	5.4.17		Fairly quiet, considerable aerial activity on both sides. Big bombardment by us on our right sub-section front. Little retaliation no damage.	
"	6.4.17		Much aeroplane activity and of our troops strewn influence on our right while on Messines communications. Bosches barrage accomplice. Relieved 12.15 AM by 16th Notts & Derbys. Entrained at Ypres for BRANDHOEK. No billets ready by 4.30 am. Reveille 10 a.m. Rain.	
"	7.4.17		Cleaning up. Recreation in the afternoon. Reg. moved in evening near ST ELOI. 7.50 p.m. Loaded Baths.	
BRANDHOEK	8.4.17		Easter day. Church Parade 10.20 am. Baths at POPERINGHE in the afternoon. Working party at night 150 unloading of shells. C.O. Lt Col W.C. Millward proceeded on Commanding Officers Course at Second Army. Lt Col. J.H.O. Gibbs T. Cassells C.O. vide Col Millward.	
"	9.4.17		Battalion Parade for C.O.'s Inspection. Remainder of morning Training of Specialists. Football in the afternoon weather very cold wet and rain.	
"	10.4.17		C.O.'s Battalion Parade. Lewis Gun training. Football in the afternoon. Weather still very bad.	
"	11.4.17		Cleaning up camp. Previous inspection preparatory to going into the line. Battalion marched off 3.0 p.m. relieved 17th Notts & Derbys in Infantry Barracks YPRES. 'Conf in Brigade support MAPLE COPSE OBSERVATORY RIDGE SECTORS. Relief complete 1.45 a.m. 12.4.17.	
YPRES	12.4.17		Training by day. Heavy working parties at night by night - day under R.Es - Brigade arrangements.	
"	13.4.17		do. do.	2nd Lt T.S.R. WOODROW joined Battalion for duty from CANADA.
"	14.4.17		do. do.	Lt Col MILLWARD returned on completion of CANADA Course. Returned R.T.O. 2nd Lt SOMERVILLE proceeded 8.17
"	15.4.17		do. do.	Relieved by 4th D. LI. at 11.15 p.m. + marched to Billets. ---- Rest day --- all officers away afternoon. Coy 10th Corps. 2nd 5th Corps. 2/Lt R.B. MASON joined on
BRANDHOEK	16.4.17		at BRANDHOEK. Reconnoitred HILL TOP SECTOR. Football in the afternoon. Heavy rain in the evening.	
"	17.4.17		Very hot. Cleaning up camp preparatory to inspecting. Handed over camp to 7th SOUTH LANCS (ammunit). By train from BRANDHOEK 9.55 pm. Detrained 1.13 to WELSH HILL TOP SECTOR. Left sub section. Very late relief.	

Army Form C. 2118.

WAR DIARY
or
INTELLIGENCE SUMMARY.
(Erase heading not required.)

Instructions regarding War Diaries and Intelligence Summaries are contained in F. S. Regs., Part II. and the Staff Manual respectively. Title pages will be prepared in manuscript.

Place	Date	Hour	Summary of Events and Information	Remarks and references to Appendices
BEG HILL TOP SECTOR Left section	18.4.17		Relief complete. 3.10AM. Quiet night 1 day. 2 Casualties on CANAL BRIDGE 4 by M.G. fire. Capt SALTER rejoined from leave in Scotland	
"	19.4.17		Quiet night. Artillery more active during day. 2nd Lts. CONWAY, DAVIS & RICE joined the Battalion for duty, posted to the 11th now the Battn.	
"	20.4.17		Quiet night. Considerable shrapnel sent over. Hostile registration on front Nieuport lines. Heavy counter battery work by ourselves.	
"	21.4.17		Very quiet all day. Full artillery activity 2 return into by Snipers. Hostile relief suspected, owing to appearance of newer younger men next morning.	
"	22.4.17		Quiet night. More activity. Hostile registration on communication trenches, 4 casualties sustained 2 killed.	
"	23.4.17		Fairly quiet all day. Considerable dug out accomplition completed this day. Inter communicated during the for Relieves 11.30pm by 14th Hants. Took over billets in Brigade Reserve on CANAL BANK E. 2nd Lt. LAPWORTH left on leave for England.	
"	24.4.17		Reveille 6 AM. Cleaning up of equipment inspection etc. Reconnaissance accompaniment of MEDT. walking parties	
"	25.4.17		Reveille 8. Training in close order. Drill Musketry etc repeated having for all men not on working parties. Heavy bombardment at 10 p.m. lasts about 30 mins. No raid reports. Reconnaissances by all Officers of left Brigade sector (LANCASHIRE FARM)	
"	26.4.17		" 9. Training Do. Working parties 2nd Lt. CLARKE returns from leave in England.	
"	27.4.17		" " " 2nd Lt. BOTTING joined for duty from England.	
"	28.4.17		" " " working parties. Cleaning up billets. Relieved by 1/1st Cambs Regt. 11.45pm	
"	29.4.17		Late relief. entrained at YPRES for POPERINGHE. From there marched to M. CAMP. all in Camp 5.0 AM. Reveille 12 noon. Cleaning up for Inspection	
"	30.4.17		Reveille 7 AM. C.O's Inspection as for G.O.C. Football recreation in afternoon.	

a.k. 15 E
2 sheet

Army Form C. 2118.

WAR DIARY for MAY
or INTELLIGENCE SUMMARY.

1st ROYAL SUSSEX REGT   XI R Sussex Regt   1/5/15

(Erase heading not required.)

Instructions regarding War Diaries and Intelligence Summaries are contained in F. S. Regs., Part II. and the Staff Manual respectively. Title pages will be prepared in manuscript.

Place	Date	Hour	Summary of Events and Information	Remarks and references to Appendices
M Camp	1/5/17		Marched 11.8.20 to WIPPENHOEK SIDING entrained 11.30 AM for ST OMER. arrived 3.0 P.M. Entrained marched to HALLINES - (BILLETS) arrived for the night.	
HALLINES & CODAUSQUES ZUDAUSQUES	2/5/17 3/5/17 4/5/17		Marched off 6.0 AM marched to ZUDAUSQUES (BILLETS) - ZUDAUSQUES (BILLETS) NOAR CADRE & BARONSHEN. Cleaning up arriving in Billets. Commenced training (Coys. in turn) 8.0 AM. The attack by platoons. Rows of turning 8.12 - 1p.m. 4p.m.	
"	5/5/17		Training during morning (Battalion in turn.) Brigadier present short criticisms rehearsal in afternoon. 1 p.m. to 9 p.m. Musketry practice on range.	
"	6/5/17		Training all day. Brigade in the attack. Brigadier & Brigade Officers ZUDAUSQUES & CORMETTE. Criticism (informal) by Divisional Commander + Staff Officers. Criticism completed.	
"	7/5/17		8 A.M. to 2.30 p.m. Continuation of firing on Range. Afternoon & evening	
"	8/5/17		Church Parade 11.15 A.M. followed by Holy Communion. Football in the afternoon.	
"	9/5/17		Platoon & Company training in the attack (Open warfare) 8 am - 4 pm. Football in the evening.	
"	10/5/17		Keeping & morning. Examination of the Town in Boys. Platoon Competition. Organized by Battalion. Running. Hat leg. work + Afternoon Battery attacked sports. 4 p.m. French.	
"	11/5/17		In the field all day. The Brigade in the attack. Brigadier Scheme MORINGHEM - ZUDAUSQUES to ABBST. Division Commander present, accompanied by Staff Officers afterwards.	
"	12/5/17		Continuation of competition amongst Platoons by NCOs & specialist officers. Games - Inter-Coys Tournaments (horse + foot gun) Holiday in the afternoon. Regimental Sports until 7.30 p.m.	
"	13/5/17		8.0 during morning. Church Parade 11.45 A.M. followed by Holy Communion. Reunion during afternoon.	
"	14/5/17		Judo at Turk in Patron Comp Scheme during morning. Remainder of Companies at Coy Commander's Schools. 4 to 6 pm Football during afternoon.	
"	15/5/17		Marched off from ZUDAUSQUES 7.0 A.M. Breakfast LONGUENESSE at 10 A.M. Rest during day. Battalion marched off 11.0 pm reached WIZERNES - CAPELLE & ZERMEZEELE at 5 AM. 11.30 AM. arrived in Billets. Rest during day.	
LONGUENESSE	16/5/17 17/5/17		Billets at night.	
ZERMEZEELE	18/5/17		Brigade March. Battalion moved off 7.30 A.M. reached WORMHOUDT 10.25 AM. Battalion Billets in WORMHOUDT area.	

A5834 Wt. W4973/M687 750,000 8/16 D. D. & L. Ltd. Forms/C.2118/13.

Army Form C. 2118.

11th ROYAL SUSSEX REGT

WAR DIARY for MAY
or
INTELLIGENCE SUMMARY

(Erase heading not required.)

Instructions regarding War Diaries and Intelligence Summaries are contained in F. S. Regs., Part II. and the Staff Manual respectively. Title pages will be prepared in manuscript.

Place	Date	Hour	Summary of Events and Information	Remarks and references to Appendices
WORMHOUDT	19.5.17		Company training during morning. 8.45AM – 12.45AM "Final Assault, Bayonet Fighting" Musketry practices. Afternoon Brigade Sports. Tea 5.0pm.	
"	20.5.17		Brigade Church Parade 10.30AM. Football in the afternoon. Officers v N.W. Books v N.W. teams	
"	21.5.17		Training during morning by Companies as before. Coys Bayonet Fighting Hand Assault & Field Camp drown off. Afternoon 2nd Lt T.A. DAVIDSON (whose is to join them) form Regiment.	
"	22.5.17		Raining all day. Lectures during Inches.	
"	23.5.17		Training & Companies during morning as before. Inspection of Coys by Brigadier also Battalion Cooks & B.H.Q. In afternoon training given in the open.	
"	24.5.17		Left WORMHOUDT during morning & Marched to PEUBLON. Training in the morning & before inspection of Rifle Bombers Bombers by Brigadier. Football during afternoon	
"	25.5.17		Training during morning as before. Inspection of Lewis Guns & Rubber by Brigadier. " " " Signallers & Company Officers, R.S.M., C.S. Majors, C.Q.M.S. & Ration Anti-patrol.	
"	26.5.17		Inspections " " "	
"	27.5.17		by Brigadier. Football Efforts during afternoon. Bivouac on the ground.	
"	28.5.17		Church Parade at 11.30AM. Football in the afternoon. Preparations for moving made.	
"	29.5.17		Reveille 1.30AM. Marched off 4.0AM. Reached D. CAMP at 11.0AM. Cleaning up during afternoon Rolling towards cleaning. Working parties under 7th Canadian Railway troops. Battalion parade as string as possible for all aspects work B.	
@ Camp	30.5.17		Working parties. Served 12 midday. March off 8.0pm. arrived HILL TOP SECTR. tests withdraw to deliver 6th	
"	31.5.17		NOTTS & SERCYS by 11.30PM.	

T. Cook Major
Comdg 11th Royal Sussex Regt

CONFIDENTIAL

Yr 16

ORIGINAL COPY.

11TH BATTALION ROYAL SUSSEX REGIMENT

WAR DIARY

— FROM —

1ST JUNE TO 30TH JUNE 1917.

VOLUME 16.

ORIGINAL COPY.

11th Batn Royal Sussex Regt.

Army Form C. 2118.

Instructions regarding War Diaries and Intelligence Summaries are contained in F. S. Regs., Part II. and the Staff Manual respectively. Title pages will be prepared in manuscript.

WAR DIARY for JUNE 1917

or

INTELLIGENCE SUMMARY.

(Erase heading not required.)

Place	Date	Hour	Summary of Events and Information	Remarks and references to Appendices
HILL TOP left sub-sector	1/6/17		Relieved 16th Sherwoods. relief complete 12.50 AM. Discharge of gas by us on Mr. Balm front. Little retaliation. Between 3 & 3.30 pm. Demonstration on 2nd Army front. Cooperation on our own front by Smoke & M.G. Barrage. Retaliation by Artillery on Support line & B.H.Q. several Casualties (11) Heavy bombardment of YPRES commenced 10.15 pm with Gas Inflammatory Shells. HORNBY TR dug in new R† front (Company) by 14th HANTS during night.	
"	2/6/17		Gas discharged over YPRES blown over own own Sector. 1 Casualty. Artillery very active both sides during night. Barrage on Support posts & CTs at Stand to 3.50 AM. lasted 50 mins. Few enemy evacuation of B.H.Q. no casualties. Fairly quiet remainder of day. Much gas actually & Gas Alarms on enemy supports by no attack.	
"	3/6/17		Both sides shelling back areas during night. Quiet day. Cleared our own front line while heavier shells meant front line. New trenches. (HORNBY'S & BELLINGHAM) registered with "Minenwerfer" by enemy.	
"	4/6/17		Fairly quiet day. Demonstration by us on 2nd Army front with Artillery 3. 3.10 am. no retaliation. Work on trenches carried on during night by 13th Gloster (Pioneers). Artillery activity on both sides throughout.	
"	5/6/17		Quiet morning. O.K. enemy active during afternoon registering trajectories with our own close supports Subaru's & men in CTs. retaliation bring fire on these areas with 77m & 15 cm & few minenwerfer on R† line. Trawley shower B.H.Q. with S.A.P. Shrapnel. Relieved by 14th HANTS. Relief complete 11.13.	
CANAL BANK EAST	6/6/17	1.50 AM	Relief complete 1.50 AM. moved into Brigade. left Reserve CANAL BANK EAST. all in Intell: 3.0 AM. Ravelli 12 o/c noon afternoon company at disposal of O.C. for clearing up inspection returning & deficiencies. Working parties under Brigade arrangements during night. Major E.N. SNEPP Norfolk Reg† joined for duty. Took over command from Major CASSELS who became 2 i/c.	
"	7/6/17		Heavy shelling during night of YPRES with gas & inflammatory shells. Gas discharged by left Brigade at 1 AM. Trained in afternoon by Specialists. Inspection of line by C.O. Working parties as usual during night. By operation on our night advances 3.10 AM. Bonifac tured advanced from billets to be in front of Minimum.	
"	8/6/17		Quiet night. Working parties met with much shelling. Training carried on during afternoon including preparation for intended raid by C Coy. Trial by F.G.C.M. of 220 J & W.R. BOTTING at G. Camp. Working parties as usual in evening.	
"	9/6/17		Heavy bombardment during night retaliation for our raid on left Brigade front. Discharge of Gas on our R† Batt[n] front (HILL TOP) Retaliation near CANAL BANK. Training in afternoon as usual Practice of raid Scheme, but raid postponed. Working parties as usual.	

ORIGINAL COPY.

11th Batt. Royal Sussex Regt.

Army Form C. 2118.

WAR DIARY for JUNE
or
INTELLIGENCE SUMMARY.
(Erase heading not required.)

Instructions regarding War Diaries and Intelligence Summaries are contained in F.S. Regs., Part II. and the Staff Manual respectively. Title pages will be prepared in manuscript.

Place	Date	Hour	Summary of Events and Information	Remarks and references to Appendices
CANAL BANK. EAST.	10/6/17		Fairly quiet night. Voluntary Communion Services. 7.30 & 9.30 Quiet day but Cornelis battery work carried out by enemy near CANAL BANK. 10 pm Battalion moved into HILL TOP Left sub sector to relieve 14th HANTS. Major Cassels proceeds to REST CAMP slightly gassed.	
HILL TOP. Left sub sector.	11/6/17		Relieved 14th HANTS Relief complete 12.40 AM. Artillery on both sides very active. Enemy troublesome during Till 6.30 AM. with heavy minenwerfer + Shelling, all calibres. Enemy seemed restless all day. R.H.Q. Shirtsides shelled between 2.30 AM & 3.15 AM. also Support Coy. Very front quiet - dull. 11th Royal Sussex Camt into Command of 13th Corps. Visit of Corps Commander along Brigade front at 12.15 pm. 2nd Lr. A. G. VIDLER returned from leave & took over command of D. Coy.	
"	12/6/17		Heavy shelling in the line during the night. also on B.H.Q. Reprisals again early morning. Gunfire upon 2nd Lt. V.R. BOTTING by C.M. duly promulgated. "Severely Censured." Relieved B. Coy for duty. Quiet day, but enemy artillery active again towards evening.	
"	13/6/17		Usual barrage on support + C.Ts early morning. 2 Explosions felt during night intonation of enemy blowing up dumps on roads Junction PILKEM. Quietest day of the Term so far. Good deal of Cornelis battery work on both sides. Rain arranged for this evening against again postponed. Capt. A.G. VIDLER evacuated with slight concussion Marker 9.05	
"	14/6/17		Weather still holding out, very hot. Enemy artillery active on our front again. Shelled in Support 10 pm. returned 3 dugouts. Indian company relief in evening C.A. Coy in front line.	
"	15/6/17		Weather still good. enemy shelling more than usual on same targets especially across on Tangle + WILLOWS (Left Coys Support). Retaliation obtained with good result. B.H.Q. subjected to intermittent shelling. Enemy very restless during night. Bombs and actually early morning + bit enemy also night flying.	
"	16/6/17		Enemy not quite so active during night, chief activity bombardment of left front with 77 mm. Enemy aircraft again active as yesterday. This out this town enemy has shown extreme nervousness in evidence by Continual Shelling with Whizbags of main C.T's + Strong points at about 5 morning during T aircraft reconnaissance at their lines. also unusual number of very lights during night. Relieved by 17th Sherwoods.	
"	17/6/17		Relief complete 12.50 AM. Battalion moved back into Divisional Reserve at E camp. all in billets 4.0 AM. Reveille. 11 AM. Cleaning up Inspection. Voluntary Services in afternoon.	

ORIGINAL COPY.

11th Batt: Royal Sussex Regt.

Army Form C. 2118.

WAR DIARY for JUNE 1917.

or

INTELLIGENCE SUMMARY.

(Erase heading not required.)

Instructions regarding War Diaries and Intelligence Summaries are contained in F. S. Regs., Part II. and the Staff Manual respectively. Title pages will be prepared in manuscript.

Place	Date	Hour	Summary of Events and Information	Remarks and references to Appendices
E. Camp.	18/6/17		Training of Specialists under Scheme submitted by Specialist Officers. 8 hrs a day. Bombing & Gunner Sections Signals. Bns arrival. Filling in area unevenly & camp extremely during night. Remainder Batt. on the Square. Capt. ALLEN on course & Capt. VIDLER from Hospital reported for duty. Took over A & D Coy respectively. 2nd Lt COLLYER joined from England reported for duty. Detailed to B.Coy.	
"	19/6/17.		Specialist training as yesterday. 2nd Lt V. WARD reported for duty from England & posted to A Coy. weather unsettled. Bathing under Brig. arrangements.	
"	20/6/17		Specialist training completed with reports. Scouts effected a cross country scheme during afternoon. The handling for more back.	
HOULLE	21/6/17		Battalion paraded ready for marching off at 8.50 AM. Marched off at 9.0 AM. Reached Poperinghe Station 10. AM. Did not entrain till 12.30 p.m. Few shells fell near Station during entraining. no casualties. Arrived WATTEN at 3.30 AM. Marched to billets in HOULLE all whilst 6.30 p.m. Major C.E CUMMINGS 12th Rl. DURHAM L. INFANTRY. Joined Battalion & took over command from Major F.N SNEPP Notts & Derby Regt. who returned to Brigade. very wet night.	
"	22/6/17		Raining. Cancelled training. Return training by means of Lectures etc in billet. Specialist under Specialist Officers. Instruction & address by C.O to all Officers in the evening & short conference on following days work.	
"	23/6/17.		March off to training area 7.30 AM. Specialists carried on training under Officers. Remainder of Batt. under Coy Officers. Whole Battn fired 2 practices on Miniature range. Staff training 7.30 – 12.30 1.30 – 4. 30 p.m.	
"	24/6/17		Sunday. Church Parade only. Men rested as much as possible. beautiful day.	
"	25/6/17		Marched off to training area at 6.0 AM. Home at training 7.0 AM to 1 PM. "THE ATTACK" by Platoons by Companies by the Battalion. The lectures took place between 11.1 pm short conference afterwards. & criticism by C.O + Lt Col Harvey. G.S.O.I 5th Army.	
"	26/6/17		Morning Revolver range practice for Officers & men. Marched off to training ground 10. AM. Hours of training 1. – 7 p.m. "THE ATTACK" by Battalion, by Companies, by Platoons. Light Artillery Brigade was present. Late return of Battalion.	

ORIGINAL COPY.

11th Batt. Royal Sussex Regt.

Army Form C. 2118.

WAR DIARY for JUNE
or
INTELLIGENCE SUMMARY.
(Erase heading not required.)

Instructions regarding War Diaries and Intelligence Summaries are contained in F. S. Regs., Part II and the Staff Manual respectively. Title pages will be prepared in manuscript.

Place	Date	Hour	Summary of Events and Information	Remarks and references to Appendices
HOULLE	27/6/17		Miniature Range Practice for all the Battalion firing of Grenades – Bombs. Revolver practice for Officers Musketry Battling Parade for all Companies. Lecture in the Evening to all Officers & Platoon Sgts. in the Brigade by Brigade MG. Officer on how to train for 1 Run in "Musketry" (to be continued).	
"	28/6/17		Scheme on training area abandoned owing to rain. Training in minor tactics especially in Musketry on lines laid down by officer in lecture given previous day. At 5.0 pm Lecture in the "Malting" near by, by the 18th Corps Commander to selected Officers from 116th & 118th Brigades on Training – Organization based on lessons learnt from "Battle of Arras" with regard to future operations. Corps Commander Lt. Genl. Sir Ivor Maxse.	
"	29/6/17		Attack scheme again abandoned owing to heavy rain during night. Platoons having on lines outlined by Coys Commander the previous day, carried out Also Battalion tested in intense digging. Demonstration of "Consuming Fire" in the attack, by the 2nd Army School of Musketry. Range attended by all Company Officers & Platoon Officers.	
"	30/6/17		Battalion marched off at 4.45 am commenced digging practice trenches at 6.30 at spot about 4 miles away. Very wet. Arrived back in billets 12.30 p.m. 2nd Lieut J. Enoy A Coy proceeded on leave to England. Tried by F.G.C.M. "C.S.M. YORKE D. Coy + Pte. HANNER D. Coy, at Rue Batt. HQrs. Charges "When on active service [illegible] an act to the prejudice of good order & discipline."	

E. E. Cummins
O.C. 11th Battn. Royal Sussex Regt.

SECRET. Copy No. 8

"C" Company, 11th Bn., Royal Sussex Regt., 116th Inf. Bde.

Ref. Map – (a) St. Julien – Sheet 28.N.W.2. Ed. 5.A.   7.6.17.
         (b) Attached Sketch.

1. "C" Company, 11th Bn., Royal Sussex Regt., will carry out a raid at an early date. The actual date will be decided later.

2. The objects of the raid are:-
   (a) To capture prisoners.
   (b) To secure identifications.

3. The part of the enemy trenches to be raided is the enemy front Line from C.15.a.32.12. to C.15.a.15.12. (approx) Point of entry C.15.a.25.10. (approx)

4. The strength of the raiding party will be :-
   1 Officer, 1 Platoon Sergt., 5 N.C.O.'s and 27 Other Ranks.

   The detail of the various parties and their tasks is as follows:-

DETAIL.	Offs.	N.C.O.s	Men	TASK.
(a) Bombing and Blocking Party. Left Party.		1	3	To Bomb and block trench to left of Point of entry to 50 yds. distance.
(b) Bombing and Blocking Party. Right Party.		1.	3.	To Bomb and block trench to Right of point of entry up to 50 yards distance.
(c) Mopping up Party. Left Party.			4.	To enter Trench and proceed to left and obtain prisoners or identification.
Right Party.			4.	To enter trench and proceed to right and obtain prisoners or identification.
(d) Centre Covering Party. (Bombers)		1.	5.	To advance to C.15.a.20.15. and cover Liason party and occupy old trench in case anything exists there.
(e) Liason Party.	1.	1.	4.	To keep communication with our trench and direction for return of raiding party. The officer will remain at point of entry with liason party. Liason Party to run a tape from point of exit to gap in enemy wire.
(f) Covering Party. Rifle Grenadiers (Left Flank) " " (Right Flank)	1. 1.	3.) 3.)		To fire volleys into enemy front Line on both flanks from "NO MANS LAND" if required and protect party from possible enemy flanking attack in NO MANS LAND

5. The raid will be supported by:-
   (a) "R" Group R.A.
   (b) The 116th L.T.M. Bty.
   (c) The 116th M.G. Coy.
   (d) The Lewis Guns of the 11th Bn., R.S.R.

6. The action of the Artillery, T.M.'s, V.M.G.'s and Lewis Guns will be as follows:-

   (1) BOMBARDMENT.
   (a) "R" Group R.A. will barrage Enemy's Front Line from C.15.a.60.20. to C.15.c.95.80. *with 18 pdrs and bombard points as under with 4-5 rows on 18 pdrs (1) C.12.a.8.0 - C.14.a.85.0 (2) between Saps 13 + 15*
   This Barrage will continue from ZERO to ZERO plus 20
   (b) The L.T.M.'s (4 Guns) will bombard as follows:-
      1 Gun on C.14.b.97.15.   1 Gun on C.15.a.50.40.
      1 Gun on C.15.a.50.15.   1 Gun on C.14.b.98.30.
   This Bombardment will continue from ZERO to ZERO plus 20.

   (ii) BARRAGES.
   (a) The V.M.G.'s (4 Guns) will form a barrage from C.14.b.80.20. along CALABASH LANE and from C.15.a.8.0. along trench to BULOW Farm and HINDENBURG FARM.
   This Barrage will commence at Zero & continue to Zero + 20
   (b) The 11th Bn., R.S.R. Lewis Guns (4 Guns) will form a barrage from C.14.b.40.15. to C.14.b.90.20. and from C.15.a.50.20. to C.15.d.9.80. Two Guns on each Flank.

   These barrages ((a) & (b)) will commence at ZERO and will cease at ZERO plus 20.

7. The action of the Infantry will be as follows:-
   (a) Position of assembly in our trenches C.15.c.25.78.
                                              (No.11 Post)
   (b) Position of assembly in NO MANS LAND C.15.c.25.85.
                                              (approx)
   (c) Time of entry into enemy's trenches ZERO plus 1 minute.
   (d) <u>Action of advance from position of assembly in NO Mans Land.</u>
   The Raiding party will form up and advance in file as follows:-

   Left Bombing Party   <-- 5 yds. -->   Right Bombing Party.
   Left Moppers.   <-- 5 yds. -->   Right Moppers.
   Centre Covering Pty.   <-- 5 yds. -->   Liason Party.
   Left Covering Pty.   <-- 5 yds. -->   Right Covering Party.

   (e) At ZERO minus 5 minutes the raiders will commence to crawl forward and will get as close to enemy trench as possible according to Light, Clouds etc. At ZERO they will rush forward and gain enemy trench as quickly as possible.
   (f) On entering enemy trench Bombing Parties and Moppers up will proceed respectively 50 yards to Right and Left.

   Centre Covering Party to C.15.a.20.15.

   Liason Party to Point of entry.

   Right and Left covering Parties will move respectively 50 yards to either flank of points of entry, *and on our side of enemy wire where they will lie down facing outwards.*
   (g) <u>SIGNAL FOR WITHDRAWAL</u> will be long blasts on the whistle and unless a prisoner is captured will be at ZERO plus 11 mins. Both Officer and Senior N.C.O. to carry whistles.
   If prisoner is captured signal will be given earlier
   (h) Action of covering Party. 4 Rifle Grenadiers on either flank to protect flanks and fire volleys into enemy trench on

(h) **Action of Covering Party** (Contd)
both flanks and our side of enemy wire where they will lie down facing outwards.

If a prisoner is captured he will be taken immediately to Officer in charge who will send him under escort (1 on each side and 1 behind) to our line via the tape.

As soon as the Officer considers he has had time to reach our line or is well on the way he will signal the withdrawal.

(i) **Moppers up** will search for indentifications papers etc.

(j) **Order of Withdrawal** will be:-
    (1) Moppers up
    (2) Bombers.
    (3) Centre Covering Party.
    (4) Liason Party.
    (5) Flank Covering Parties.

(k) **Casualties** if any, will be brought back by Moppers up and Bombers.

8. A Time Table is attached.

9. ZERO hour will be notified later.

The Password will be notified later to all concerned daily by O.C. 11th R.S.R.

10. Watches of all concerned will be synchronised at 4.0.p.m. and again at 10.0.p.m. under arrangements to be made by O.C., 11th Bn., Royal Sussex Regiment. *This will not be done by telephone*

11. ACKNOWLEDGE. *The Rendezvous after the Raid will be at Headquarters Rt Support Coy. Left Front Batln in Coney St*

14. *The Code name for this raid is JOHNSON*
It is proposed (ordered) that Johnson should start to-night *It is proposed (ordered) to carry out the raid to-night*

7.6.17.
                           Lieut-Colonel,
              Commanding, 11th Bn., Royal Sussex Regt.

Copy No. 1 to..........
    " " 2 to..........

OTHER ARRANGEMENTS.

O.C., "C" Company will arrange to cut a gap in our wire at about C.15.c.25.80. (opposite No.11 Post) as soon as it gets dark. He will also mark out the position of assembly in No Mans Land by means of two lines of sandbags as soon as he has cut the gap in our wire.

He will place a guard of two men at far end of sandbags and another two men at far side of gap in our wire to ensure that no enemy patrol discovers this. These men will be withdrawn as soon as raiders take up position of assembly.

RENDEZVOUS, after the raid will be at Headquarters, Right Support Company in CONEY STREET.

PASS WORD   "CANAL"

Dress. Steel Helmet, Box Respirator on chest, 1 slung bandolier, Rifle, fixed bayonet - no sling.
4 Bombs each man - 2 in each lower pocket of jacket.
Bomber Parties. Two men of each party carry bucket of 10 bombs.
RIFLE BOMBER PARTIES. Two men each carry bucket of 6 Rifle Bombs.

                           Lieut-Colonel,
              Commanding, 11th Royal Sussex Regiment.

"C" Company, 11th Bn., Royal Sussex Regt., 116th Inf. Bde.   SECRET.

Ref. Map - (a) St. Julien - Sheet 28.N.W.2. Ed. 5.A.   7.6.17.
          (b) Attached Sketch.

1. "C" Company, 11th Bn., Royal Sussex Regt., will carry out a raid at an early date. The actual date will be decided later.

2. The objects of the raid are:-
    (a) To capture prisoners.
    (b) To secure identifications.

3. The part of the enemy trenches to be raided is the enemy front line from C.15.a.32.12. to C.15.a.15.12. (approx) Point of entry C.15.a.25.10. (approx)

4. The strength of the raiding party will be :-
    1 Officer, 1 Platoon Sergt., 5 N.C.O.'s and 27 Other Ranks.

The detail of the various parties and their tasks is as follows:-

DETAIL.	Offs.	N.C.O.s.	Men	TASK.
(a) Bombing and Blocking Party. Left Party.		1	3	To Bomb and block trench to left of Point of entry to 50 yds. distance.
(b) Bombing and Blocking Party. Right Party.		1.	3.	To Bomb and block trench to Right of point of entry up to 50 yards distance.
(c) Mopping up Party. Left Party.			4.	To enter Trench and proceed to left and obtain prisoners or identification.
Right Party.			4.	To enter trench and proceed to right and obtain prisoners or identification.
(d) Centre Covering Party. (Bombers)		1.	5.	To advance to C.15.a.20.15. and cover Liason party and occupy old trench in case anything exists there.
(e) Liason Party.	1.	1.	4.	To keep communication with our trench and direction for return of raiding party. The Officer will remain at point of entry with liason party. Liason Party to run a tape from point of exit to gap in enemy wire.
(f) Covering Party. Rifle Grenadiers (Left Flank) " " (Right Flank)		1. 1.	3.) 3.)	To fire volleys into enemy front Line on both flanks from "NO MANS LAND" if required and protect party from possible enemy flanking attack in NO MANS LAND.

5. The raid will be supported by:-
   (a) "R" Group R.A.
   (b) The 116th L.T.M. Bty.
   (c) The 116th M.G. Coy.
   (d) The Lewis Guns of the 11th Bn., R.S.R.

6. The action of the Artillery, T.M.'s, V.M.G.'s and Lewis Guns will be as follows:-

   (i) BOMBARDMENT.
       (a) "R" Group R.A. will barrage Enemy's Front Line from C.15.a.60.20. to C.15.c.95.80. *with 18 pdrs. - and bombard points as under with 4.5 hows.* This Barrage will continue from ZERO to ZERO plus 20 *(1) C.12.a.8.0. - C.12.a.8½.0½ (2) between Saps 13 + 15*
       (b) The L.T.M.'s (4 Guns) will bombard as follows:-
           1 Gun on C.14.b.97.15.   1 Gun on C.15.a.50.40.
           1 Gun on C.15.a.50.15.   1 Gun on C.14.b.98.30.
       This Bombardment will continue from ZERO to ZERO plus 20.

   (ii) BARRAGES.
        (a) The V.M.G.'s (4 Guns) will form a barrage from C.14.b.80.20. along CALABASH LANE and from C.15.a.8.0. along trench to BULOW Farm and HINDENBURG FARM.

        (b) The 11th Bn., R.S.R. Lewis Guns (4 Guns) will form a barrage from C.14.b.40.15. to C.14.b.90.20. and from C.15.a.50.20. to C.15.d.9.80. Two Guns on each Flank.

        These barrages ((a) & (b)) will commence at ZERO and will cease at ZERO plus 20.

7. The action of the Infantry will be as follows:-
   (a) Position of assembly in our trenches C.15.c.25.78.
                                          - (No.11 Post)
   (b) Position of assembly in NO MANS LAND C.15.c.25.85.
                                          - (approx)
   (c) Time of entry into enemy's trenches ZERO plus 1 minute.

   (d) <u>Action of advance from position of assembly in NO Mans Land.</u>
       The Raiding party will form up and advance in file as follows:-

       Left Bombing Party   <- 5 yds. ->   Right Bombing Party.
       Left Moppers.   <- 5 yds. ->   Right Moppers.
       Centre Covering Pty. <- 5 yds. ->   Liason Party.
       Left Covering Pty.   <- 5 yds. ->   Right Covering Party.

   (e) At ZERO minus 5 minutes the raiders will commence to crawl forward and will get as close to enemy trench as possible according to Light, Clouds etc. At ZERO they will rush forward and gain enemy trench as quickly as possible.

   (f) On entering enemy trench Bombing Parties and Moppers up will proceed respectively 50 yards to Right and Left.

   Centre Covering Party to C.15.a.20.15.

   Liason Party to Point of entry.

   Right and Left covering Parties will move respectively 50 yards to either flank of points of entry, *and on out side of enemy wire where they will lie down facing outwards.*
   (g) <u>SIGNAL FOR WITHDRAWAL</u> will be long blasts on the whistle and unless a prisoner is captured will be at ZERO plus 11 mins. Both Officer and Senior N.C.O. to carry whistles.

   (h) Action of covering Party. 4 Rifle Grenadiers on either flank to protect flanks and fire volleys into enemy trench on

(h) **Action of Covering Party (Contd)**
both flanks and our side of enemy wire where they will lie down facing outwards.

(h) If a prisoner is captured he will be taken immediately to Officer in charge who will send him under escort (1 on each side and 1 behind) to our line via the tape.
As soon as the Officer considers he has had time to reach our line or is well on the way he will signal the withdrawal.

(i) **Moppers up** will search for indentifications papers etc.

(j) **Order of Withdrawal** will be :-
  (1) Moppers up
  (2) Bombers.
  (3) Centre Covering Party.
  (4) Liason Party.
  (5) Flank Covering Parties.

(k) **Casualties** if any, will be brought back by Moppers up and Bombers.

8. A Time Table is attached.

9. ZERO hour will be notified later.

10. Watches of all concerned will be synchronised at 4.0.p.m. and again at 10.0.p.m. under arrangements to be made by O.C., 11th Bn., Royal Sussex Regiment.

11. ACKNOWLEDGE.

7.6.17.
Lieut-Colonel,
Commanding, 11th Bn., Royal Sussex Regt.

Copy No. 1 to.......................
   "   " 2 to.......................

OTHER ARRANGEMENTS.

O.C., "C" Company will arrange to cut a gap in our wire at about C.15.c.25.80, (opposite No.11 Post) as soon as it gets dark.
He will also mark out the position of assembly in No Mans Land by means of two lines of sandbags as soon as he has cut the gap in our wire.
He will place a guard of two men at far end of sandbags and another two men at far side of gap in our wire to ensure that no enemy patrol discovers this. These men will be withdrawn as soon as raiders take up position of assembly.

RENDEZVOUS, after the raid will be at Headquarters, Right Support Company in CONEY STREET.

PASS WORD   "CANAL"

Dress. Steel Helmet, Box Respirator on chest, 1 slung bandolier, Rifle, fixed bayonet - no sling.
4 Bombs each man - 2 in each lower pocket of jacket.
Bomber Parties. Two men of each party carry bucket of 10 bombs.
RIFLE BOMBER PARTIES. Two men each carry bucket of 6 Rifle Bombs.

Lieut-Colonel,
Commanding, 11th Royal Sussex Regiment.

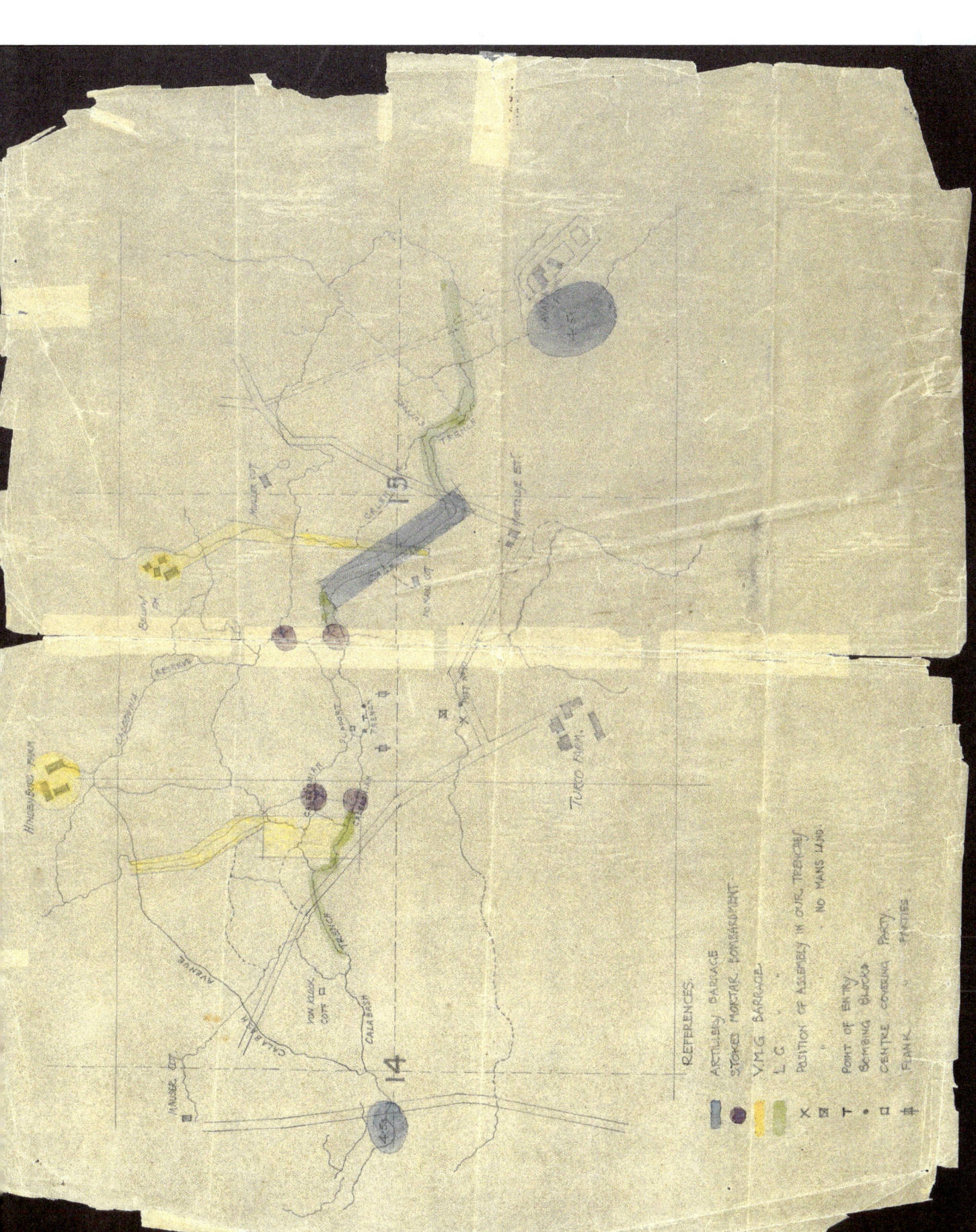

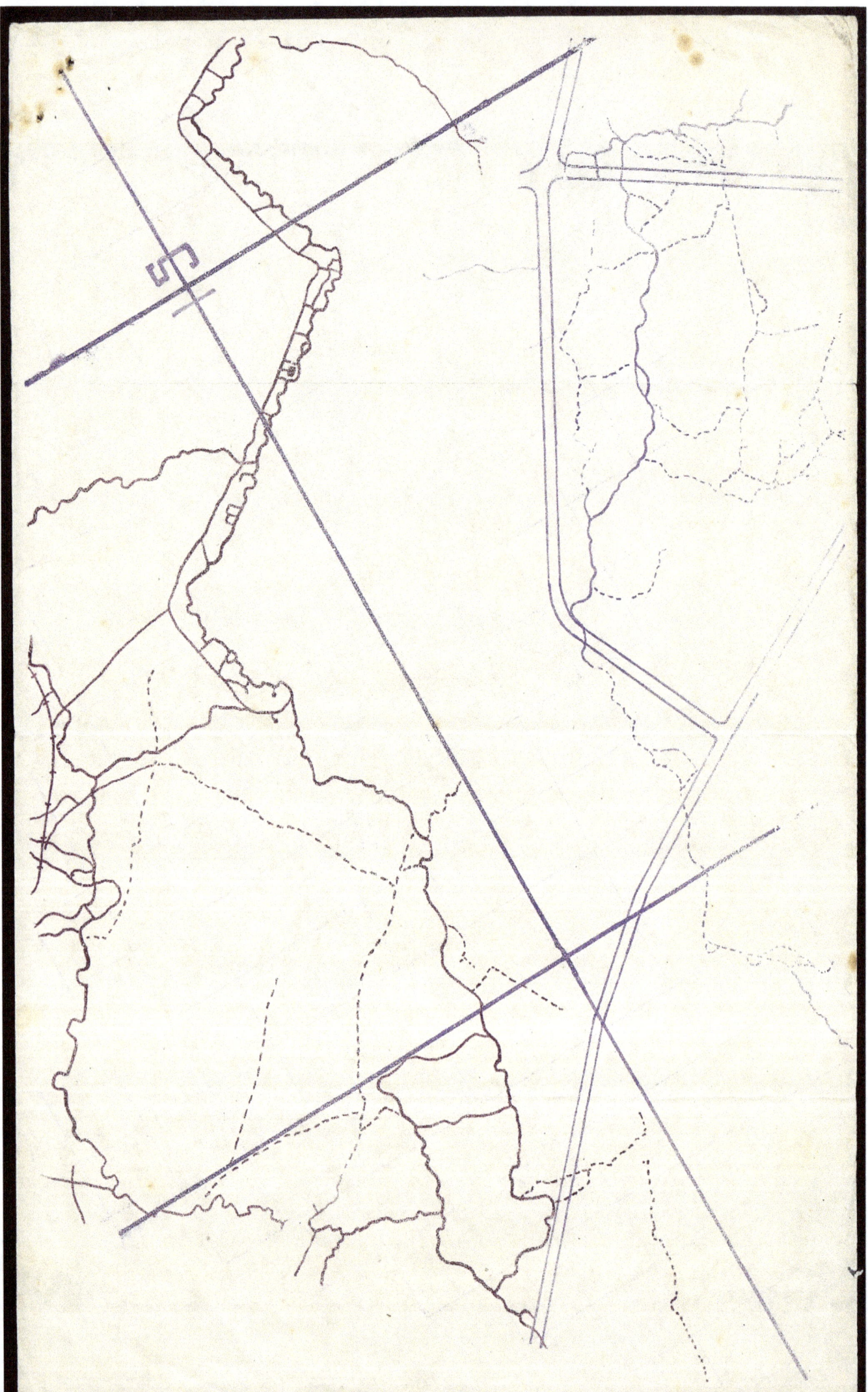

Original

11 R Hussars

1/6/30

17. E
Nathans

Army Form C. 2118.

WAR DIARY
or
INTELLIGENCE SUMMARY.
(Erase heading not required.)

Vol 17

Place	Date	Hour	Summary of Events and Information	Remarks and references to Appendices
HOULLE	JULY 1st		Church Parade 9.45. Battalion marched out to Range, fired 2 Practices. 1st class 3 fires. Bright day. Compt. Commander + C.O. left for Corvee (Special) infantry operations at Corps school. Battalion on parade on Digging of Practice Trenches 8 till 11 am. Returned at 2 pm. 227 CHESTER returned to Hospital sick smoke.	
"	2nd		Battalion engaged on digging of trenches 8 am till 1 pm. Reconnaissance of route & trench system by officers, runners, scouts & guides during digging. Returned to billets at 3 pm.	
"	3rd		Musketry practice during morning on Miniature Ranges. During afternoon continuing digging of practice trenches. Further reconnaissance of trench system by Companies under guidance of runners, scouts.	
"	4th		Training of Companies in Musketry. Bombing, Hermes in Map Reading. Bathing of all the Battalion. Officers returned from Grenade Course.	
"	5th		9am till 12 noon. Bright day. Training of Companies individually on practice trenches in face of Barrage cases of direction. Evening 7 till 6.30 in the Matories. Lecture by C.O. on future operations.	
"	6th		Morning 9 am till 12 noon. Practice attacks under barrage time by the Battalion on practice trenches. Short interview by C.O. to all Companies afterwards. Returned to Billets 2 pm. Fine Day. Afternoon - Brigade Gymkhana of Transport etc. Tours and Practice on Range 7.30 am till 12 noon. Rendezvous practice.	
"	7th		Sunday. Church Parade at 9.45 am. Conference of Intelligence Officers under Brigade Major. Colo. - Conference of Compys Commanders under C.O. Many Thunderstorms during night.	
"	8th		Battalion left Billets 8 am marched to Assembly trenches on practice ground for Brigade practice of the attack. We assembled at 11.30 am. Zero hour 12 noon. Parties carried out under Turin Hate with dummy barrage. Machine fired 1.45 pm. Our operation closed at 2.30 am. Criticism by C.O. on ground to all Companies. Return march 3 pm - all in Billets 4.30 pm. Major W.C. MILLWARD reported from Grenade Course. 227. V. WARD left to join 9th Royal Lancers.	
"	9th		Training in Billets - Musketry, Grenade Throwing etc also lectures on future operations by Section officers. Fine Day. Commanders. Evening 7 - Lecture to Runners and signalling details by Intell. officer.	
"	10th			
"	11th		Brigade attacks. Zero 11 am. Will Range achefore in conjunction with 11th Hf. Brigade attacks. Criticism afterwards. Fine Day.	

Army Form C. 2118.

WAR DIARY
or
INTELLIGENCE SUMMARY.
(Erase heading not required.)

Instructions regarding War Diaries and Intelligence Summaries are contained in F. S. Regs., Part II and the Staff Manual respectively. Title pages will be prepared in manuscript.

Place	Date	Hour	Summary of Events and Information	Remarks and references to Appendices
HOUTLE	Jun 12th		Training under Coy. arrangements in morning. Short periods for rest during afternoon. Battalion marched off at 11-15 p.m. for night operations in Sector Trenches.	
"	13th		Divisional practice under actual attack conditions during hours of dawn. Zero hour 4-10 a.m. Breakfast served at 3 a.m. all Lewis gun men men carried on Mules. Carrying parties organised & practised. Operations closed at 8 a.m. All in Billets 10 a.m. Bathing by Companies during day. Remainder rest. 2nd Lieuts C.L. BARLOW and R.H. ELLIS joined from England for duty.	
"	14th		Coy. Drill 8-10 a.m. then marched to Houtkerke. Very stormy, attacked with rain. 2nd hour 11 a.m. Divisional practice of the attack under actual conditions. Operation finished 3 p.m. Men came in very wet.	
"	15th		Sunday. Church Parades under Brigade arrangements at 10 a.m. followed by Holy Communion. 2nd Oly. Paying out by Companies. Evening. Preparation for moving off back to forward area.	
C. CAMP.	16th		Returned by Train from WATTEN. Marched off 7-10 a.m. Arrived POPERINGHE 11-30 a.m. and proceeded to C. Camp. Lorry transit to head up. Had 9-30 train. Everybody was killed thirteen. Quite a quiet night in spite of numours that the Camp was Shelled. Working parties carrying S.A.A. etc. at night. 2nd/Lt. NAYLOR went on leave.	
C. CAMP.	17th		Wet day. 2nd/Lt. W. Lewis wounded and 2/Lt. W. B.deck taken away during of Brigade Bombing Officer. Companies training 4 hours a day. Musketry. P.T. Lecture on the attack. Practicing Model of Trenches. Working party not very successful during afternoon owing to slump. Was blown up. Working parties at night. A. Coy went up to CANAL BANK to work for Artillery at 7-30.	
"	18th		Raining in the morning. Musketry. P.T. Pistol practice. Musketry. Lecture by Coy. Officer. Coy & CSM. Lecture very Short. No Company. No change rifle. Corps by H.V. C. in Naval Gun. Since very Short. A. Coy. CANAL BANK from Coy during morning. Of Col. Kilshaw infantry night here on CANAL BANK. No working parties at night.	
"	19th		Musketry day. Rain followed training in morning. Lt. Col. CUMMINS proceeded to Field Ambulance. Kept W.C. unwell. Gd. over Battalion with Major J. Cavell on 2 I/c.	
"	20th		Special day. After a very quiet night. Our Artillery giving them hell on. Rumour that Air Raid at Gun that had been knocked out. Late had been shell for 2 hours. A. No. aeroplane flew out back to Poperinghe. Lays bombs struck tube in far direction of MANZEATINGHE. Chilo Casualty. Working party 250.	

A5884 Wt W4973/M687. 750,000. 8/16 D. D. & L. Ltd. Forms/C.2118/13.

WAR DIARY
or
INTELLIGENCE SUMMARY.
(Erase heading not required.)

Army Form C. 2118.

Place	Date	Hour	Summary of Events and Information	Remarks and references to Appendices
C. CAMP	July 21	-	Very fine day. Reconnaissance of tracks to be used on X/Y night. C. Coy. relieved A. Coy. in CANAL BANK. 2/Lt. HARRISON wounded in thigh. Good deal of shelling during early hours. Jerrying large railhead dumps put up by O.C. during the night.	
"	22nd		Beautiful day. 14th and 15th R.I.R., 13th R.I.R., 1 Brigade H.Qrs. arrived about 9. to A 30. Camps. Very close billeting. Aeroplane activity - Artillery enormous. 2/Lt. CONWAY with patrol to ravines detailed to examine wire on the Battle front until the dawn. Quiet night - no working parties.	
"	23rd		Training and drawing of bombs, extra S.A.A. etc to L.T. following for stores. Large working parties during night at CANAL BANK. 2/Lt. CONWAY out to Boyl. Reported knowing whole patrol.	
"	24th		Coy. training during day and working parties under Brigade arrangements. Enemy shelling Camps & ammunition dumps intermittently during day & night. Hostile aeroplane active during night - dropping bombs on ammunition dumps in the vicinity. Company training etc. C-Coy in CANAL BANK sustained severe casualties to O.Rs.	
"	25th		Particulars, casualties &c. Reconnaissance of Model trenches by all ranks. Some of 2 Bombs per man and 50 extra rounds of S.A.A. except specialists. Company training & Inspections - preparing for offensive - going into action and reviewing roles of rest of Bn. to.	
"	26th		Training under Company arrangements. Inspection of Companies in fighting Order. Battn. under 2 hours notice to move up to the line ready to reinforce. that all Books is examined, his front line system. Inspection of field dressing etc, and deficiencies completed. Hostile aeroplane active during night - Bombing ammunition Dumps to. 3 O.Rs. wounded by Bomb at Transport Lines.	
"	27th		Final arrangements before going into line, and inspection by C.O. of kits thrown. 2/Lt. NAYLOR returned from Leave. Lecture to all ranks by C.O. before proceeding to Hilltop Sector. Battalion moved up & took over HILLTOP SECTOR from 6th Lincolns.	
"	28		Battalion paraded at 8.30 p.m.	

Army Form C. 2118.

WAR DIARY
or
INTELLIGENCE SUMMARY

(Erase heading not required.)

Instructions regarding War Diaries and Intelligence Summaries are contained in F. S. Regs., Part II. and the Staff Manual respectively. Title pages will be prepared in manuscript.

Place	Date	Hour	Summary of Events and Information	Remarks and references to Appendices
HILLTOP	July 29.		Fairly quiet day. Enemy shelling C.T.'s & front line - 3 Casualties. To-duck for aerial activity own bombardments incessant all day long.	
"	30.		Enemy Artillery gain very active - 7 Killed, 6 wounded. Battalion moved up into Battle position late this evening. H.Qrs moved to BILGE TRENCH. Bow Knives & Field Guns kept up a continuous barrage all day.	
"	31.		Fairly light. Bombardment continued till 1 hr before Zero. All received hot meals ready for attack by 2 a.m. Barrage commenced 3.50 am Hostile Barrage opened on Front Line & Bilge Trench 1 hour before - Attack progressed well - Yellow & Blue Line taken with few Casualties. B.H.Qrs moved into German trenches in Dry Cut. During afternoon D Company's moved up in close support of 1/4th Hants. Bosch put in abortive attempt of counter attack - nothing happened. Enemy shelling incessant all night - 2/Lt W J Collyer killed. 2/Lt's F.W. Vice, Hayst C. ALLEN wounded. About 150 Casualties amongst O.R. Battle still continuing.	

W. J. Holloway Major
2nd I/C 1/4th Royal Berks Regt

SECRET.

6.6.

11th Batt. Royal Sussex Regt.

Herewith please find copy of
our Operation Orders

[signature]
& Adjutant.
for O.C. 12th Batt. R. Sussex R.

12TH BATTALION,
ROYAL
SUSSEX REGIMENT.
No. 7409
Date 23-7-17

SECRET.

OPERATION ORDER.   12th Bn. Royal Sussex Regt.

Reference Map ST. JULIEN 1/10.000 (SECRET) Sheet 28 N.W.2. Edn 5A

INFORMATION.

   1. (a) The 39th Division is the Right attacking Division of the XVIII Corps.

     (b) The 116th Infantry Brigade is the Right attacking Brigade of the 39th Division.

     (c) The 12th Bn. Royal Sussex Regt. is the Right attacking Battalion of the 116th Infantry Brigade.

BOUNDARIES.

The Battalion Boundaries on the right - a line drawn from Junction of PRATT STREET and CAVAN TRENCH (C.21.c.7.1) through BELLE VUE to CHEDDAR VILLA (C.17.c.7.0) and on the left a line drawn through Junction of FINCH STREET and CAVAN and FORWARD TRENCHES (C.22.c.3.5½) to CROSS ROADS (C.22.c.6.8) through CANADIAN DUGOUTS round N.W. Corner of Moat at MOUSE TRAP FARM and bearing N.E to C.17.c.0.4.

OBJECTIVES.   The Battalion has three objectives:-

   1. The YELLOW Line.   Parts of CALIBAN TRENCH, CALIBAN SUPPORT and CALIFORNIA TRENCH, within the Battalion boundaries.

   2. The RED Line.   CALIBAN ROW, PART OF CALIBAN RESERVE, within the Battalion boundaries.

   3. The BLUE Line &   CALIFORNIA RESERVE and TRENCH
      the DOTTED BLUE   running N.E. side of MOUSE TRAP FARM
      Line roughly from   within the Battalion boundaries.
      C.17.c.7.0 to C.17.c.0.4

The Battalion will attack on a two Company Front, and each Company on a two platoon front.
Dividing line between companies - a line drawn from C.22.c.5.3 to C.17.c.4.3½.

LIAISON.   "D" Company will detail one N.C.O and six other ranks to form a Liaison Post at C.22.d.80.99 (Junction of Southern Boundary with German Front Line.

        "C" Company will detail one officer and twenty five other ranks to capture CHEDDAR VILLA (C.17.c.7.0) and form a liaison post there.

        Both these posts getting into touch with troops of the Division working on our right.

COMPANY OBJECTIVES.

"D" Company will attack and capture the YELLOW and RED Lines on the Right advancing in two waves from the Assembly Trenches - HOPKINS and ARMYTAGE Trenches.

The objective of the first wave will be the RED Line
" " of the Second wave will be the YELLOW Line.

Bombing parties for dealing with CALIFORNIA DRIVE and CALIFORNIA AVENUE will be detailed by the first wave.

When the BLUE waves have passed through to attack and capture the BLUE and DOTTED BLUE LINES, "D" Coy. will move forward in support.

On the capture of the BLUE and the DOTTED BLUE LINES "D" Company will start making artillery bridges over the German Front Line System of Trenches.

"C" Company will attack and capture the BLUE and the DOTTED BLUE LINE on the right, and will advance in Artillery formation from assembly in CAVAN TRENCH extending on crossing HOPKINS TRENCH and moving forward in two waves, passing through the YELLOW and RED Lines.

No. 10 Platoon of the Second Wave will be responsible for dealing with the BLUE LINE (CALIFORNIA RESERVE) and when completed, moving forward to the DOTTED BLUE LINE and assisting in consolidation.

A Bombing party will be detailed by "C" Company to work up CALIFORNIA DRIVE to the DOTTED BLUE LINE.

No. 12 Platoon will occupy CHEDDAR VILLA and consolidate it and act as liaison party with the troops on the right.

Another strong point will be consolidated by "C" Company on its Front, adjacent to the DOTTED BLUE LINE.

"A" Company will attack and capture the YELLOW and RED Lines on the left, advancing in two waves from assembly in HOPKINS and ARMYTAGE Trenches.

The objective of the first wave will be the
RED LINE, CALIBAN ROW. and CALIBAN RESERVE.

The objective of the second wave will be the YELLOW LINE, CALIBAN TRENCH and CALIBAN SUPPORT.

Two Bombing parties will be detailed by the first wave to deal with CALIBAN ROW and CALIBAN RESERVE and communicating trench from C.11.b.5.1. to C.11.b.7.5.

When the BLUE waves have passed through the RED Line for the attack on the BLUE and the DOTTED BLUE Lines, "A" Coy. will move up in support.

If not required to assault, the BLUE or the DOTTED BLUE Line, this Company will immediately reorganise and be held in readiness to support the attack on the BLACK LINE if called upon to do so.

"B" Company will attack and capture the BLUE and the DOTTED BLUE LINES advancing in Artillery Formation from assembly in CAVAN TRENCH extending on crossing HOPKINS TRENCH and moving forward in two waves passing through the YELLOW and RED Lines.

No. 5 platoon will be pushed forward close under the Barrage to capture MOUSE TRAP FARM immediately the RED LINE is taken.

The remaining platoons advancing and capturing the BLUE and the DOTTED BLUE LINES.

No. 8 platoon dealing with the Northern part of CALIFORNIA RESERVE.

Nos. 5 and 8 platoons will move forward and assist in the consolidation of the DOTTED BLUE LINE when they have dealt with MOUSE TRAP FARM and CALIFORNIA RESERVE.

Two strong points will be consolidated by "B" Company on its front and adjacent to the DOTTED BLUE LINE.

Each Company will detail a Carrying Party of one N.C.O and seven O.Rs to carry from Battalion Dump up to Company Dumps.

Each Lewis Gun Team will carry up 16 loaded Lewis Gun magazines and 16 more per gun will be carried up by the Carrying Party.

Lewis Gun and S.A. Ammunition will be carried to Company Dumps where empty Lewis Gun magazines should be filled by members of the Lewis Gun team.

BATTALION HEADQUARTERS - old Right Company Headquarters in BILGE TRENCH.

BATTALION FORWARD COMMAND POST - near road at South entrance to MOUSE TRAP FARM, where Battalion H.Qs will move on capture of the BLUE and the DOTTED BLUE Lines.

Distance between waves will be forty yards, closing up as objectives are reached.
Barrage Map attached.

                         sd. W. COOTE BROWN.
                             Lieut.Colonel, Commanding.
                             11th Bn. Royal Sussex Regt.

19.7.17

TIME TABLE to accompany ORDER No. _____

Time	Infantry	L.T.M's	V.M Guns	Lewis Guns	Rifle Grenadiers	Artillery	Remarks
Zero less 45'	Advance to Post N.M.						
Zero less 15'	To move out to a point on N. Man's land						
Zero less 5 mints	Commence crawling forward						
Zero	Rush forward to Enemy Trench	Open fire	Open fire	Open fire		Open fire	
Zero plus 1 minute	Enter Enemy Trench				Open fire		
Zero plus 5 minutes	Infantry leave enemy trench and get back to our line				Finish firing & return to our trench by party of Lewis guns		
Zero plus 20	—	"Cease firing"	"Cease firing"	"Cease firing"		"Cease firing"	

Army Form C. 2118.

WAR DIARY
or
INTELLIGENCE SUMMARY.
(Erase heading not required.)

Instructions regarding War Diaries and Intelligence Summaries are contained in F. S. Regs., Part II. and the Staff Manual respectively. Title pages will be prepared in manuscript.

Place	Date	Hour	Summary of Events and Information	Remarks and references to Appendices
3rd Battle of YPRES	1st Aug 1917		The Battle Continued – It rained heavily all night & continued through the day. Reinforcements were sent through to consolidate the new Blackline. Potted Black line was constituted by the Dotted Black, Solid Black lines abandoned. The new Headquarters Coys, 2 Coys in Potted Black line were at Shrapnel Corner & Junction Dug outs. Camp reserve in Cafe Belge dug outs. Enemy shelled during whole night with heavy HE plus with gas around Kitchener Wood, Kitchener Wood, Hampshire Farm & along Black line. Artillery cooperation very good.	
		7.30pm	Orders were received to relieve 11th Hampshire in line of 11th Sterenbeek dotted Black + Solid Black lines. Relief completed 3am on 2nd. Casualties not known. Only 2 Casualties.	
"	2nd Aug 1917		Disposition after the relief was: Advanced Company Hampshire Dotted Black line. 2 Platoons on left in front. 2 Platoons + H.Q on right. 11th Hampshires left on Blackline Hq. Held 12 Sub Deblaize line. Starting Headqrs: East side of valley, Railway Embkt. E of the Sterenbeek. 1 Coy Hants + Coys Rifles attached. Complition unknown at present. During advance Tank + Bde went with Signallers + ranging Battn moved up not up to the enemy fire. Signallers followed up from Gordon House throughout the whole time laying cables, & took part in fighting. Sec. Lieut A.C. Hunt & Sec Lieut Lidbrook RAM were all the time helping by about 20th KRRC 11th 2nd Bde 2nd Bde West along the whole front.	
		1.15pm	Relief was completed. 3rd Coys Hampshire bivouacked at Caesar line. 1st Aug were relieved by 14th AIF Tasking the 2nd 4th Battalion.	
	3rd Aug	10.30am	Battn in the relief moved back into Dugouts on the Canal bank in Divisional Reserve. Battn relieved by 3.30am.	
			Battn at ± midday moved overland from Bde 5 miles back by road, marching past the School Camp, St Jean O/S Brisset Farm, arrived at Russells Camp, Saragin Farm, Barracks Station YPRES + Elverdinghe. + Brielen Pontoon.	
SCHOOL CAMP	4th Aug		Remained at Camp. The whole of the day was spent on cleaning up + Reorganising.	
	5th Aug		Reform + Conference on whole + examination rows at the Burgdial of Company. Continuation of Reorganisation.	
	6th Aug		Russell's 7 am. Morning was devoted to continuation of Reorganisation for the occupation of the new Line. Russell 4 pm. Afternoon was devoted to Route march + tomorrow in to Reserve. During the afternoon advances & moving part of Kenora Camp to Caestre proceeding to Bailleul Railway. Russell 7am...	
	7th Aug		Resting 7am. Morning devoted to Reconnaissance for all purposes. Carried on to more Route March + Tactics training & Games.	
	8th Aug		Revelle 4.30am. Transfer of Coys to continue. Fell in at 6.30 + moved back marching then to the good roads. They had some during the afternoon the receive of Brigadier before leaving for the XVIII Corps.	
"			Revelle 4:30am. March off 6:30am. B Coy Bn Barbed wire Brigade & 1st Army L.R. Balloons Service. March by Bus to Meteren at 9:15am. A 9:15am day 13 Bus leaving at little Strat.	
METEREN	9th Aug		Revelle 7am. Divisional Commander inspected the Bde. Congratulated & Remarked on the dignified exercises, schoolwork which the Bn has done. The Bn was remarked to their more preliminary attacks rest day move Monday.	
"	10th Aug		At 2 am the Bde was inspected by the 2nd Army Commander. Congratulating the Battalion on their fine work. AFC was also inspected the unit trenches & Officers of Staff giving them some insight of the future. A 2 pm Draft of Cols & Cpl from II Corps rejoined Line XIII Bn to assist.	
			(General resigned in the afternoon.) General service for U.S.A. National service & move in. Lt Worcester 12 assist of men in the Neighbourhood course proceeded for 9 Corps. General Journal at Youryvount...	
	11th Aug		The morning was spent in reorganisation + Inspection of the Line. The 3rd Suffolks were down in B Coys left. W/o Gerry + Hanson & B Coys left. Centrer & then combined. The Back from the 3rd Suffolks in the afternoon ... the after rain & morning had proved very during. B Coys Read to all the rest the Div. Now the S Batt fighting. 6th Wellingtons.	
	12th Aug	6am	Reveille at 6am. March to Meteren by Motor Bus arrived 11:30am. B. R. Burn & Capt Fisher.	
SPOIL BANK	13th Aug		Reorganising this morning. The usage in hanging up for the Line. An Inspection made were all the Companies ... to check the Batt Dressing & Stock. At 3pm moved off to the support sector. A very quick relief in a few shells firing. During the night starting to the No Shocky Dug-out + Battalion HQ in Spoil Bank, coming off the Ypres Comine Road in line.	

At 12 midnight Gerry fired two gas shells. No gas. Very busy firing |

WAR DIARY
or
INTELLIGENCE SUMMARY.
(Erase heading not required.)

Army Form C. 2118.

Place	Date	Hour	Summary of Events and Information	Remarks and references to Appendices
SUPPORT. LEFT SUBSECTOR HOLLEBEKE	AUG 14		Quiet day. Enemy fairly quiet. Capt Salving ME took over 2/3 in Comm and 2/3 in comm and Lieut Adm. Capt Herbs in comm during relief of companies. During the night Capt Fountain with his Company shelled by the main Army area at many different parts by enemy aeroplanes, returning to the front line. Two Lewis gun teams & M.G.E.O. if 13 at 3 pm a Lewis was very near by Its a German aeroplane. The Company then worked on the front and back support trenches to improving the dugout few casualties.	
"	AUG 15		Improvement of Mule Track continues also electric working on the Company positions where noted shelters in trenches study owing to the large number of front in between them positions vacuum rated by the front line. He was up Seven casualties during the day. gained supplies, supplying drainage swampy sub typ course in the R.M. Banks.	
"	AUG 16		Work in trenches & mule track & carrying and & spares up to front line in preparation for relief of the first line Bde 8m from Camraderie during the night 16.	
"	AUG 17		Advance parties proceeded to the front line & the Welsh Battalion moved up at 3:50 3 Coy Comming Front line, A the B the in support near Imm D at right relief Bn was Enemies on our Right. At 3 am Right Front Coy in charge went with Lieut Bouvert & Coy in Reserve in the North Chateau Lieut O'Neill & 13th RSR & N'W to both as crossed the Little Creek is very many men to the hammock the Battn approach the Kenney bodies ne gel but no one we have by this man in with enemy alone so blasted. Wing & shot total crowd in.	
HOLLE BEKE LEFT SUB SECTOR	AUG 18		A fairly quiet day. The front line was shelled a little during Mule Track was contin't a brisk shelled ne morning of the relief killed. Heavy shelling of most areas during the morning. Two casualties.	
"	AUG 19		Another quite day with the exception of heavy shelling of back area & special attention being paid to OAK DUMP. Recieved of SMOA sent away make up of 3rd Coats ught Prussians were again shelled during the afternoon but easy far and infrared by front communication and enemies of rather difficult his infreviate message as at deposits at daylights 8/2 WOODWAY & Proceeded to & Corps Gunns course. Hot cheeked out our new rates of 2/3 Capt from X.A.P.M. 2 Gas alerts during the night to 5.9 + 4.2 + 4.5 at the Junction of the BESSIEGE.	
"	AUG 20		Nothing very much doing. A certain amount of electrical shelling rounds slowly of whole extend. The great relief knack in Hayes he movement to the Passive Coy, Partole again the front Both informed by the 18th Hampshire Reg being many rolled out by the 18th Hampshire Reg Relief completed at 11.30 pm. Before coming down from front on the Canal Bank near Lock No 6 Bde A Cross the gutt Camera by the monthly staff of the frames. On Relief the Battalion went again into the Support position in SPOIL BANK & the OLD GERMAN Huts.	
"	AUG 21			
SUPPORT LEFT SUBSECTOR HOLLEBEKE	AUG 22		Dispositions slightly altered. A Coy occupying Bogsand & SpoilBrk with the SPOIL BANK unfortunately ranked the Railway Station spoil bank with the Submarine Shack h suffered 6 casualties in which the 16th ARMY had carried out hastily at night to break lay in shelter on the track took line the material Relieved by the 16th RIFLE BGE. Lt YOUNG Bell - Releif completed quick and duly + a most pleasant walk back to ROB'S WOOD CAMP. Great Antelantin Taken again shelling during the relief of three Platoons being detailed to take Sond & Spoilbank by many of our friends to watch he Country. The BATTERY Groups to Runstalla.	
"	AUG 23			
RIDGE WOOD CAMP	AUG 24		Revilles 7am Cleaning up - followed half of Refreshments. The Sand bags by all Ranks were Enjoyable. A Cot infact were being treated 3' x 2' 6" was been lectured against from aeroplane bombs from Messrs gum & count mounted for Anti Aircraft defence. Lt WORCESTER USA made Several lectures & Capt GLOSTER returned from Leave.	

WAR DIARY or INTELLIGENCE SUMMARY

Army Form C. 2118.

11 R Sussex 116/39
9/8/18

Place	Date	Hour	Summary of Events and Information	Remarks and references to Appendices
RIDGE WOOD CAMP	Aug 25		Cleaning & smartening up. Companies completed the second days in of Bn. under officers. Return in ordinary from lines for the section of the Bde for Brigade and was visited by GOC.	
"	Aug 26		Shelled by a hostile 4.2" gun during the early hours of the morning – two men wounded. Companies did 3 trainings in Small Squads during the morning. Rests & recreation in the afternoon	
"	Aug 27		Advance parties proceeded to the line arriving at 2 a.m. A very wet night. The Companies getting ready, supper at 7.30 p.m. Battalion entrained & left Dominion Camp to move up by the line. Band played as at 7.30 pm in the army area & also 11 to 12 when 116th 117th 118th Bdes saw better relief. Marched past Nep + from Rly the whole time.	
RIGHT BATTN LEFT BDE	Aug 28		Dispositions as per wire. D Coy. L. FRONT COY man and Reach. no ration wish Chuckboards. B Coy R FRONT COY. A Coy SUPPORT COY on W side of a railway embankment & B Coy in RESERVE. Bn HQ in all Coy HQ S& Capt the SUPPORT COY were in CONCRETE dugouts very strong but not all occupied as the first line was not reachable by day. any the SUPPORT & RESERVE Coys could be reached. A very quiet day with practically no shelling – no casualties.	
"	Aug 29		A very lovely day when drill of the battalion's quietly. Gunboats were obtained & the rations & hot meals given got well into working order & everybody feeling much happier in consequence. The support & reserve Coys were supplying men and equips, rest samples, & the support Coy impound dugouts + shelters in the SOMERBY EMBANKMENT. The trench train which were manned & constantly working moved about the enemy dugouts, which were mainly visible in the hedge in front from this bunting were sent out at night to reconnoitre the railway embank line to find if possible a Captain on the embank.	
"	Aug 30		Owing to the wind which still continued to blow having what because much driven very little enemy traffic from our own artillery was noted obscuring the enemy in the afternoon the 4.5" Hows did a very good shoot on the enemy's concrete dugouts several direct hits being seen. At night several patrols were sent out and obtained upon amount of information concerning the enemy's dispositions.	
"	Aug 31		Relieved by the 16th HIGHLAND LT INFY. 10.20 p.m. Z army guide taking effective to Hussar Le Quint. No casualties at cell during this tour from Battn HQ D Coy went to Rifle Reserve lines. B Coy at the Trump-war Bluff. A Coy at Spoil Bank Tunnels C + D Coys + Bn HQ in GORDON TR + CONVENT LANE near YPRAMETREELE.	18 E 3 sheet

F. Hossack Major
H. H. R Pierce

11th Bn R Sussex R · Original · SEPT. 1917. 116/39

WAR DIARY or INTELLIGENCE SUMMARY
Army Form C. 2118.

Vol 19

Place	Date	Hour	Summary of Events and Information	Remarks and references to Appendices
CORDON TR VOORMEZEELE	SEPT 1		On Divisional Reserve. 2 Coys at VOORMEZEELE. 1 Coy SPOIL BANK. 1 Coy PROVOSTS GUARD. Very quiet day. Working parties at night.	
"	SEPT 2		Grassy rather windy all day & being fired on with any mind. Shared with MV gun at JULIAN. Working parties at night. Recently by the SCHOOL WATSON & relieving the RIDGE WOOD CAMP.	
RIDGE WOOD CAMP	SEPT 3		Cleaning & Smartening up. The Battn in ??? returned to Arms through the night. R/Lt C ?? BLUNDEN MUELLER to 2ND ARMY WIRELESS COURSE.	
RIDGE WOOD CAMP	SEPT 4		REORGANISATION & Rest. Football during the afternoon. Being very active work for Platoon during the night. No casualties.	
"	SEPT 5		Continuing at ditto. Visit of Coy Commanders during the morning for party of 2nd Ren?? to DICK. Buff & Research. A ??? looking much better for the guiding time & rest.	
"	SEPT 6		Bath ?? looking much better for the guiding time & rest.	
"	SEPT 7		RECONNAISSANCE of MT SORREL SECTOR by Officers & NCOs. ADVANCE parties to MT SORREL as ???? suddenly receives ? move out ??	
"	SEPT 8		Batt'n moves off 5/pm to relieve 1/1 CAMBS in MT SORREL SECTOR - very quiet relief - completed 9.30pm Bnhd HQ BASIN CO'S KHIVE HOUSE during the night.	
MT SORREL	SEPT 9		Fairly quiet piece of line but ??? mines area run. Coys of Infantry down going in to the coming SKON. DISPOSITIONS from hrm 13 Coy SUPPORT, A COY RESERVE C & D Coys ~ MT SORREL TUNNELS. RMR ?? Coys working Camps ???? + HORSEIN	
MT SORREL	SEPT 10		SACQUEREES Identity of a gnd shd army 5th Lanft numbers of Kicks being made & communications to line ?? up. Moving ??? in front line at night. No casualties.	
MT SORREL	SEPT 11		RESERVE Coys working to?? hard Carrying Timber to the TUNNELLERS. A Bn TR THE 4/5 DIV CASUALTIES 1.	
MT SORREL	SEPT 12		2/Lt LAWTHER attached on 6th ARMY Co COMMANDERS Course. Relieved by 7 KRRC Relieved ?? in dugouts at CONVENT LANE Rest & Cleaning up. Small working parties to RKES DUG OUT ???	
VOORMEZEELE	SEPT 13	SEPT 14	On Div Reserve in dugouts at CONVENT LANE Rest & Cleaning up. BAGLOW invalided on 1/CORPS GEN COURSE. 1/4 EUSTWOOD to BE B & R 23 REST.	

A 5834 Wt. W4973/M687 750,000 8/16 D.D.&L.Ltd. Forms/C.2118/13.

Army Form C. 2118.

WAR DIARY
or
INTELLIGENCE SUMMARY.
(Erase heading not required.)

Instructions regarding War Diaries and Intelligence Summaries are contained in F.S. Regs., Part II. and the Staff Manual respectively. Title pages will be prepared in manuscript.

Place	Date	Hour	Summary of Events and Information	Remarks and references to Appendices.
SHRAPNEL CNR. FOREST SECTOR.	15		Bn paraded at 8 p.m. and marched to BRIGADE HEADQRS. NOM R.S.s in LARGA WOOD TUNNELS. Relief complete 6 p.m. Very wet day - arrived heavily draggled. Enemy retaliation was slack. Bdy retaliated being distroyed by tracks though the night by 1.O.R. trenchen.	
	16		Our guns very active. Special practice barrages at 10 a.m. and 6 p.m. Aeroplanes were kept busy registering and NOT one hostile though the shelled ZILLEBEKE rather H.E. and shrapnel. Working parties supplied from 1 O.R. trenchers.	
	17		Not very shelling by our artillery, practice barrages at 5.30 a.m. and 3 p.m. Enemy guns retaliated THOMPSON'S DUMP. Working parties —	
	18		Shelling still heavy on both sides. Bn relieved by 17th CRR and marched to ASCOT CAMP VIZERTURE. Relief advance parties & the left along afternoon. A shell burst in rear of timber sat'd camp, killing 7 O.R., wounding Snipit. Class R. Eng B. and ORs also wounded. Bn arrived camp at 11.2 p.m. Enemy were searching for 1st 93.OTS. Hevel 500 new road. Bn. wounded 1 Bar CAPT CULTRA & ORs.	
		2 p.m.	at practice ground L.S.B. during forthcoming operations. L.B. attacked and L.H.S.O.R. guns B.C. Q.M. STAFF N.4 on tour.	
ASCOT CAMP	19		Reveille 10 a.m. Rest & cleaning.	
	20		B.O's inspections Coy (saving) Recreation in afternoon.	
	21		The same, also Baths.	
	22	4 p.m.	Bn moved to BEGGAR'S REST into huts just before Bn left ASCOT CAMP	
BEGGAR'S REST MENIN ROAD	23	3 a.m.	Intense fire B was rather 4 a.m. Bn proceeded into support in CLONMEL COPSE.	
	24		Bn role over front line immediately S of MENIN ROAD, relieving 8th Y.&.L. Heavy bombardment throughout the night.	
	25		In the early morning enemy attacked on a wide front and was unsuccessful on our left K.A. Our Capt. CAREW counter-attacked our division front & gave the enemy no chance, inflicting heavy casualties and wide NOMANS LAND. To meet things of this party afterwards be supported our left flank by direct. He return from a dugout on the road our front trigger again was warm. Enemy's shelling and his infantry, violent and our casualties were heavy.	
	26		The HQ Bdu including 13th R.S.R. and 14th HANTS with 1 platoon in 11 R.S.R. attacked our left attacks yesterday actions shelling a considerable SOS trigger position.	
	27		Enemy shelling died out our H.Q. dugout killed CAPT GATEMILL (B.MO.) the F.OO. and SDR. Battalion on relieved by 13 R.S. and went back to 30 FORT CORPSE. D Company hurried had to return to close supports Bn finally moved back to 1805 HOUSE this (am still known as a BRIGADE	
Mt. BEGREN	28		Arrival at camp 5 a.m. Rest and cleaning. Estimated casualties of this war 10 officers 195 OR.	
	29		Visit by Major General & four of his Staff	
	30		Adm. CHURCH PARADE CO's inspections.	

M Kelsey Millward Lt. Col.
ONSG 11th R. Sussex R.

TIME TABLE to accompany ORDER No _____ Copy No 2.

Time	Infantry	L.T.Mˢ	V.M. Guns	Lewis Guns	Rifle Grenadiers	Artillery	Remarks
Zero less 45'	Assemble at Post No 11						
Zero less 15'	To move out to assembly point 112 "No Man's Land"						
Zero less 5 minutes	Commence crawling forward						
Zero	Rush forward to Enemy Trench	Open fire	Open fire	Open fire		Open fire	
Zero plus 1 minute	Enter Enemy Trench				Open fire		
Zero plus 11 minutes	Infantry leave enemy trench and get back to our line				Finish firing and return to our trenches in rear of Raiding party		
Zero plus 20	—	Cease firing	Cease firing	Cease firing		Cease firing	

CONFIDENTIAL

11TH BN. ROYAL SUSSEX REGT.

WAR DIARY

— FOR —

1ST October 1917 to 31st October 1917

VOLUME 20.

WAR DIARY or INTELLIGENCE SUMMARY

Army Form C. 2118.

Place	Date	Hour	Summary of Events and Information	Remarks and references to Appendices
KOKEREELE (STAFFORD CAMP)	1.10.17		C.O's inspection of coys during morning. Reorganization of coys: training of S/Bts in the afternoon, rest and recreation am) to consent by Turches. At about 9 pm enemy aircraft dropped bombs on fifth Stand vtg at Road field. Killing 11 and wounding 15 ORs. Weather fine.	
	2.10.17		Section and platoon training. 2.30 p.m. G.O.C. 39th Div'n inspected the Bttn. in the field of 12th R.S.F. and presented decorations in connection with the ST JULIEN battle, starting with the G.O.C to Lt Col MILLWARD. He complimented the Brig. Genl. on commanding such an efficient Bttn., and then inspected the Transport Lines. Dessert by Turches.	
	3.10.17		Physical, specialists and Sec. Section training. C.O.'s lecture to officers on Bttn. training 2.30, 2.30 p.m. Baths. — ST JANS CAPELLE. Night operations 7.30 — 8.30 p.m. — movements in Box respirators. Dull weather.	
	4.10.17		Training conts. 2/Lts E.DAVISON, R.C.M. WIGSBERY-SMITH, A.G.A. INDIA & W.G.P. CALDICOTT promoted Lieutenants. Draft 7-10 ORs joined.	
	5.10.17		No leather. 2 coys firing on the rifle range in the morning. Lt BURR seconded to England.	
	6.10.17		Marching and Respirators 5.30 a.m. Inspection by Br Genl HORSLEY. 9 a.m. Gas demonstration and tests 10 a.m. Sports arranged for the battalion caring to inclement weather.	
	7.10.17		Raining again. Divine service. C.of E. 11 a.m. 2/Lt WHITING joined Bttn.	
	8.10.17		Training again. C.O. Coys firing on the range. Lt MAYCOCK vacated leave. His duties as T.O. being subsequently taken over by Capt. G. SALTER. Capt. G.A.ALLEN rejoined Bttn and was with HQ. Hot day.	
	9.10.17		5 a.m. Route march. HQ. fired on Range. Inoculation by M.O.	
	10.10.17		Training conts. Range used by S Coy and still details. 25 O.R's assumed on Reinforcements.	
	11.10.17		8.30 a.m. Route March. 2-3 pm Battalion drill at the Double. 2/Lt LAMBORTH granted leave. Service range limit for 13th & American North D.O.R.O and an Reconnaissance.	
	12.10.17		Physical, ordinary & Box breathing. Sections on toilets and tea. Platoon training 6.7 pm. Nights of Bon Respirators.	
	13.10.17		Baths and Musketry. Football etc. in afternoon. Route march. Roystock practices completed. Orders to move on 14th received. Party under S.BURNHAM reconnoitered camp near VIERSTRAAT. Working party attacked to Rifle Bde Gr GALARY. Great guns of East, NE and rain.	
	14.10.17		Sunday. Divine service. More postponed. Lts J.B. J.G BUTLER joined Bttn. Parade at 3 Coy Western Front. C.O. 2/I/C obtained reconnoitred up to the line, No also slightly hindered by having to form through an open block. 12 BUNDAY Tubes and Tram Motor rubles to COATHAM STREET TUNNELS. Lt Col G.G HARRISON rejoined the 13th. 11 ORs reinforcements.	
	15.10.17		Getting up and inspection during the morning. 2.45 p.m. Bttn marched to Embussing position near Road and took lorries to GUM BANK — Shine marched in CHAPS TO MEDIC'S ST TUNNELS. Transport lines moved to BEAVER CAMP REMINGEL.	

Signed Lt Col.
Comdg 11th Royal Sussex

E.B.

Army Form C. 2118.

WAR DIARY
or
INTELLIGENCE SUMMARY.
(Erase heading not required.)

Instructions regarding War Diaries and Intelligence Summaries are contained in F.S. Regs., Part II. and the Staff Manual respectively. Title pages will be prepared in manuscript.

Place	Date	Hour	Summary of Events and Information	Remarks and references to Appendices
CANADA STREET TUNNELS near ZILLEBEKE	16.10.17		Day spent in cleaning tunnels, building latrines, re-arranging accommodation and burying dead. Enemy quiet (for this sector).	
	17.10.17		Advance parties turned to the front line at dawn. Bn relieved 12 R.S.R. AFM DAM S. of TOWER HAMLETS; relief complete by 8 pm. Rain depressing. B, C, & D in front line, left to right. A in support. In quiet relief followed by intermittent shelling on both sides. Rain after mid-night.	
TOWER HAMLETS RIGHT	18.10.17		Our Artillery and M.G. Barrage at 5.30 am. Enemy replied. Fire detached at 6.0am reopened at 8.10 am. Artillery fairly active on both sides during the day. Enemy sent over thousand gas shells into Sanctuary mid-night and 3 hours. Ten D dropped bombs near Bn H.Q. & front line. Bn H.Q. round junction N. 6 to the steep side of BODMIN COPSE. Enemy fire at 8pm. 2/Lt GRANT and 2 ORs wounded.	
	19.10.17		Patrols out during night, but ground too churned up for any accurate information. Artillery quiet. Enemy prisoners afterwards including 2 ORs wounded. Bn relieved during the night 19/20 by 17 KRRC. Reconcentration of our forward posts was observed by the enemy who (who?) a great number of very lights and opened a barrage with Mint rifle grenades, killing 1/Lt KEANE, split No 9 who was first up, but enemy firing did not keep up.	
Near VIERSTRAAT	20.10.17		Weather wet going difficult over ice duckboards. On reliefs, Bn marched to BOIS CAMP 3/0 J.D S.E. of the BRASSERIE. Rest refitting. Building parapets round tents. Lt. BOOKER - HISSEY joined. Lt. LIMBURY-BUSS and OLIVE went on leave. Fire worker 25 Ch. reinfts.	
	21.10.17		Sundry Divisional Inspections. Baths at KEMMEL CHAV. Enemy aeroplanes dropped bombs in vicinity at dawn. Training under Coy. arrangements. Advanced parties sent to next billets but shortly recalled. A fly pond R.E. Travellers at VIERSTRAAT in working party.	
	22.10.17		2/Lt. P.A. IRBY joined. B.P., as also T.R.R. J.7. Lt. CL BROWN prior promotion to rank. Capt.'s leave franch on completion of 18 months commissioned service.	
CARNARVON CAMP	23.10.17		Bn moved bus KEMMEL, LOCRE and CANADA CORNER to CARNARVON CAMP, parading 12.45 pm and arriving at 4.1 pm. This bomb had previously been used as horse lines and was in a very muddy and comfortless state. Raining most of the day.	
Near RENINGHELST	24.10.17		Camp cleaned, most hints, moved up. Tents trenched up: Baths drawing. Enemy planes near recent was 16 nights. Reinforcements 2 ORs.	
	25.10.17		Cpls of land and men still rifle's piece in the Bay 2 Cpn. frost on Rifle Range. Training programme cont.?	
	26.10.17		Rain all day next evening D route march cancelled. Quiet night. Reinforcements 2 O.Rs.	
	27.10.17		First Baths at WESTOUTRE. Training. L/Cpl DAVIES and L/Cpl STURGEON went on leave to U.K.	
CHIPPEWA CAMP	28.10.17		Advance party left CARNARVON CAMP at 10 am. Bn paraded 1.40 pm and marched via CANADA CORNER to LA CLYTTE to CHIPPEWA CAMP arriving 4 pm. Bn billeted in huts. Publication of names of numbered for gallantry on 26th Sept. and subsequent days in 16 NCO's and men (M.M.)	Appendix A Appendix B
	29.10.17		Weather fine. Training as per programme. Camp improvements carried out.	
	30.10.17		Training cont? Heavy bomb dropped close to camp 11.30 pm	
	31.10.17		During the month, 50 part of the pioneers me, Bn had a new allotment of 7 for day. Many who were ink came in were not due to the in March 1916 and SOMME HILL wth it was now unable to get their leave.	CB

Lt-Col
Comdg. 11th R. SUSSEX REGT.

APPENDIX A

11TH Service Battalion Royal Sussex Regiment.

AFTER BATTALION ORDERS
by
Lieut-Colonel W.C.MILLWARD. D.S.O. Comdg.

245. **HONOURS & AWARDS.**

Under authority granted by the Field Marshal-Commanding in-Chief, the General Officer Commanding Xth-Corps has awarded the following decorations to the undermentioned N.C.O,s. and men for gallantry and devotion to duty:-

THE MILITARY MEDAL.

15834	L/Cpl.	W. SALMON.	11th Bn. R. Sussex R
1016	A/Sgt.	J. WATSON.	do.
773	Pte.	G. AVIS.	do.
6871	Cpl.	J. KEYS.	do.
16586	Pte.	C. BINGHAM.	do.
2665	L/Cpl.	H.J. BAKER.	do.
15819	Pte.	F. CHANDLER.	do.
990	L/Cpl.	W. ELPHICK.	do.
13200	"	V. DEEPROSE.	do.
15682	Pte.	C. BLUNDEN.	do.
15224	"	B. FAULKNER.	do.
738	"	W.E. SHEARING.	do.
5979	"	J. DUNNINGHAM.	do.
185	L/Cpl.	G. GUILDFORD.	do.
20450	Pte.	C. MASON.	do.

The Commanding Officer heartily congratulates the recipients of the above decorations.

(Sd) W.C.F. CALDWELL.
Lieut. A/Adjt.
28/10/17.   11th Bn. Royal Sussex Regiment.

BAR TO MILITARY MEDAL.

307 Pte. H.E. FISHENDEN. 11th Bn. R. Sussex Regt.

APPENDIX B

11th Service Battalion Royal Sussex Regiment.
PROGRAMME OF TRAINING FROM 29.10.17 TO 4.11.17.

29.10.17.
- 7.30 a.m. to 7.45 a.m. Foot Rubbing.
- 9.0 a.m. to 10.30 a.m. Instruction in Consolidation of Shell-Hole.
- 10.30 a.m. to 11.30 a.m. Platoon Training.
- 11.30 a.m. to 11.45 a.m. Break.
- 11.45 a.m. to 12.45 p.m. Company Training.
- 12.45 a.m. to 1.0 p.m. Box Respirator Drill.
- 2.0 p.m. to 4.0 p.m. Specialists Training.
- 5.15 p.m. to 5.30 p.m. Foot Rubbing.

30.10.17.
- 7.30 a.m. to 7.45 a.m. Foot Rubbing.
- 9.0 a.m. to 9.30 a.m. Bayonet Fighting.
- 9.30 a.m. to 10.30 a.m. Platoon Training.
- 10.30 a.m. to 11.0 a.m. Battalion Drill.
- 11.0 a.m. to 11.15 a.m. Break.
- 11.15 a.m. to 12.15 p.m. Instruction in Consolidation of Shell-Hole.
- 12.15 p.m. to 12.45 p.m. Bayonet Fighting.
- 12.45 p.m. to 1.0 p.m. Box Respirator Drill.
- 2.0 p.m. to 4.0 p.m. Specialists Training.
- 5.15 p.m. to 5.30 p.m. Foot Rubbing.

31.10.17.
- 7.30 a.m. to 7.45 a.m. Foot Rubbing.
- 9.0 a.m. to 1.0 p.m. Route March.
- 2.0 p.m. to 4.0 p.m. Specialists Training.
- 5.15 p.m. to 5.30 p.m. Foot Rubbing.

1.11.17.
- 7.30 a.m. to 7.45 a.m. Foot Rubbing.
- 9.0 a.m. to 10.0 a.m. Instruction in Consolidation of Shell-Hole.
- 10.0 a.m. to 11.0 a.m. Platoon Training.
- 11.0 a.m. to 11.15 a.m. Break.
- 11.15 a.m. to 12.15 p.m. Company Training.
- 12.15 p.m. to 12.45 p.m. Battalion Drill.
- 12.45 p.m. to 1.0 p.m. Musketry.
- 2.0 p.m. to 4.0 p.m. Specialists Training.
- 5.15 p.m. to 5.30 p.m. Foot Rubbing.

2.11.17.
- 7.30 a.m. to 7.45 a.m. Foot Rubbing.
- 9.0 a.m. to 10.0 a.m. Instruction in Consolidation of Shell-Hole.
- 10.0 a.m. to 11.0 a.m. Platoon Training.
- 11.0 a.m. to 11.15 a.m. Break.
- 11.15 a.m. to 12.15 p.m. Company Training.
- 12.15 p.m. to 12.45 p.m. Box Respirator Drill.
- 12.45 p.m. to 1.0 p.m. Musketry.
- 2.0 p.m. to 4.0 p.m. Specialists Training.
- 5.15 p.m. to 5.30 p.m. Foot Rubbing.

3.11.17.
- 7.30 a.m. to 7.45 a.m. Foot Rubbing.
- 9.0 a.m. to 1.0 p.m. Route March.

4.11.17. CHURCH PARADES.

W. COLSEY MILLWARD,
Lieut-Colonel.
Comdg. 11th Bn. Royal Sussex Regt.

28/10/17.

CONFIDENTIAL.

11th BATTALION ROYAL SUSSEX REGIMENT

WM 21

WAR DIARY

FOR

1ST NOVEMBER TO 30TH NOVEMBER 1917

VOLUME 21.

WAR DIARY or INTELLIGENCE SUMMARY

Army Form C. 2118.

Place	Date	Hour	Summary of Events and Information	Remarks and references to Appendices
CHIPPENA CAMP	1.11.17		Bn. arrived back to Camp between 1.30 + 2 A.M. having been on working party under R.E. carrying RE materials to BODMIN COPSE. Rather spoilt by sun shining all heat in return. Arrived at 11 A.M. Practice on a REPLICA for the future attack on the MOUND. Capt Tyler accompanied the Bn. from the 1st OX & BUCKS L.I. – also 1st/5 D Coy. – Conduct on the showing very exemplary.	
"	2.11.17		B & D Coys practices on REPLICA during the morning + after dark before the Brig. noted General orders to move up the line on the 5th day. Capt A.G.A. VIDLER + Capt G. SALTER proceed to England for 6 months instructors Course. 2Lt LINDSLEY BUFF. 2/Lt OLIVE + 2/Lt SUTLER rejoined from leave.	
"	3.11.7		Divine Service. Cleaning up + preparation for the move. The Batn paraded at 8 A.M. + took lorries to SHRAPNEL CR. Harries to the line + relieved the 4/5 BLACKWATCH in the TOWER HAMLETS. Rr. Subsector. Relief completed 11 A.M.	
TOWER HAMLETS Rt. Sub Sector	4.11.17		Three Coys in front line (A.C.D.) which consists of a french broken in trench. B Coy in a trench in support. Heavily shelled especially MOUND + at 4.45 A.M. Bn. Carr (Hq Bty) Army (MT BTTY) only.	
"	5.11.17		Another Army barrage at 6.30 A.G. + Rifle fire very heavy during the night. Enemy shelling the back areas in retaliation. Several casualties. Mule part from brought up rations rate. Start Bank to forward 2000 x E of BODMIN COPSE.	
"	6.11.17	6AM	The Batn put up a smoke Barrage to mask the nothern SUFFIELWELT in conjunction with the assault in PASSENDAELE. GOLDEVA HOEK C.H.C. An Army Barrage was put up at the same time. They [?] afterwards Batn. was relieved [?] night by the 12 Rd Surrey R. – Very quiet relief – completed 12 midnight.	
Support BODMIN COPSE	7.11.17		The Batn in relief provided for support positions in BODMIN COPSE. 2 Coys in BRITR BODMIN COPSE + 2 Coys in SWIRIN + another 2/Lt HARRIS IN O.C. Coy + C.S.M. SWIRIN + another N.C.O. Killed by a 5.9" shell which hit dug out cry. Bn. relieved by the 17th K.R.R.C. + marched to GODEZONNE Camp near	
GODEZONNE Camp	8.11.7		VIESRAAT X Rds. arriving 3.30 P.M. Bn. held in the [?] 1.30 P.M. Bn. [?]	

2449 Wt. W14957/M90 750,000 1/16 J.B.C. & A. Forms/C.2118/12.

Army Form C. 2118.

WAR DIARY
or
INTELLIGENCE SUMMARY
(Erase heading not required.)

Instructions regarding War Diaries and Intelligence Summaries are contained in F. S. Regs., Part II. and the Staff Manual respectively. Title Pages will be prepared in manuscript.

Place	Date	Hour	Summary of Events and Information	Remarks and references to Appendices
CHIPPEWA CAMP.	9.11.17		PUBLICATION OF HONOURS + AWARDS. D.S.O. Capt. P.L. CLARK. DCM No 2251 Sgt A Pickford. M.C. 2/Lt. T.H. DYKE. No 555 Sgt F Howley 2/Lt A.B. MCCOROW. No 6346 Pte H. Silverstein M.M. Sgt. H. Wiseman	
"	10.11.17		Coys at Disposal of Coy Commanders for cleaning up + cleaning up + kit + foot inspections. 2/Lt STURGEON rejoining Battn from leave. Battn Concert in the evening.	
"	11.11.17		Physical Training. Platoon + Coy Training. Bn Rev. + saluting Drive. Rain at intervals. Lt. N.C.F. CALDWELL Posted to Instead. Lt + QM SWTAIN took over duties of Adjutant.	
"	12.11.17		SUNDAY. Divine services during the morning. Bath day + some Canin. MAJOR/Lt. Col. STURGEON being O.C. of 2nd in Command of. Schools Course. CADT C.A. ALLEN. M.C. 1/Lt CHESTER being appointed as O.C. Bn. Concert Party 2nd DAVIES 155th New Command of D. Coy. Presentation of Awards for Bn Officers SEPT 25-27 by Brigadier General C. CowdR Doll at CHIPPEWA CAMP from 7AM. to NOON (800 men Bathed) Rest + Recreation in the evening. Bn Concert in the evening. Bn Concert Party Show BD.	
"	13.11.17		Morning devoted 15 Cleaning up the Camp. At 1.30pm the Battn Marched to BEDFORD HD in Bed. Reserve arriving at 5.20 pm. Camp Kitchen was in a very muddy + wet condition. 2/Lt STURGEON appld TOWN MAJOR. HEDGE ST TUNNELS. 2Lts MEO. SQUIRES, RIDER + DINGLE joined the Battn. 2/Lt J.R. BUTLER 155th New Command R.A. Coy vice 1/Lt CHESTER.	
BEDFORD HOUSE	14.11.17		Morning devoted to rest + cleaning up – making Butts improving Sanitary arrangements Generally Cleaning up the Camp. 4.15 pm Battn went to working party to front line Carrying + laying Ammerican S.T. + making trenches mud in the R.E's.	
"	15.11.17		Bn returned from WAS Party 4 am. Casualties. 2/Lt DAVIES Died of Wounds Took key dufficult. Gas Room 2/Lt DAVIES Mortally injured R.W. 12.30 pm. Proper orderly of Capt. Morning the office room.	

Army Form C. 2118.

WAR DIARY
or
INTELLIGENCE SUMMARY

(Erase heading not required.)

Instructions regarding War Diaries and Intelligence Summaries are contained in F.S. Regs., Part II. and the Staff Manual respectively. Title Pages will be prepared in manuscript.

Place	Date	Hour	Summary of Events and Information	Remarks and references to Appendices
BEDFORD CAMP	16.11.17		B Coy Paraded 3.45am for work, party went to 19 Bn. Pioneers – 3am 2 Platoon each of A.C.D Coys went to front line for Revetting + carrying U. Frames.	
"	17.11.17		Early morning. Same working parties for Revetting. Gas Precautions taken in the Camp.	
"	18.11.17		Same working parties as on the 16th – 1815am 18 15am Horsle Plume night Rooms held in observation Balloon – Grieve deceased in Parachute. 11am Holy Communion. Work + Improvement of Camp Continues.	
"	19.11.17		Working parties same as on the 16th – "Very Showery". Work + much Shelling. 1.30 pm the Batn. marched to SCOTTISH WOOD" Camp – arrived 2.30pm + occupied huts vacated by 13 R. Sussex 12. who moved to BEDFORD HQ. "RUMSTARS" (the Concert Party) in the Evening. Concert by the 167th	
SCOTTISH WOOD CP	20.11.17		Companies at disposal of Coy Commanders during the day for cleaning up Re-work on Camp Improvements. – Very Stormy night.	
"	21.11.17		Baths for the Bn. 7am – 12noon – Drill + Training in Day. Gassed. Cadet DREW rejoined Batn from Div HTR. Appointed to A. Coy. Men for Sgts + Cpls Stripes.	
"	22.11.17		Inspection by C.O. of Coys in Huttents in Morning. – In Harness – Buss to HQ21 SICK in MORELAND AV. The C.O. Congratulated the Batn on their good work consolidating the Line + Trans Railway Training – Lt. MAYCOCK returned from Leave	
"	23.11.17		Training –	
"	24.11.17		Training hunter Trophy Programme Arranged – Party left for new billets by Lorry from EIZENWALLER – Barn Bn keen RKRSRKIE clearing in afternoon – 2 Lt BARLOW SICK (contd)	

Army Form C. 2118.

WAR DIARY
or
INTELLIGENCE SUMMARY
(Erase heading not required.)

Instructions regarding War Diaries and Intelligence Summaries are contained in F.S. Regs., Part II. and the Staff Manual respectively. Title Pages will be prepared in manuscript.

Place	Date	Hour	Summary of Events and Information	Remarks and references to Appendices
	25.11.17		The Bn. paraded at 9.30.A.m. & marched to EIZENWALLER. Subtraining at 10.45.a.m. Subtrains to GODAESVELDT arriving 12.45 pm. - Marched to WINNEZEELE arriving 4 pm in Billets - billets very scattered.	
WINNEZEELE	26.11.17		Coys at Disposal of Coy Commanders for cleaning up. 2/Lt DAVIDSON returns from leave.	
"	27.11.17		9 am - 11 am. Physical Training - Coy & Platoon Training - 2/Lts BADCOCK & BROOKES returned from Brigade School. 2/Lt STURGEON from Town Major HEDGE ST. Lt BADCOCK proceeds to leave - Coys to move on 28th for work in the forward area.	
"	28.11.17		Advance Party left at 9 am. for POTEDZE. Physical Training. Borrowing Platoon Training &C during the morning. Reception during the afternoon. Capt HOWSON proceeds on leave. Capt MOIR proceeds to Bell Hrs. G. Capt. BREN taking over duties of 2nd in Command: & 2/Lt. BUTLER duties of Adjy.	
	29.11.17		Bn. Paraded at 5.30 a.m. marched to GODAESVELDT & entrained at 6.55 am for YPRES. Arrived YPRES 10 am & marched to Camp between YPRES & POTIJZE. Accommodated in Tents.	
POTIJZE	30.11.17		Working Parties Commenced. A + B Coys. majority of 1st Reinf. Draft. Remained at WINNEZEELE on light Railways with the Canadian Railway Coy. C + D Coys + 1/2 B.H.Q. Detail parade at 6 a.m. for work in areas near ZONNEBEKE, carried an improvement of Camp 10 pm. for same work. Detail which was in afternoon Coal detail	

2449. Wt. W14957/Mgo 750,000 1/16 J.B.C. & A. Forms/C.2118/12.

CONFIDENTIAL

11th BATTALION ROYAL SUSSEX REGIMENT Vol 22

WAR DIARY

FOR

1st DECEMBER TO 31st DECEMBER 1917

VOLUME 22

Original

Army Form C. 2118.

WAR DIARY
or
INTELLIGENCE SUMMARY
(Erase heading not required.)

Instructions regarding War Diaries and Intelligence Summaries are contained in F.S. Regs., Part II. and the Staff Manual respectively. Title Pages will be prepared in manuscript.

Place	Date	Hour	Summary of Events and Information	Remarks and references to Appendices
POTIJZE	1-12-17	4 a.m. 10 a.m.	Batt. on working parties 2 shifts of 4 hours each, first party leaving at 4 a.m. & the second party at 10 a.m. working under Canadian R.E's making & repairing roads & railway to front line. Details engaged on camp improvements. Cold & wet day. 2/Lt DINGLE passed to England.	
"	2-12-17	"	Same working parties as before. Second party left work earlier owing to hostile shelling at C.A.G. BURGESS went on leave. Very windy & cold day. 4 O.R's reinforcements. 2/Lt Wright J.A. (Part IIB Lt. M.B.) Struck off strength.	
"	3-12-17	"	Same working parties as before. Work on camp improvements continued. Hostile aircraft overhead.	
"	4-12-17	"	11.30 p.m. 2 midnight dropping bombs in a neighbouring camp & causing several casualties amongst Middlesex Regt. Same working parties as before. Camp improvements continued. Flaps & boards for tents arrived. Snow & sleet in morning.	
"	5-12-17	"	Same working parties as before. Camp improvements continued. Flap boards put down. Batt. ordered to hold itself in readiness to move back on the 8 inst. 7.30 a.m. hostile aircraft passed over camp & dropped bombs in (RE Vicinity also between 10.30 & 11 a.m. & during night. Baths in YPRES 2.45 to 4 p.m. Bright day but cold & frosty.	
"	6-12-17	"	Same working parties as before. 3 men wounded on working party. 2.30 p.m. advance party (5 new inlists. 3.30 p.m. hostile aircraft passed over camp & dropped bombs, no damage on acct of R.lgs. Points & one a lot was killing 10 & wounding 10.	
"	7-12-17	4	Same working parties as before in 4 shifts commencing 3 a.m. 40 men. 7 p.m. 40 men. 11 a.m. 80 men. 2.30 p.m. 40 mins. Then	
"	8-12-17	4.30 a.m.	Reveille 4.30 a.m. 8.10 a.m. Batt. paraded & marched to ST JEAN Station entrained at 8.40 & reached GODSWEIDE at	
WINNEZEELE	9-12-17	10 a.m.	10 a.m. Marched to WINNEZEELE arriving 12.30 p.m. 18 O.R's reinforcements Batt. Dull day with some rain. Divine service. Parade service 10 a.m. on football ground. Capt airport of Capt Commanders for cleaning up etc. Transport proceeded to raw Billeting Area. 2/Lt MED proceeded on Bombing Course at X Corps Schools	
"	10-12-17	5.30 a.m.	Reveille 5.30 a.m. Batt. paraded at 8.45 & marched to Cp DESWELDE Station entraining at 11.45 a.m. Arrived at NIELLES & Larry entered en route & arrived LES & LT LIMBERY-BUSE discharged from hospital 7 O.R's reinforcements (Canada)	
SENINGHEM	11-12-17		2/Lt BARROW C.B. to England sick 2/Lt PINCHES J.A. to England sick	
"	12-12-17		Training programme commenced. P.T. Platoon & Coy training & Batt drill at the double during the morning Recreation & football in the afternoon	

2449 Wt. W14957/Mgo 750,000 1/16 J.B.C. & A. Forms/C.2118/12.

Army Form C. 2118.

WAR DIARY
or
INTELLIGENCE SUMMARY

(Erase heading not required.)

Instructions regarding War Diaries and Intelligence Summaries are contained in F. S. Regs., Part II. and the Staff Manual respectively. Title Pages will be prepared in manuscript.

Place	Date	Hour	Summary of Events and Information	Remarks and references to Appendices
SENINGHEM	13-12-17	8 A.M.	Batt. fired on rifle range during morning parading at 8 a.m. & firing from 9 a.m. till 1 p.m. Baths in afternoon.	
"	14-12-17	8.30 A.M.	2/Lt WHITING & CHRISTIE rejoined the Batt. from courses & posted to C & D Coys respectively. 8 O.R's reinforcements. Batt paraded 8.30 a.m. & marched to G.H.Q ranges which were improved & extended. Intensive dripping practised	
"	15-12-17	4 A.M.	Lewis gunners fired on range 2.30 p.m. Cross Country run. Dull & muggy day with rain. Reveille 4 a.m. Batt paraded 5.30 a.m. & marched to X Range near LUMBRES & fired from 9 a.m. to dusk. 5 prizes to be given for the best shots. 2/Lt CHESTER rejoined the Batt. from course & posted to B Coy. 2/Lt BADCOCK returned from leave & posted to A Coy. MAJOR LEWIS returned from course. CAPT DREW appointed Sports Officer.	
"	16-12-17		Divine Service in morning - Casuals who had not fired paraded 5.30 a.m. & fired on range 8 & 11 a.m. Baths 8 am to 12 noon & 1 to 4 p.m. Cross country race arranged for hat cancelled. Tie in football Competition between D Coy & Football Competition. Cold day with snow in evening.	
"	17-12-17	8.30 A.M.	Batt paraded 8.30 a.m. & proceeded to X ranges. Firm from the h/p 11-12.15 at 200 & 300. Brigade Signalling Communication Scheme arranged for but not carried out for some reason. Lt Col C. LOWTHER promoted B20 to A Co's L-men for xmas festivities. Snow on ground.	
"	18-12-17	6.30 A.M.	Reveille 6.30 a.m. 8.0 a.m. Batt paraded & marched to training ground practised attack against a skeleton enemy. Brigade Communication Scheme carried out. Cross country race in afternoon. Inter Coy boxing competition. C Coy beat A Coy. Cold fine day.	
"	19-12-17	9 A.M.	Batt paraded on short range. Firing commenced 9 a.m. Batt. Signalling Scheme continued.	
"	20-12-17	10 A.M.	G.O.C's inspection of Coys commencing at 10 a.m. The G.O.C. expressed himself highly pleased with the turn out especially of R.W.R. Bright fine day. Coys country race. Home competition in the afternoon. Lt Col G. BURGESS returned from leave.	
"	21-12-17	11 A.M.	Batt inspection by Divisional General. Batt paraded at 11 a.m. Presentation of medals & bands afterwards by Afternoon. The General expressed himself very pleased with the turn out. Afternoon A.R.L. Coys played off ties in football.	
"	22-12-17	9 A.M.	Final L-types country race. Bright day. Lt CAMPBELL & 2/Lt A.R.NORRIS & draft of 20 O.R's joined the Batt. Batt fired a short ranges commencing at 9 a.m. Lewis gunners also fired. Numbers parties carried out. MAJOR HUNTINGDON & PARTRIDGE visited the Batt on the range. Leave on leave men advised on P.T. & Bayonet fighting. Col. MILLWARD went on leave. Semi Finals & Final of Tug of War	

2449 Wt. W14957/M90 759,000 1/16 J.B.C. & A. Forms/C.2118/12.

WAR DIARY or INTELLIGENCE SUMMARY

Army Form C. 2118.

Place	Date	Hour	Summary of Events and Information	Remarks and references to Appendices
SEVINGHAM	23-12-17	11:30 A.M.	Parade Service in Transport Field at 11:30 A.M. Football matches etc in afternoon. LT. COL W.C. MILLWARD D.S.O. MAJOR F. Cassel's & Capt. C. LAPWORTH 2/LT (R.V. ELLIS L.R.A.M.S. STEVENSON mentioned in despatches	
"	24-12-17		Capt. at disposal of Coy. Commander for Platoon & Coy. Training, musketry, an assault course & kit inspection. Preparation of Ave Reparation of Personnel Gas N.C.O. posture by 2nd I/c. In charge of Coy 2nd I/c. Sport taken in afternoon. Capt. ANON returned from leave - 2/LT NEO returned from course. The cd m T.O.R's joined the Bn.	
"	25-12-17	10 A.M.	Christmas Day. 10 A.M. Church Parade in Transport field. 11:30 A.M. Football match Officers V Sergeants 2/17 CHRISTIE to hospital sick. 2/LT WHITING granted leave to wear badge of Rank & Leave in completion of 18 months commissioned Service. LT C.A.G. BURGESS Appointed additional Acting Capt with effect from 17 inst.	
"	26-12-17		1917 Warmer in morning with ground clear of Snow. Snow again in evening. Snow at intervals during the day. 2 hrs. Regtl. Coy. L. Platoon drill & training in morning. Snowball fights in the afternoon. having order to move on 28th inst. to Area occupied 4/17 to date.	
"	27-12-17	9 A.M.	Snow fairly thick. Regt. proceeded to short ranges commencing firing 9 A.M. Lewis practice on entrenched course	
"	28-12-17	8:45 A.M.	Recovery practice for Off's & NCO's 1st & No.5 of Lewis gunner teams. Bullet party left for new area under 2/LT WHITING. 116th Inf Brigade made advance on billets to SELLES in order to follow the 117th Inf Brigade to come in. Batt. paraded at 8.45 A.M. & marched to SELLES arriving 12:15 P.M. Marching very difficult owing to the frosty condition of the roads. Motor transport started later & couldn't manage the journey & returned to SEVINGHAM with Blankets	
"	29-12-17	9 A.M.	Batt. paraded at 9 A.M. & marched back to SEVINGHAM arriving at 1 P.M. Travelling again difficult. 2/LT CHESTER & ELLIS went on leave. Motor Transport left for SIEGE FARM in the morning. Breakfast at 11 P.M.	
"	30-12-17	11 A.M.	Batt. paraded at 12:30 A.M. & marched to WIBERNES Station arriving at 6 A.M. spending very difficult & tiring. Entrained then & travelled to ELVERDINGHE Station. Thence marched to SIEGE CAMP. Motor transport arrived late at night.	
SIEGE CAMP	31-12-17	7:30 A.M.	S.O.S. message sent at 7:30 A.M. STAND TO under cancelling same arrived in Quick Succession. LT. KINSERY. & sigs N. Coy. Commander proceeded to reconnoitre the line at 10 A.M. Regimental Transport arrived 12:30 P.M. & signal communication with transport lines completed during the afternoon. Coys. at disposal of Coy. Commanders for P.T. Musketry & L.G. Hostile aeroplanes passed over camp between 5 & 6 P.M. & dropped bombs in the near vicinity.	

31.12.17

Major
Commanding 14 Bn L/S Regt

Confidential

Vol 23

a.n. 23E

11th Service Battalion, Royal Sussex Regiment

WAR DIARY
— for —
JANUARY 1918
(VOLUME 23)

Army Form C. 2118.

WAR DIARY
or
INTELLIGENCE SUMMARY
(Erase heading not required.)

Instructions regarding War Diaries and Intelligence Summaries are contained in F. S. Regs., Part II. and the Staff Manual respectively. Title Pages will be prepared in manuscript.

Place	Date	Hour	Summary of Events and Information	Remarks and references to Appendices
SIEGE CAMP	1.1.18	9 A.M.	Fresh north. Specialist Training. Classes from 9-12 & 1.30 - 3.35 P.M. L.G. & R. Grenade, Scout & Snipers	
"	2.1.18	9 A.M.	& Lewis Classes. Capt C.A. ALLEN returned from Base H.Q'rs	
"	3.1.18	"	Physical Training 7-10 A.M. Specialist Classes continued 10.15 - noon & from 1.30 - 3.30 P.M.	
"	"	"	Firing on Range 9 A.M. - 1 P.M. Specialist Classes cont'd. Finals of Boxing contests. 11 Pte H. non Serwt P.C.977	
"	4.1.18	"	Major LEWIS proceeded to Tank Corps. Capt DREW takes over 2nd I/C	
"	5.1.18	"	Physical Training & Specialist Classes as before. Staithes Bakery classes commence	
"	6.1.18	6 A.M.	Baths 9 A.M. - 12.noon. Physical Training & Specialist Classes cont'd. L.G. Classes fires on Range 2.30 - 3.30 P.M.	
"	7.1.18	11 A.M.	Divine Service. Cap't Parade Service 11 A.M.	
IRISH FARM CAMP	8.1.18		Morning devoted to cleaning up in preparation for move. B's marched to IRISH FARM (hence to HORACE CAMP) for work in front line under R.E.'s except W.O. details who stayed at IRISH FARM	
A. MOROCCO CAMP	9.1.18		Working parties cont'd	
"	10.1.18		Working parties cont'd	
"	11.1.18		Capt C.H.G. BURGESS to Hospital sick. Working parties cont'd	
"	12.1.18		Working parties cont'd. Lt BLUNDEN returned from course. 3 O.R's wounded in working party	
"	13.1.18	10 A.M.	Capt Privates Service in IRISH FARM CAMP. 2nd Lts J N MARTIN A & S Gunner W W CARTER join'd Batt'n. Hostile hands passed over camp at night. About 40 VALENTINES taking over duties of M.O. for some days	
"	14.1.18		Snow in early morning. Capt proceeded to IRISH FARM CAMP from R.E's Advance party to take over.	
			Other afternoon 2nd Lt's DAVIDSON STANDBY & URQUHY proceeded on II Corps General Court 2nd Lt MEIR on R.I.A Instructors	
IRISH FARM CAMP	15.1.18	3.15 A.M.	Gleaning up during the morning. 8.15 P.M. B.B. proceeded Kinswick in relief. Sub sector LEFT BATT HERWOOD BRIG. during very ordinary. When trenchward the NORTH Regt Batt relief (the rest campsite still serviced	
TRENCHES	16.1.18		A.B. Coy's respective posts in front line. D Coy in Support, gun Reserve, 1.B Batt R.S.R. in early H.Q. Fairly quiet and during the day. no casualties. Our mined & blue 14.1 Front Line communications. Cut ground still very heavy. Trip any night during the night out & trip pay all front line trenches	

2449 Wt. W14957/M90 750,000 1/16 J.B.C. & A. Forms/C.2118/12.

WAR DIARY
or
INTELLIGENCE SUMMARY

(Erase heading not required.)

Army Form C. 2118.

Place	Date	Hour	Summary of Events and Information	Remarks and references to Appendices
TRENCHES	17.1.18		CAPT ALLEN went to ascertain the state of the LEKKERBOTERBEEK & found it to be quite impassable. Snow lasted early in the morning & rain all day. Considerable artillery activity on both sides. At about 12 noon four hearers at 5 P.M. Ruled bay valley.	
	18.1.18		Rain washed out every mealy, artillery on both sides more active during (the morning). Batt. relieved by the 14 Gr. WARDS later afterday to A. B & C Coys proceeded to HUB TOP FARM LD Coy to the STEEN BECK & A11 in action. 10 P.M. no casualties.	
HILLTOP FARM CAMP	19.1.18		Rest & cleaning up. Hostile artillery active round the end of the camp especially on batteries. Hostile planes active & Coy relieved D Coy in the STEEN BEEK during the afternoon.	
"	20.1.18		Voluntary Church service. Foot was established in camp. Special fatigue parties held clearing of equipment, huts etc. & Coy relieved B Coy in the STEEN BEEK.	
"	21.1.18		Foot continued & fatigue parties cont. during morning. Hostile shelling of the camp during the afternoon. 6.30 P.M. Batt marched to MENIGE station & entrained for RAILWEX STN then marched to SCHOOL CAMP.	
SCHOOL CAMP	22.1.18	9 A.M.	Morning about 11 P.M. cleaning up & C.O. inspecting sanitary conditions of camp (not visiting huts etc.). Batts 6.15 PM 2ND LT GIBBS	
		6 O.R.'s joined the Batt. D Roll in the evening		
"	23.1.18	9 A.M.	Parade. Inspection of kit, equipment etc. Fatigue over new service lines. Recreation in & afternoon. Numerous	
"	24.1.18	9 A.M.	devoted to reorganisation of platoons, lectures, cleaning of equip. etc. 12.0 noon CO's inspection. Review from in the afternoon. LT. WHITING transferred from A to D Coy as 2nd I/C	
"	25.1.18		Coys at disposal of Coy Command to complete cleaning up etc. 7 hour's close order drill. 2 a.m.'s drill. parade (?)...	
"	26.1.17	10.15 am	Reveille 6.30 am. Chilly morning. 10.15 am. Batt. paraded & marched to PROVEN STATION. Entrained at 12.15 from & marched to MERICOURT L'ABBÉ, a halt being made for about 3/4 hour at TINQUES where Tea was supplied. On detraining at MERICOURT N° 100 am. Batt. marched to BILLETS at CHERSY QUILLY in the II. Army Area, arriving at 5 am the 27th Inst. A Coy and 16 O.R.s from C. Coy provided the Detraining Party, the whole Party &c Group, having preceded the Batt by an earlier train. These men were much hindered by the troops of the Division having been engaged in the YPRES Salient for some a year, and they were glad to get & on entirely new from... Capt. C. LAPWORTH went on leave.	

Army Form C. 2118.

WAR DIARY
or
INTELLIGENCE SUMMARY
(Erase heading not required.)

Instructions regarding War Diaries and Intelligence Summaries are contained in F. S. Regs., Part II. and the Staff Manual respectively. Title Pages will be prepared in manuscript.

Place	Date	Hour	Summary of Events and Information	Remarks and references to Appendices
CHERISY GILLY	27-1-18		Reveille 1.30 p.m. Breakfast 2.30 p.m. Afternoon devoted to cleaning up.	
"	28-1-18		Bright day. Reorganization of Platoons. Inspection of kit and Equipment and issuing of deficiencies. Baths at CHERISY. Letters by 2nd Lt. & W.O. on Foot-Exertions to all officers, followed by lectures to Company Comrs and their Subordinates. Football match in afternoon v 3rd Bns South Wales Borderers. Result winning by 2 goals to 2. Battalion inspected by Commandant Depot in evening.	
"	29-1-18		Reveille 4.45 for ???. Breakfast ??? morning. Capt DYER with 89 Snipers carried out a Reconnaissance of the line. Parties of Rapid loading Bn Lewis Guns Drill and Lectures during morning. Concert in afternoon. A Bombing Show in evening took given by Lieutenant DYER. Lt. RA K.C. MILLWARD returned from leave.	
"	30-1-18	12.30 p.m	Battn paraded at 12.30 p.m. and marched to CORBIE arriving 4.30 p.m. Entrained at 6 p.m. & travelled to PERONNE arriving 10.30 p.m. Marched to HAUT ALLAINES arriving 12.30 a.m. next morning. Rt. proceeded on fatigue, carrying Bags. Capt A. CROSSWELLER returned from leave.	
HAUT ALLAINES	31-1-18	9.30 a.m	Neuville. 9.30 a.m. Breakfast 10 a.m. Rest and cleaning up. Billets & fatigue Day. Afternoon ???? up for new ????.	

Philip Millward
Lt. Colonel.
Commandg. 12th Bn R. Sussex Regt.

ESTIMATE: 1 HR

CONFIDENTIAL

11TH BN. ROYAL SUSSEX REGT.

WAR DIARY

FROM

1ST FEBRUARY TO 28TH FEBRUARY 1916.

(VOLUME 24)

24 E

Army Form C. 2118.

WAR DIARY
or
INTELLIGENCE SUMMARY.
(Erase heading not required.)

Instructions regarding War Diaries and Intelligence Summaries are contained in F.S. Regs., Part II. and the Staff Manual respectively. Title pages will be prepared in manuscript.

Place	Date	Hour	Summary of Events and Information	Remarks and references to Appendices
HAUT ALLAINES	1/2/18		Bn. moved into forward area by train. 2 Coys and B.H.Q. at 9 A.M. and 2 Coys at 1 P.M. Relieved 12th Bn. Royal Scots GOUZEAUCOURT left Centre Sector - Bn. in Reserve - B.Hq. REVELON FARM - Weather fine - frosty	
REVELON FARM.	2/2/18		C.A. ALLEN and Lieut & QM. B.F. SWAIN proceeded on leave. Bn. employed in carrying out improvements to Billets etc. 2nd Lieut. A.R. NORRIS proceeded on course of musketry - Weather thick.	
	3/2/18		Bn. relieved 1/4th HAMPSHIRE REG.t in left sub-sector - Lieut relief - 2nd Lieut. MEO returned from G.H.Q. Lewis Gun course at LE TOUQUET.	
LINE.	4/2/18		Situation quiet - Weather fair - 2nd Lieuts. H.M. GEARY, H.J. MANGER, H. ETHERION joined Bn.	
	5/2/18		Bn. employed in improving defences etc. - E.As. bombed FINS area - Slight shelling of front line. 1 O.R. killed.	
	6/2/18		Working parties - LIEUT. J.C. WHITING to Hospital (Sick) - Light shelling of back area.	
	7/2/18		2nd Lieuts. J.R. BAKER, J.R. HADDON, E.J. HEMSLEY, A.W. NEALE, E.L. WEALE, LIEUT. P.D. WILMOT, CAPTS. H.C.T. ROBINSON, T.H. FENTON, L.A. BAKER, W. JACK FAST + 200 O.Rs. joined from 12th R. Sussex Reg.t	
	8/2/18		Usual trench routine - Situation quiet & weather fine. 2nd Lieut. A. BROOKER joined from 1st R. Munster Fus. Companies employed working parties etc. Quiet day. LIEUT. BURTON joined Bn. from H.A.C. 2nd LIEUT. E.C. PIPER proceeded on V. Army course.	
	9/2/18			

Army Form C. 2118.

WAR DIARY
~~INTELLIGENCE SUMMARY~~
(Erase heading not required.)

Instructions regarding War Diaries and Intelligence Summaries are contained in F. S. Regs., Part II. and the Staff Manual respectively. Title pages will be prepared in manuscript.

Place	Date	Hour	Summary of Events and Information	Remarks and references to Appendices
REVELON FARM.	10/2/18		Day quiet. Battn. relieved at night by 13th R. Sussex Regt. and 1/1st Herts. - moved to Bde. reserve at REVELON FARM. - One company at HEUDICOURT.	
	11/2/18		Cleaning up, usual inspections, baths at HEUDICOURT. - Working parties at night. - Weather fine - Capt. J.R. BUTLER proceeded on leave to U.K.	
	12/2/18		Bn. employed together with 14th R. Sussex, 13th R. Sussex and R.E.s in wiring in no man's land. All parties returned about 2 A.M. Casualties NIL. 45 ORs. joined Bn. from Reinforcement Camp.	
	13/2/18		Cleaning up & foot rubbing parades and inspections preparatory to going into line.	
LINE.	14/2/18		Bn. relieved 1/1st Herts Regt. in left sub. sector - Guint relief - C.O. proceeded on Course & attached to Corps Artillery. - LIEUT. E.C. BLUNDEN took over duties as Adjt. - VII Corps Commander visited forward area - Weather fair.	
	15/2/18		Quiet day, slight shelling at intervals - Companies employed at night on working parties, cable burying, & improvement of Defences. - LIEUT. W.C.F. CALDWELL proceeded to U.K. for 6 months tour of duty.	
	16/2/18		Day fine & aircraft busy - Slight shelling - working parties at night for companies and B.H.Q. cable burying & trench digging - Enemy aircraft bombed Woodpost lines and FINS area. 2 ORs. wounded slightly and 1 HD. RIDER 1 MULE wounded.	

Army Form C. 2118.

WAR DIARY
or
INTELLIGENCE SUMMARY.
(Erase heading not required.)

Instructions regarding War Diaries and Intelligence Summaries are contained in F. S. Regs., Part II. and the Staff Manual respectively. Title pages will be prepared in manuscript.

Place	Date	Hour	Summary of Events and Information	Remarks and references to Appendices
LINE	17/2/18		Day fine - Enemy artillery active - Damage slight - Working parties at night employed on carrying and digging trenches. 1 O.R. killed	
	18/2/18		Weather fair - Working parties at night improving defences - C.O. returned from Artillery course - Capt F.H. FENION took over command of 116 L.T.M.B.	
	19/2/18		Weather fair - Day quiet - Working parties at night.	
	20/2/18		Day fine - Enemy artillery active - Coys and B.H.Q. employed at night on cable burying and trench digging. Casualty 1. O.R. killed.	
	21/2/18		Weather stormy. Situation quiet - Working parties by Coys & B.H.Q. at night. LIEUT & QM. B.E. SWAIN took over duties as Adjutant.	
	22/2/18		Day quiet - Battalion relieved at night by 1/1st HERTS Regt and moved into Brigade Reserve at REVELON FARM. - LIEUT E.C. BLUNDEN M.C. proceeded to U.K. for six months rest.	
REVELON FARM	23/2/18		Weather fair - Baths at HEUDICOURT allotted to Bn - Remainder of day cleaning up and refitting. LIEUT. THORNTHWAITE J.N. transferred from 13th Bn. P. Sussex Regt - 2d LIEUT'S G. STURGEON, P.A. URBAN and J.A. DAVIDSON transferred B. Sussex - Brigade schools reopened - 2d LIEUT. V.R. BROOKER proceeded to Bde School as L.G. instructor - CAPT E.L. WEALE posted to, and took over command of B Company.	

Army Form C. 2118.

WAR DIARY
or
INTELLIGENCE SUMMARY

(Erase heading not required.)

Place	Date	Hour	Summary of Events and Information	Remarks and references to Appendices
REVELON FARM.	24/2/18		Weather fine - Coys and B.H.Q. on day and night working parties employed on improving defences - Troops in billets carried out Box Respirator drill & musketry. - LIEUT. G. MAYCOCK M.C. proceeded on 14 days leave to U.K.	
	25/2/18		Weather fair - Day and night working parties - Box respirator drill and musketry - CAPT. C. LAWORTH posted from B to C Coy. - LIEUT. H.V. BADCOCK, 2nd LIEUTS. C.T. SQUIRES and 2nd LIEUT. HEMSLEY proceeded on course at VII Corps Schools - MAJOR R.C.A. ALLEN returned from leave and took over duties of 2nd I/C.	
	26/2/18		Weather Showery - Foot rubbing parade and visual inspections before moving into line - Relieved 1/1st HERTS. Regt. in Left Sub Sector - Enemy artillery active - shelling transport - 2nd LIEUT. H.M. GEARY proceeded to 5/1st Army Schools on musketry course - 75 O.R's joined from Reinforcement Camp. 2nd LIEUT. J.W. MARTIN appd. Intelligence Officer.	
LINE.	27/2/18		Weather fine - Our artillery fairly active - Raids by Right and Left Bdes. during night - Enemy artillery retaliated on our front - Casualties 3 O.R's wounded, 1 remained at duty.	

Army Form C. 2118.

WAR DIARY
or
INTELLIGENCE SUMMARY.

(Erase heading not required.)

Place	Date	Hour	Summary of Events and Information	Remarks and references to Appendices
LINE.	28/2/18		Weather changeable - Enemy aircraft fairly active - Shelling by our and enemy artillery - CAPT. P.F. DREW M.C. proceeded on leave - LIEUT. R.G.K. LIMBERY-BUSE proceeded to U.K. for 6 months rest. Casualties 2 O.Rs. killed 2 O.R. wounded. 2ⁿᵈ LIEUT. HADDON was wounded by a fragment of our A.A. shells.	

116th Inf.Bde.
39th Div.

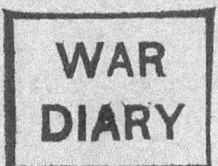

11th BATTN. THE ROYAL SUSSEX REGIMENT.

M A R C H

1 9 1 8

March 1918

Vol 25

War Diary

11th Batt'n Royal Sussex Regiment.

VOLUME 25.

25 E.
8 sheet

WAR DIARY
or
INTELLIGENCE SUMMARY

(Erase heading not required.)

Place	Date MARCH 1918	Hour	Summary of Events and Information	Remarks and references to Appendices
GOUZEAUCOURT	1		Battalion in Louis at Gouzeaucourt Centre Section. Heavy Artillery Bombardment on left lasting two hours. Little enemy activity on our own front. Everybody standing to. Clear bright day. Snow at night. Working party of details of officers at night. Left Coy extended its front taking over 6 posts from 1/1 Cambs Regt. Relief complete 12 mn. No casualties. n 15th HdQrs reconnoitred Pilgrims Commanication arranged so that move could be made at short notice in case of enemy attack. 2/ Lieut NORRIS Returned from course. 2 R.G.C. LIMBERY BUSE proceeded to ENGLAND on 6 months loan of duty.	
"	2nd		Weather dull. hail. Snow fell during morning - Divis.l. Brigadier Generals visited the lines. No enemy activity during day. Considerate artillery activity during evening. Enemy blew up derelict Tanks opposite Right Battalions Front. Left Coy HdQrs moved from QUENTIN REDOUBT to CHALK PIT. 1 O.R. Wounded.	
"	3rd		Quiet day. Weather milder, but not good for Observation. Into Coy Relief after dark. Our Artillery active from dusk till midnight. 2/Lieut M.C. OLIVE and H.J. MANGER returned from 2 2.6 Field Coy R.E. R.S.M. BIRD. Wounded at duty.	
"	4		Enemy Artillery very active at morning "STAND TO". 2 O.R.s wounded by shell. Weather dull. 2/Lieut 1. MED Returned from R.A.	
"	5		This bright day. Observation good. Enemy shelled SUNKEN ROAD at Battn H.Q. at intervals during morning owing to movement 2 ORs Wounded. Our artillery active during day.	
"	6		Enemy raised front at 4-30 AM on left H.Q. Entire posts of Right Battalion & Captured 2 ORs. Heavy hostile artillery barrage between our front line & Bn HQ. Remainder of day fairly quiet. Battalion relieved by 1/1 Herts Regt at night. Relief very quiet after relief. Battn. at REVELON FARM.	

WAR DIARY
or
INTELLIGENCE SUMMARY

(Erase heading not required.)

Instructions regarding War Diaries and Intelligence Summaries are contained in F. S. Regs., Part II and the Staff Manual respectively. Title Pages will be prepared in manuscript.

Place	Date	Hour	Summary of Events and Information	Remarks and references to Appendices
REVELON FARM	7th		Battalion engaged in clearing up - Baths at HEUDICOURT - Musketry. Respirator Drills. Enemy shelled back areas during day. - Caps C.A. ALLEN M.C. appointed A/Major whilst 2nd in Command, effect from 16.1.18. Capt J.R. BUTLER proceeded to Brigade schools as Instructor.	
"	8th		Weather fine. A, B & D. Coys practised raid on Courcé in morning & again at night. Enemy shelled back areas at intervals. Enemy bombing aeroplanes active at night. Lieut C.R.G. BURGESS rejoined from Hospital. Lt J.J. CHESTER proceeded to ENGLAND on 6 months' tour of duty.	
"	9th		Practice of Raid on Courcé during morning. Rain on enemy front line carried out by D.Coy at night. Left assembly point 11PM. Majority of party surprised by uncut wire & a number entered enemy front line posts which were found unoccupied. Not coming having retired when our Artillery barrage started. Our men withdrew at 11-15 PM. Enemy artillery very quiet during operations. 1 O.R. Missing. A & B Coy carried out Box Respirator Drills in dark.	
"	10th		Battalion "STOOD TO" at 4AM. in answer to supposed "S.O.S." Signal from front line. Preparation for move into the line made during the morning & at night Battalion relieved 1/1 Herts Regt. Very quiet relief. Enemy shelled REVELON FARM during evening. No CASUALTIES. Wiring of Battalion front carried out during night.	
GOUZEAUCOURT	11th		Bright day. Companies resisted [?] or repairing communication trenches. Artillery on both sides very quiet during day. At night our Artillery carried out harassing fire on known targets. Wiring further Battalion front completed during this night.	
"	12th		Reported that enemy had been cutting gaps in wire on our front. Additional patrols sent out at night by front line Companies. Coys employed in repairing trenches during morning. Quiet during day. Battalion relieved at night by 4 Bn South African Infantry. Omit relief 18th marched to AX Lining FINS - HEUDICOURT at night by 4 Bn South African Infantry. On relief 18th marched to AX 205 Sorting trenches to GURLU	

2449 Wt. W14957/M90 750,000 1/16 J.B.C. & A. Forms/C.2118/12.

WAR DIARY
or
INTELLIGENCE SUMMARY

(Erase heading not required.)

Instructions regarding War Diaries and Intelligence Summaries are contained in F. S. Regs., Part II. and the Staff Manual respectively. Title Pages will be prepared in manuscript.

Place	Date	Hour	Summary of Events and Information	Remarks and references to Appendices
GURLU WOOD	12"	—	WOOD. in G.H.Q. Reserve. Draft of 15 Signallers joined Battalion	
GURLU WOOD	13"		Warm sunny day. Battalion engaged in cleaning up. Band played during afternoon. LECTURE by Dr. IRVINE on AMERICA in Y.M.C.A. Hut. 2/Lt R.V. ELLIS proceeded on Lewis Gun Course VII Corps School.	
GURLU WOOD	14		Battalion marched to HEM. Billets in tents. Weather conditions fine. Foot inspection in evening. 2 Lt. N.C. DIVE proceeded to ENGLAND on 6 months tour of duty.	
HEM.	15"	3-30 P.M.	Battalion employed on working party at G.H.Q. Salvage Dump. Returned at 3-30 P.M. Reconnaissance of Corps front by C.O. & Officers. Weather fine. Capt H.M. TYLER proceeded on leave to U.K. Capt J.R. BUTLER to Hospital sick	
HEM.	16"		Battalion on working party at G.H.Q. Salvage Dump. Weather fine. Football matches in evening. Conclusion of Battn Knocking-out competition. Draft of 12 O.R.s joined Battalion. 2/Lt E.C. PIPER returned from Course.	
"	17.	7-30 A.M.	SUNDAY. R.C. service at 7-30 A.M. 2 Coys employed on unloading Ballast trains at Salvage Dump. Baths for remainder of Battn. Reconnaissance of Corps front by Officers. N.C.Os carried out 2/Lt V.R. BROOKER transferred to Machine Gun Corps proceeded to England. Football matches in evening.	
"	18"		Battalion engaged on work at Salvage Dump. Reconnaissance of Corps front by Officers. PICCOT Baths for 2 Coys. Football matches in evening. Lieut. Col. W.C. MILLWARD D.S.O. went to Brigade as G.O.C. (temporarily)	

WAR DIARY or INTELLIGENCE SUMMARY

(Erase heading not required.)

Place	Date	Hour	Summary of Events and Information	Remarks and references to Appendices
HEM.	19"		Working parties as on 18th. Rain at intervals all day. Reconnaissance of Corps front by all officers who had not previously been. Actg. Divisional Brigade Generals visited & inspected the Camp. CAPT H. CRASSWALLER R.A.M.C. returned from leave. 2/Lt H. HEMSLEY attached 116 L.T.M. B.	
"	20"		Working parties as on previous day. Officers + 50 O.Rs. attended the funeral of Brig. Genl. G.A.S. CAPE C.M.G. at PERONNE leaving Camp at 9.15 A.M. Capt P.F. DREW & Leather duck. 2/Lt. G.V. STURGEON proceeded on leave & 2/Lt. Capt P.F. DREW returned from leave.	
"	21st		Working party as on previous day. At midday orders were received to move. Parties recalled. Battalion marched off at 2.30. at CLERY. Details to be left out of line were sent with transport to GURLU WOOD. Battalion proceeded in Motor Lorries to the support of the Munster Fusiliers at VILLERS FAUCON. Battalion detrained 1 mile from the village & marched to a sunken road where they rested for 3 hours. Here the Battalion took up a position in support S. of the level crossing in front of VILLERS FAUCON. From this position A + C Coys were sent to reinforce the front line. B. Bn. H.Q. + B + D. Coys remained in support. 2/Lt. I. MED missing.	
VILLERS FAUCON.	22nd + 23rd-	7 A.M.	C. Coy took part in a counter attack which dislodged the enemy but were forced to retire owing to being outflanked on their right. About 11 A.M. the Battalion were ordered to withdraw + take up position 400 yds behind the village. This position was held until the 1/1 Herts Regt had passed thro, when the Battalion reorganised and withdrew to GREEN LINE in front of TINCOURT WOOD - here the Battalion reorganised and took up a position on a ridge on the left of BUSSU behind TINCOURT WOOD. 13th R.S.R. on right 1/1 Herts on left. 13th R.C.R. were outflanked + forced to retire, covered by our fire	

WAR DIARY or INTELLIGENCE SUMMARY

Place	Date	Hour	Summary of Events and Information	Remarks and references to Appendices
BUSSU	23rd		About 9AM. Battalion withdrew to a position on high ground N. of ST DENIS & at 3 P.M. we were forced to relinquish this position to MT ST QUENTIN. Well this position for 2 hours allowed transport to withdraw to CLERY. Then withdrew up SOMME VALLEY following the River at BUSCOURT. Later Bat'n received orders to march to Bois St Gyr at FEUILLERES. 11PM. Bat'n orders to cross River at FRISE take up position at HEM RIDGE. Officers wounded Major C.A. Allen, Capt L.A. Baker, Capt C.A.E. BURGESS, Lt. P.A.M. B.E. SWAIN – Missing Capt A. CRASSWALLER and 2Lt A. BROUGER. Wounded 2Lt J.R. BAKER. 2Lt HETHERTON (missing)	
HEM	24"		Battalion hope held position until the LEICESTERS had passed thro' then withdrew to FEUILLIERES. Instructions received to collect stragglers & report at HERBECOURT. Where Major Genl FEETHAM gave instructions that we should take up position at HEM under Lt. Col. W.C. MILLWARD. at 4 pm we withdrew to CURLU where Battalion were relieved by 35" Division. Transport at CAPPY. Killed. Capt W.J. FAST. Wounded 2/L.M. 2Lt J.W. GIBBS CAMPBELL. MISSING Capt. C. LAPWORTH, 2Lt A.R. NORRIS. 2Lt J.W. MARTIN. 2Lt J.W. GIBBS	
"	25th		Battalion moved by route march via SUZANNE and CAPPY to CHUIGNOLLES when remainder of day was spent in reorganising – C.O. 2/Lt J.A. Davidson, Lieut P.D. WILMOT Missing.	
CHUIGNOLLES	26"		7AM. Battalion moved forward took up position in reserve at WOOD S.E. of CHUIGNOLLES Joined by the 13 R.I.R. & Ill. Herts Reg'. Later withdrew thro' CHUIGNOLLES to Valley N. of PROYART where the Brigade assembled & proceeded to a Ferme in the AMIENS Road N. of HARBONNIERES – took up position S. of Main Road supported by 4 V.M.G's. Lewis A.H.E. GUNNER and E.C. PIPER killed.	
	27"		At midday 118 Bde passed thro' our position & proceeded in direction of BOYONVILLERS. At 3 pm the 8" Division launched unsuccessful counter attack & were now front. Transport moved from HAMEL to GENTELLES re-establishing the PROYART- FRAMMERVILLE Line.	

WAR DIARY
or
INTELLIGENCE SUMMARY

(Erase heading not required.)

Place	Date	Hour	Summary of Events and Information	Remarks and references to Appendices
	28"		At 9 A.M. Battalion recd. orders to withdraw thro' HARBONNIERES where we joined the 11th Herts. from winning thro' CAIX to CAYEUX. Here the Division concentrated at 12-noon. The Brigade then took up position on high ground facing MIENCOURT which was occupied by the enemy.	
	29"		1 A.M. Orders recd. to withdraw to IGNAUCOURT where Battn. rested two daylight later took up position in sunken road due N. of AUBERCOURT. At 10 a.m. Ordered to take up position in sunken road South of COURCELLES. Here Battn. was joined by the 13th R.S.R. Lt. Col. W.C. Millward D.S.O. (A/Brig. Gen.) Wounded.	
	30"		5 A.M. Enemy attacked Battn. on right. Forces then to retire. We formed a defensive flank south held on until 7 am when enemy got behind our right flank forces us to withdraw through AUBERCOURT to this Army line N.W. of village. Held this position till 11 A.M. when enemy enfilated us from high ground on other side of River. Finally forced us to retire to sunken road VILLERS BRETONNEUX - AUBERCOURT road. At 12 noon we withdrew to line held by 13 Gloster on high ground immediately in front of BOIS de HANGARD. 2/Lt F. BURTON Wounded. 2/Lt C.T. Squires (missing)	
	31		Consolidated this hill in previous day. Battn. was relieved by the 16th Division. Lt. M.H. Bedford & 2/Lt R.V. ELLIS rejoined Battalion. Capt. P.F. Drew. M.C. Comdg. Offr.	

Brown Capt.
Comdg. 11th Royal Sussex Regt.

2/Lt. J A Davidson

11" R. Sussex Rgt.

1918

116/39.

NOT FOR VISITORS

Extracts from Diary of 2/Lieut.J.A.Davidson,
"B" Coy. 11th R. Sussex Regiment,
116th Brigade (Br.Gen.Montague Hornby),
39th Division, Fifth Army.

March 21st, 1918. During the night and early morning there seemed by the continuous distant rumbling noise to be a big straffe on somewhere. Our horses arrived about 8.30 a.m. and after a hurried breakfast we started gaily off. There were 6 of us, and Capt. Drew was senior of the party. The guns were still thundering in the far distance. We rode for nearly two hours towards the front line, the noise of the guns increasing in intensity all the time, until we met a Colonel riding who stopped and asked us where we were off to. We told him and he replied that our errand was hopeless as the Bosch big offensive had started. He ordered us to report for instructions to our Brigade H.Qs. who were at Gurlu Wood, so we broke off to the right across country. I had been managing my horse pretty well I thought but feeling awfully sore and stiff began to think reconnoitring by lorry or even on foot preferable. We got to Brigade H.Qs. about 12 noon and decided to give our horses a rest as we had ridden about 18 miles. I was one of the first to dismount. Things seemed busy at Brigade, runners coming and going. I was only too glad to lie on the grass whilst Drew reported. After about 20 minutes he returned and said we had to go straight back to camp. I soon realised my stiffness and soreness when I got up and was helped into the saddle again, and now we started off pretty quickly. I managed to follow along and keep them in sight until after about an hour Drew and those in front disappeared down a valley. There was one other chap near me about as much of a novice at riding as myself, and we walked our horses along together. At the crest of the hill we saw down in the valley the other horses cropping the grass and Drew and the others sitting down and we joined them at a canter and found they were having lunch and I was dammed glad of another rest. We had quite a good rest here, but it did'nt seem to help my soreness and I only felt stiffer than ever when we got up to go on. However, we had only about another hours ride before us and then the camp, and the thought of tea and a stretch on my bed helped me to bear my discomfort, but my heart fell when the camp appeared in sight for everyone seemed rushing about packing up and in the general confusion there was no sign of tea, but I was lucky to get a whisky before the bottle was packed away in the Mess box. I had of course my box-respirator revolver and Water bottle on me and I found that Fox (my batman) had packed all my things and only saw my valise being carried off to the transport waggons that were waiting. Weary, sore and "fed to the teeth" I took command of my platoon which had fallen in ready to march off and we joined up with the other companies of the Battalion. Here whilst at a few

minutes "stand easy" the Sergt. in charge of the
Canteen came along and I was able to get from him a
packet of 50 cigarettes as my own had practically run
out, and how thankful I was later that I had these.
After passing the ruins of Cléry (see map at end of
volume) and about 3/4 of an hours March we fell out
on the side of the road and the cooks soon had tea going
for the men so I was at last able to get some by
borrowing Fox's mug. Here we rested for quite half
an hour when a motor despatch rider brought up orders.
Certain officers, N.C.O.'s and men were detailed to be
left out of the show in the usual way and Capt. Weab
being one of these, the Command of the Company passed
to Capt. Burgess, with myself as second in command and
2/Lt.Piper. Reorganisation took some little while and
presently several motor lorries turned up into which
the men were placed and I took a front seat next to
the driver with the last of the men of my company.
We had a good long drive nearly up to Aizecourt and it
was just beginning to get dusk when we began to meet
motor ambulances and lorries returning from the front
packed full of wounded which made us realise what we
were in for. In the distance we could see shells
flashing as the shrapnel burst in the air, and just out
of range of these shells the lorries stopped, the men
were bundled out and marched off in small parties across
the fields. Piper and Burgess led but presently the
latter joined me in the rear. Shells soon began to
burst all around us but we all got through without

a scratch to the shelter of a dip in the ground and
then to sunken road which led us to just outside
Villers Faucon. Here we halted, the men occupying big
holes dug in the bank of the road with an N.C.O. in
charge of each party and we officers got into a mud
hut which was pitch black and we dared not strike a
light, as shells were still falling around and we did
not know quite where or how near the Bosch might be.
A Sergt. came to tell us that one of the mens rifles
had gone off, the bullet passing through his calf, it
was a question of whether it was a self inflicted wound
and I had to go out and get details and witnesses before
sending him down to a dressing station. We now settled
down for a rest in our shelter and still sore I was just
munching with a bit of bully beef in one hand and a
lump of bread in the other when a chit came from the
C.O. that sentry groups were to be posted at the cross
roads in the village of Villers Faucon and at the level
railway crossing beyond/ that after posting these I was
to take back word to B.H.Q. as to their exact positions.
I got the two parties together, took them out to the posts
giving them details of their duties and hurried to
report to Burgess and then on to B.H.Q. which I found
was in a dug out in a small quarry close by. Maj.Allen
who was acting C.O. then detailed me to go with two
runners to act as Liason Officer with the 13th Sussex
who were in the railway cutting on our left. As an
extra man I took my batman (Fox). He proved quite
useful and I was very glad to have him with me in the
time that followed. Unfortunately I went off without

11th Royal Sussex Regt.   21/3/18.

The 13th R. Sussex Regt. are in the railway cutting
two companies each side of their B.H.Q. which is about
400 yds. from roadway level crossing.

    They are standing by waiting further orders.

    An Officer here tells me that our BROWN LINE
is strongly held by us.

    I am remaining here until I receive further
orders. Am sending this back by one of your runners
and one of my N.C.O's.

                      (Sgd). J. A. DAVIDSON, 2/Lt.

                                B. Coy.

Runner.
11.30 p.m.
Railway cutting.

taking any rations with me. Passing my two
Sentry groups, I walked up the railway cutting, passing
an enormous 16 inch Naval gun mounted on a railway
truck, this I thought had no business to be there with
the Bosch as close and I wondered whether I could in
any way disable it before it fell into their hands;
however I am glad I did'nt attempt anything for during
the night some daring R.Es. brought up an engine quietly
and managed to haul it away which was pretty good work.
I found the 13th Sussex dugout, reported to Maj. Robinson
and was told to make myself comfortable and get some
sleep. I reported to my C.O. my exact position by one
of the runners and turned in for a sleep on the ground,
but about 3 a.m. I was woken up by the fact that the
13th were changing their head quarters to tunnel
dugouts in some large chalk quarries. I reported
the change of position by runner and followed sleepily
along. At the new quarters I got about another hours

March 22nd. sleep but the 13th had breakfast about 4 a.m.
As things were getting lively outside, and I was able to
cadge a bully beef sandwich from their mess cook and
realising how hungry I had been and not knowing where or
how the next meal might come I sneaked a tin of bully
and put it in my box respirator case which for the next
9 days I treated as a reserve larder and always tried by
scrounging about to keep one tin there.

The night had been fairly quiet except for shelling
but at dawn the Bosch renewed the attack.
Maj. Robinson sent me to take command of a small party
of men who had come back withour line of trenches.
I found they were from an Irish Regt. and had apparently

been driven back by the Bosch; they were about 20 strong and I had just told them off to man the position when one of there own officers turned up and of course he took them over. The quarries were now being pretty heavily shelled and slightly to my right rear I could see men engaged in rifle fire, so I went further along the trench to the left where I knew the Herts Battn. of our Division were. Here I found Lt. Eve whom I had met at the Millam course and I stayed and helped him. Away on our right front we could see the Bosch marching up in close formation and I longed for our artillery to open up on them but altho Eve telephoned the information back, giving the map reference, no response came, in fact our artillery was practically silent and we saw some of our planes about. About 11.30 a.m. we saw our men at the Quarry retiring and a telephone message came through that we were to retire too. Fox and I went along the trench for some way hoping to find a communication trench leading back, for we saw men retiring across the open being shelled with shrapnel and falling in bunches killed and wounded, a pitiful sight. We could find no trench back and so had to go over the open chancing the shells and often nearly stumbling over the dead who lay in the long grass. I soon lost touch with the Herts and found myself alone with Fox, so as soon as we were well out of the range of the shells, I set about trying to find my battalion but it was a hopeless tack, altho I met two of our men who had quite lost their way.

All I could glean was that Brigade H.Q. had been at
Gurlu Wood and I started to try and make my way there
as best I could across country. I finally arrived there
about 5 p.m. after having wandered about for miles,
pretty fagged out, with torn puttees and looking pretty
much like a tramp. I found Capt. Bolton, the Staff
Captain, and he told me the Battalion had been in
action and had retired to Tincourt about an hours
walk from Gurlu nearer the front but much further over
to the right. I had ½ an hours rest and he gave me a
whisky and a pocketful of army biscuits, as I was
beastly hungry and they were all he had. Brigade had
retired but he had remained behind to see after rations
which he hoped would be round that night. Three other
of our men had straggled in and so after rest I marched
the men off to Tincourt to reach which Bolton had
indicated the way; after some enquiries I found that
Battalion, with Capt. Lapworth now in command, Maj. Allen
and Capt. Burgess both having been wounded, and I was
given command of "A" Coy. with Lt. Piper and Burton
under me. The company's position was about the
centre of the Battalion's front, in a trench marked
out by the R.Es. but hardly a foot deep and showing
hard white chalk. We were ordered to dig ourselves in,
no easy job in the hard stuff as we only had six spades
for the whole company and practically all the men had to
simply use there entrenching tool. It was useless to
try and make a proper trench so I told each man to make
a hole for himself and then afterwards if there was time
to try and connect these up.

It was now practically dark except for a misty moon but the men worked fairly well for two hours when rations having arrived I let them knock off. Fox got me a little tepid bully beef stew which I was thankful for and I sent back a short, hurried letter to the wife by the quarter master Sergeant (Stone) just to let her know I was O.K.

My right flank in a tiny valley was about 200 yards from the next company and I put a strong Lewis gun post there to guard this gap, sentries were told off and I felt there was nothing much else to be done. Fox lent me his waterproof sheet as he was sharing one with a pal and I settled down for a rest. I think I must have dozed for a little while and when I woke up there was a thick damp mist and I was shivering and my teeth chattering with the cold. I walked around to find Burton shivering too so we kept on the move to try and get warm, visiting the sentries etc., but we did'nt seem to get much warmer. About mid-night a note came from the C.O. (Lapworth) saying

March 23rd. he wanted to see Company commanders at 1 a.m. and I sent my runner back with the messenger with a note asking Lapworth whether he could spare us a wee drop of rum or whisky. Like an angel he sent his flask back and the spirit put new life into us. At 1 a.m. I went to B.H.Q. returning the flask and to meet the other company Commanders (Fast, Baker and Campbell). Lapworth read out orders he had received for us to take up a new position near Bussu about a mile and a half further back; the 13th Sussex were going too and we were to meet Maj. Robinson at 3.30 a.m., so that we had to have our men ready to move off at 3 a.m.

Going back I called my sergeants together, gave them
the necessary orders and at the specified time when all
was serenely quiet we vacated the line and marched off to
Bussu. The line here was only marked out with tape
but we got a few more spades and started to convert old
shell holes into posts. My positions was on the top
slope of a valley side with the 13th Sussex on my right
and the other companies of my Battalion extending on my
left across the valley and up the opposite side. I had
a little bit of a trench and impromptu dugout for my
Company Head quarters and this I occupied with Lt.Burton
Sergt. Clarke (acting Coy. Sergt, Major, a stout fellow)
and two men with Fox. The Coy. Mess Cook had found a hollow
just behind and here he managed to boil us some tea on
a tommys cooker which was wonderfully welcome with cold
bully and biscuits for breakfast at about 6 a.m. after
being up all night. I put out an advance observation
post of a Corpl. and four men to watch our front and give
warning but we had a good field of fire in front of us
and I felt we could not very well be surprised. I borrowed
some field glasses from one of the men who said he had
found them, my own having been packed up in the hurry in
my valise and through these I presently saw figures advanc-
towards us in the distance. I passed along word to stand
ready but not to fire until I gave the order and it was
lucky I did so for as the figures approached nearer I saw
they were British Tommies. They came through our lines
very excited saying the Bosch had broken through again
and were coming in thousands. I told all to keep a good

look out and shortly after my men forming the advance observation post came running back saying the Bosch were advancing in small parties about 600 yds, in front of their post. I kept a good look out along my front with the glasses until I saw figures moving as though crawling in the grass on my right. I pointed these out to Burton and Sergt. Clark who both had rifles and when the figures had crept a little nearer they opened fire. One figure threw up his arms and disappeared and the others kepts low and out of sight. Other figures appeared further over to the left and sniping became general on both sides. The figures we had just seen got up and dashed forward a few yards but we were ready for them and I think most of them were knocked out. I now got word that the 13th Sussex on my left were retiring and looking across the valley on my right I could see our own men going back in small parties and considerable firing going on. I opened pretty heavy fire on anything visible and as soon as I thought the 13th had got well away gave the order for my men to retire, by posts from the left, my own little group being the last to leave and then we ran for bullets were coming over pretty thick but we were lucky in having cover close behind us. We hurried along through trees on the hillside for about ½ a mile until I found Col. Phillips of the Cambs. who had reorganised stragglers on a new position. About 20 men were digging themselves in on the level ground and on slight hill each side I could see other men taking up position.

I was sent with about a dozen of my men up the hill
on the right and just as I was going, one of my men
passed with a wounded and roughly bandaged right hand.
It was impossible for him to use his rifle and he
looked on the point of dropping with fatigue and pain
so I took his rifle from him and ordered him to get
back and find an aid post so that he could get his
wound properly dressed. Scrambling through under
growth and a few trees I got to the crest of the hill
which I found held by about 30 men with several officers
I got my men as a sort of support line about 30 yards
behind these and crouching down low to keep out of view
of a Bosch plane which was flying close to us we waited
developments. I could see across the valley to my left
but only about 50 yds in front of me as the ground
sloped away steeply. Things were pretty quiet for
about 20 minutes and I was getting cramped and stiff
when a Bosch Machine gun opened fire on the men in front
of me killing and wounding several although the bullets
passed well over my head. Those left in the front line
fired a few rounds and then came bolting back, three
falling hit as they did so and many of my men joined
in an disorderly and panically flight, altho I did
my very best to stop them. However I had three or four
stout fellows with me, one with a Lewis Gun although he
only had one drum of ammunition, and seeing that from
our position we had good cover to get away I decided to
stay on a bit and see what happened, After a minute or
two, which of course seemed to me an age, a big head
of a Bosch in his tin hat appeared above the crest of
the hill. One of my men fired and I think must have hit

him, then three other heads appeared, I quickly picked out one, and remembered he wore glasses, fired and killed him for he threw up his rifle as he fell forward, the others I think met the same fate from my men's fire. I knew we should be very hotly pressed very soon and probably attacked on our right flank but we stayed on and fired at the next two heads that appeared and then I told the men to withdraw as quickly as they could, half way down the hill side amongst the trees.

11th Royal Sussex Regt. 22/3/18.

I have noted your present position and will inform
the 13th Battalion O.C. The 13th Battalion H.Q. has
moved to the Quarry at E.18.c.85.60. using the same
dugout tunnel as the 1/1 Herts. I will keep you
imformed of any movements. 1/1 Herts line approx.
F.7.a.91 to F.8.c.24.

(Sgd), J.A.DAVIDSON,
2/Lt.
B. Coy.

Runner.
6.40 A.M.
22/3/18.

11th R. Sussex Regt.   23/3/18.

The 16th Rifle Brigade have just passed through our lines retiring.

Have posts told off and am digging in.

Have sent out listening posts to 300 yds.

(Sgd). J.A.DAVIDSON,
2/Lt.
O.C. A.Coy.

Runner
8. 55 A.M.
23/3/18.

11th R.Sussex Regt.   23/3/18.

Stragglers of Dublin Fusiliers passed through my line state their Battalion is fighting a rear guard action in the wood immediately to my centre front. Wounded man of Hants says Bosch advancing in mass formation.

(Sgd). J.A. DAVIDSON.

Forward listening post has good mile ground in front of command.

9.15 A.M.
23/3/18.

11th R.S.R.   23/3/18.

Listening post states that he sees enemy advancing in massed formation with right in front of wood to my centre front.

Stragglers say that enemys cavalary is in action.

J.A. DAVIDSON,
2/Lt.
O.C. A. Coy.

9.25 A.M.

11th R. Sussex.   23/3/18.

Machine gun fire has been enfilading on right flank.

Keeping in touch with 13th.

    Sending your note re 2 Platoons on to "C" Coy.

                    (Sgd). J.A. DAVIDSON, 2/Lt.

                    O.C. A. Coy.

11 A.M.

116th Brigade.

39th Division.
Composite Brigade

Became "A" & "B" Cos. No.1 Composite Battalion 11.4.18

11th BATTALION

ROYAL SUSSEX REGIMENT

APRIL 1918.

SECRET 17

1b/39 April 1918

JM 26

26 E
7 sheet

WAR DIARY

11th (S) Bn Royal Sussex Regt.

Volume XXVI

Army Form C. 2118.

WAR DIARY
or
INTELLIGENCE SUMMARY
(Erase heading not required.)

Instructions regarding War Diaries and Intelligence Summaries are contained in F.S. Regs., Part II. and the Staff Manual respectively. Title Pages will be prepared in manuscript.

Place	Date	Hour	Summary of Events and Information	Remarks and references to Appendices
CLEARY.	1st APRIL 1918.	—	Battalion in Rest Billets at CLEARY. Day devoted to Reorganization and cleaning up. COMMAND. C.O. Capt. P.F. Drew, M.C. 2nd i/c Capt. H. Amor, M.C., Adjt. Capt. E.L. Weale, M.C., 'A' Coy. Lieut. H.V. Backoor, 'B' Coy. 2/Lieut. J.A. Davidson, 'C' Coy. 2/Lieut. R.V. Ellis, 'D' Coy. 2/Lt. H.M. Geary.	
CLEARY.	2nd		Battalion paraded at 9 a.m. and marched to billets at AUMONT, a distance of 20 kilometres.	
AUMONT	3rd		Battalion paraded at 8:30 a.m. and marched to billets at AMATRE, a distance of 18 kilometres.	
AMATRE.	4th		Day devoted to cleaning up, taking of deficiencies and collecting late of Casualties.	
AMATRE.	5th		Day devoted to cleaning up refitting and reorganization. Casualties reported. 20 Officers and 300 O.R.'s killed, wounded & missing.	
AMATRE.	6th		Battalion paraded at 9.30 a.m. and inspected by Brigadier General WYATT, Commanding 118th Infy. Brigade. Bn. highly complimented on its good work in the Somme battle by B.O.C.	

WAR DIARY
or
INTELLIGENCE SUMMARY

(Erase heading not required.)

Army Form C. 2118.

Place	Date	Hour	Summary of Events and Information	Remarks and references to Appendices
AMATRE.	7th		Battalion paraded at 8.a.m. and marched to EMBLEVILLE. (25 Kilometres) Roads very bad and men very tired on arrival in Billets.	
EMBLEVILLE.	8th		Battalion paraded and inspected by Company Commanders. Rifle exercise and Physical Drill. Consignment of new clothing and equipment received and issued.	
EMBLEVILLE	9th		Battalion paraded at 1.a.m. and marched to EU Station. At 5.a.m. entrained for ARQUES. Arrival at ARQUES at 12 noon and marched to TATINGHEM. Arrival 3.0.p.m. Companies billeted in Barns and houses in the village. 2/Lieut: P.H. Urban reported from leave.	
TATINGHEM.	10th		Day spent in cleaning up and refilling. Draft of 20 arrived and posted to Cos. Capt: J.H. Reid, Stanyan returned from leave and sent to 2nd Army School. At 9.0.p.m. Orders received for Battalion to proceed to ST OMER and entrain for VLAMERTINGHE.	
TATINGHEM.	11th		Battalion paraded at 2.a.m. and entrained at ST OMER for VLAMERTINGHE. Length 6 Miles and 5.30 U.R.'s. Marched from VLAMERTINGHE to TORONTO CAMP and rested for remainder of day. Battalion formed into two companies (A & B) of the 1st Battalion, 87th Composite Brigade. Capt: G.E. Whitfield.M.C. in Command and Capt: P.J. Day. M.C. second in command. Heavy artillery firing during afternoon. Weather fine.	

Army Form C. 2118.

WAR DIARY
or
INTELLIGENCE SUMMARY

(Erase heading not required.)

Instructions regarding War Diaries and Intelligence Summaries are contained in F. S. Regs., Part II. and the Staff Manual respectively. Title Pages will be prepared in manuscript.

Place	Date	Hour	Summary of Events and Information	Remarks and references to Appendices
TORONTO CAMP.	12th		Battalion moved by train and Route march to OTAGO CAMP. Remainder of day resting. Camp shelled during the afternoon. Artillery active on both sides. Weather fine.	
OTAGO CAMP.	13th		Battalion under 1/2 hours notice to proceed to line. Enemy artillery active. Weather dull.	
"	14th		Day spent in reequipping and resting. Weather fine. Slight artillery activity	
"	15th		Battalion moved to VOORMEZEELE. Dinners on the march. Companies proceeded to various positions and commenced construction of new line of defence.	
DORMEZEELE	16th		Enemy very active on night Bn. H.Q. shelled. Weather fine.	
"	17th		Companies still engaged in strengthening defences. Bn. H.Q. again shelled.	
"	18th		Some positions B.H.Q. heavily shelled during night with H.E. Plans for takeover.	
"	19th		Enemy artillery and aircraft very active. Otherwise quiet day. Weather fair.	
"	20th		Weather changeable and slight snowstorms. Shared artillery activity. E.A. active during night.	
"	21st		Weather dull. Enemy artillery active during day. Bn. H.Q. moved to ENZENWALLE at night.	
ENZENWA- LLE CHATEAU (Support line)	22nd		Weather fine. Enemy artillery active and Bn. H.Q. shelled. Few casualties	

WAR DIARY
or
INTELLIGENCE SUMMARY

(Erase heading not required.)

Army Form C. 2118.

Place	Date	Hour	Summary of Events and Information	Remarks and references to Appendices
IZENWAELE CHATEAU (in't line).	23rd		Usual artillery activity on both sides, especially on Right. Armstrong S.A. carried out wire. Weather fine.	
"	24th		Artillery active especially on our front. Bn. H.Q. shelled. Major Slayter took over command of Bn. and Capt. Drew command of A Coy. Showery.	
"	25th	2:40 a.m.	Violent Artillery activity immediately followed by Enemy attack, which was repulsed. Casualties fairly heavy. Violent shelling of Bn. H.Q. Weather dull.	
"	26th		Very heavy enemy shelling. Bosch attack still held. Casualties very heavy. 2/Lt. Brodeup, M.M. took over acting Major & 2/Lt. Ratcliffe Killy. The enemy's heavy casualties in storming the BRASSERIE capturing 2 Prisoners of 3rd M. Grens. and myself. Heavy shelling. Attack still held. Enemy attempts very active. Battalion relieved at night by 1st Kings Liverpools and Confederine moved to Support positions. Bn. H.Q. at Dickibusch Ridge.	
SUPPORT LINE.	28th		Battalion in same positions. Heavy shelling of Front line during day. Quiet night. Capt. R.V. Ellis officer while on reconnaissance.	
D⁰ " - "	29th		Continued heavy shelling of our positions by the enemy. Our Artillery very active. Battalion relieved at night by 2nd Princess, and proceeded to Devonshire Camp.	

Army Form C. 2118.

WAR DIARY
or
INTELLIGENCE SUMMARY
(Erase heading not required.)

Instructions regarding War Diaries and Intelligence Summaries are contained in F. S. Regs., Part II. and the Staff Manual respectively. Title Pages will be prepared in manuscript.

Place	Date	Hour	Summary of Events and Information	Remarks and references to Appendices
DEVONSHIRE CAMP	30th		Battalion resting all day.	

R. Prin, Captain,
Comdg., 11th R. Sussex Regiment.

CONFIDENTIAL

11th BATTALION ROYAL SCOTS REGIMENT

Vol. 27

WAR DIARY

FOR

MAY 1918.

VOLUME 27

Army Form C. 2118.

WAR DIARY
or
INTELLIGENCE SUMMARY
(Erase heading not required.)

Instructions regarding War Diaries and Intelligence Summaries are contained in F. S. Regs., Part II. and the Staff Manual respectively. Title Pages will be prepared in manuscript.

Place	Date	Hour	Summary of Events and Information	Remarks and references to Appendices
DEVONSHIRE CAMP.	1-5-18		Battalion merged into two Companies. Morning devoted to cleaning up and reorganization. Battalion with other Units formed into the new No 1 Composite Battalion. 39th Divisional Composite Brigade. Moved in the afternoon to H.21.d. in Reserve Positions. Returned to DOMINION CAMP for two hours and returned to line later.	
	2-5-18		During day considerable artillery and aerial activity on both sides. Weather fine. Fairly quiet evening. Our artillery carried out heavy bombardment during night.	
	3-5-18		Artillery very active on both sides throughout the day. Enemy constantly shelling back areas. Weather fine. Battalion relieved by the 10th Bn Worcester Regt at night, and proceeded to Brigade H.Qrs where the men bivouaced for remainder of the night.	
	4-5-18		Battalion proceeded by March Route to ST JAN TER BIEZEN (M.CAMP) arriving at 5.30 p.m. Remainder of day devoted to cleaning up. Capt H.M. TYLER. attached to 1st Bn. 305th Inf Regt A.E.F. as Company Commander. 1/Lieut J.A. DAVIDSON attached to 1st Bn. 305th Inf Regt A.E.F. as Lewis Gun Officer. 2/Lieut R.A. URBAN attached 2nd Bn. 305th Inf Regt A.E.F. as Company Commander. Lieut H.M. GEARY. attached 3rd Bn. 305th Inf Regt A.E.F. as Company Commander.	
M. CAMP.	5-5-18.		Battalion moved off at 2.30 p.m. and proceeded by March Route to ROUSBRUGGE Station entraining for AUDRUICQ at 8.30 p.m. Weather very wet.	
NIELLES-LES-ARDRES.	6-5-18.		Battalion detrained at AUDRUICQ at 4.0 a.m. and proceeded in G.S. Wagons & Limbers to Billets in NIELLES-LES-ARDRES. Arrived in Billets about 6.0 a.m. Hot Breakfast provided and remainder of day devoted to sleep and rest.	

2449 Wt. W14957/Mgo 750,000 1/16 J.B.C. & A. Forms/C.2118/12.

WAR DIARY
or
INTELLIGENCE SUMMARY

(Erase heading not required.)

Army Form C. 2118.

Place	Date	Hour	Summary of Events and Information	Remarks and references to Appendices
NIELLES-LES-ARDRES.	7-5-18.		Day devoted to refitting, reorganization and general cleaning up. Baths allotted to Battalion the whole day. Weather fine.	
NIELLES-LES-ARDRES.	8-5-18.		Companies at disposal of Company commanders. Morning devoted to Rifle Inspection, Physical training and Arms Drill. Remainder of day spent in general cleaning up.	
NIELLES-LES-ARDRES.	9-5-18.		Training carried out during morning as on previous day. Signalling Classes also commenced. 2/Lieut. A. BROOKER proceeded to 2nd Army Lewis Gun School for 12 days course.	
NIELLES-LES-ARDRES.	10-5-18.		Training carried on from 9a.m. to 12.0 noon. Drill - Musketry - Bayonet fighting. - Box Respirator Drill - Bayonet Practice. Capt. G. SALTER M.C. rejoined Battalion from 6 months duty in ENGLAND.	
NIELLES-LES-ARDRES.	11-5-18.		Usual training carried out as on previous day. No parades during afternoon. Weather fine.	
NIELLES-LES-ARDRES.	12-5-18.		Church Parades for all ranks at 11.30 a.m. in front of CHATEAU. Football match against 13th Platoon in afternoon. Capt. G. SALTER. M.C. took over duties of Second in Command. Capt. H. AMDN. M.C. took over command of C. Company.	
NIELLES-LES-ARDRES.	13-5-18.		Training carried out from 9.0.a.m. to 12.30 p.m. Drill - Musketry - Bayonet fighting, - Arbering - Gas Helmet Drill - Ceremonial Drill & March Past. Some rain during day. Lieut. F.G. ARMITAGE and Lieut. J.F. BAKER rejoined from 116 L.T.M. Battery.	
NIELLES-LES-ARDRES.	14-5-18.		Usual training carried out from 9.0.a.m. to 12.30 p.m. Weather dull but fine.	

Army Form C. 2118.

WAR DIARY
or
INTELLIGENCE SUMMARY
(Erase heading not required.)

Instructions regarding War Diaries and Intelligence Summaries are contained in F. S. Regs., Part II. and the Staff Manual respectively. Title Pages will be prepared in manuscript.

Place	Date	Hour	Summary of Events and Information	Remarks and references to Appendices
NIELLES-LES-ARDRES	15-5-18		Training carried out as usual during morning. Lieut F.E. ARMITAGE took over command of "B" Coy. 2/Lieut J.R. BAKER posted to "B" Coy. for duty. Weather fine and warm.	
NIELLES-LES-ARDRES	16-5-18		Usual training continued during morning. Weather fine and warm.	
NIELLES-LES-ARDRES	17-5-18		Training continued as on previous days. Capt H.C.T. ROBINSON rejoined Battalion from 39th Divisional Headquarters and took over Command of "D" Company.	
NIELLES-LES-ARDRES	18-5-18		Usual training carried on. Major A.E. ANDREWS joined Battalion from 11th Bn. Hampshire Regt. Weather fine and very warm.	
NIELLES-LES-ARDRES	19-5-18		Church Parade. No training carried out during day. "D" Coy provided working party of 15 men for work on Brigade Gas Ground at GUEMY. Football match against 13th R. Kings R. in evening. Divisional Studio gave free performance to this Battalion at 6.30 p.m. Major A.E. ANDREWS assumed Command of the Battalion. Capt P.F. DREW M.C. took over duties of Second in Command. Capt G. SALTER M.C. took over command of "B" Company.	
NIELLES-LES-ARDRES	20-5-18		Usual training continued. Weather fine and hot. "D" Coy provided working party as on previous day. A v B. Coys. provided working party of 2 officers and 80 men for work under 225th Field Coy R.E. on Range at GUEMY. Haversack Rations taken. Party returned about 4.0 p.m. 2/Lieut E.J. HEMSLEY proceeded to ROUEN in charge of party of details from 11/8 Infantry Brigade. Orders received for Battalion to be formed into a Cadre training Battalion for instructing American Units, surplus personnel and transport to be despatched to Base Depot about the 23rd inst.	

2449 Wt. W14957/Mgo 750,000 1/16 J.B.C. & A. Forms/C.2118/12.

Army Form C. 2118.

WAR DIARY
or
INTELLIGENCE SUMMARY
(Erase heading not required.)

Instructions regarding War Diaries and Intelligence Summaries are contained in F.S. Regs., Part II. and the Staff Manual respectively. Title Pages will be prepared in manuscript.

Place	Date	Hour	Summary of Events and Information	Remarks and references to Appendices
NIELLES-LES-ARDRES.	21-5-18.		Baths allotted to Battalion from 8.0am to 12.0noon and from 1.0pm to 4.0pm. Training carries on when companies not bathing. C. & D. Companies provided working party of 2 Officers and 80 men for work on GUEMY Ranges. Weather very fine and warm.	
NIELLES-LES-ARDRES.	22-5-18.		Divisional Commander inspected Battalion with the 13th R. Irish. R. at 11.0am in front of the CHATEAU. Medal Ribbons presented to recent recipients of honours. Remainder of day devoted to general cleaning up and settlements preparatory to the Battalion being dis-banded. "A" & "B" Coys. provided usual working party for GUEMY Ranges. Weather fine and hot. 2/Lieut. A. BROOKER returned from Course at 2nd Army Lewis Gun School.	
NIELLES-LES-ARDRES.	23-5-18.		Surplus Personnel despatched to ETAPLES. Roll Call and Parade at 7.30 a.m. Entrained at AUDRUICQ Station at 2.40 p.m. 6 Officers and 367 Other Ranks proceeded under Capt. H.C.T. ROBINSON. Remainder of Battalion forming Battalion Training Staff proceeded to billets at LICQUES at 6.0 pm. Weather fine with high wind.	
LICQUES.	24-5-18		Day employed in re-organising Training Staff and arranging billets. Lieut. G. MAYCOCK. M.C. with 38 Other Ranks (Surplus Transport Personnel) proceeded to ETAPLES by march route. 2/Lieut. E.J. HEMSLEY returned from ROUEN. Weather very wet - heavy rain the whole day.	
LICQUES.	25-5-18		Reorganisation continued. Weather dull but fine.	
LICQUES.	26-5-18		Lieut. J.C. WHITING and Lieut. E.J. HEMSLEY proceeded to ETAPLES. with party of Other Ranks. Entrained at AUDRUICQ Station. Weather fine & warm. Lieut. C. GRAINGER. M.C. joined Battalion for duty as Quartermaster from 10th B. Bed. Surrey Regt. Lieut. J. JONES. M.C. temporarily acting as Quartermaster returned to 13th B. Lin. R. Baths allotted to details from 2pm to 3pm.	

2449 Wt. W14957/M90 750,000 1/16 J.B.C. & A. Forms/C.2118/12.

Army Form C. 2118.

WAR DIARY
INTELLIGENCE SUMMARY
(Erase heading not required.)

Place	Date	Hour	Summary of Events and Information	Remarks and references to Appendices
LICQUES	28/4/18 28/5/18		Battalion standing by pending arrival of American Units. Weather fine and warm.	
LICQUES	29-5-18		Muster Parade and Inspection by the C.O. on the square near the Church at 9.0 a.m. Weather very fine and warm.	

LICQUES	30/5/18 31/5/18		Battalion standing by in Billets awaiting arrival of American troops. Weather unifromwarm The following Decorations were awarded during the month.
			
			BAR TO MILITARY CROSS
			    Capt. H. AMON. M.C.
			
			THE MILITARY CROSS
			    2/Lieut. J. A. DAVIDSON.
			    2/Lieut. E. J. HEMSLEY.
			
			THE DISTINGUISHED CONDUCT MEDAL
			  No 20400 R.S.M. H.M. BIRD. No 1766 Sgt. A. GOLDEN.
			  2446 Pte. C. HENHAM. 2235 L/Cpl. T. STEVENS
			  593 A/Cpl. C. SPRUNT. 14923 2/Cpl. J. A. BARNES.
			  4336 Pte. A. HARVEY.
			
			BAR TO MILITARY MEDAL
			  No 1084 L/Cpl. C. J. PERRY. M.M.	

Army Form C. 2118.

WAR DIARY
or
INTELLIGENCE SUMMARY
(Erase heading not required.)

Place	Date	Hour	Summary of Events and Information	Remarks and references to Appendices
	3rd June 1918.		THE MILITARY MEDAL.	
			No. 1290 R.Qr. S. BOYS.	
			4822 " W. HUNT.	
			17333 Pte. P.A. GRISTON.	
			1953 " B. HOLDER.	
			17388 " O.C. MORRIS.	
			5926 Cpl. T. BURCH.	
			16944 L.Cpl. W. LUXFORD.	
			14488 L.Cpl. W.H. SPEARS.	
			15513 Pte. W.J. ANDERSON.	
			395 " H.T. NORMAN.	
			131 " E.M. SINGLE.	
			6854 " J.F. BRINKHURST.	
			17345 " A.C. TAYLOR.	
			6426 C.S.M. D.G. HONEYSETT.	
			14044 Pte. C.T. MILTON.	
			H.E. Brown Lieut. Colonel.	
			Comdg. 11th Bn. Royal Sussex Regt.	

CONFIDENTIAL

11TH BATTALION ROYAL SUSSEX REGIMENT   Vol 28 / T͟e͟ / 39 / XXXX

28 E
6 sheets

— WAR DIARY —

FOR

1ST TO 30TH JUNE 1918

(VOLUME 28)

Army Form C. 2118.

WAR DIARY
or
INTELLIGENCE SUMMARY

(Erase heading not required.)

Instructions regarding War Diaries and Intelligence Summaries are contained in F. S. Regs., Part II. and the Staff Manual respectively. Title Pages will be prepared in manuscript.

Place	Date	Hour	Summary of Events and Information	Remarks and references to Appendices
LICQUES	1-6-18		Battalion affiliation with 2nd Bn. 305th Inf. Regt. and 2nd Bn. 306th Inf. Regt. A.E.F. from 12 noon today. Capt. G. SALTER. M.C. rejoined from 2nd Army into Bn Comdr. Capt. H AMON M.C. attached to 9th Bn. Black Watch as Instructor.	
LICQUES	2-6-18		Bands allotted to Battalion from 2.0pm to 3.0 p.m. Weather fine and hot. 5 Active Ranks supplies to Training Establishment. disposition to Base.	
LICQUES	3-6-18 to 5-6-18		Training of American Battalion commenced. Musketry, Bomb, Mortars, Bayonet fighting etc. complete schemes. Also practising Company in the attack. Weather warm and fine ( )	
LICQUES	6-6-18		Orders received for all American Units of 77th American Division to leave this area. Lewis Guns, Rifle various stores handed over for safe custody by American Units.	
LICQUES	7-6-18		All Instructors attached to 305th and 306th Infantry Regiments A.E.F returned owing to their Battalions having left the area.	
LICQUES	8-6-18 to 10-6-18		Battalion standing by awaiting arrival of new American troops.	
LICQUES	11-6-18		All Officers +N.C.O. Instructors paraded at LA SOLITUDE Range for Revolver Light by Instruction under Serj. STEVENS. (A.G.S) Parade lasted from 9.30 a.m. to 12.30 p.m. Capt. P. F. DREW. M.C. and an Instructor proceeded to Second Army Area for advent Instructors.	

Army Form C. 2118.

WAR DIARY
or
INTELLIGENCE SUMMARY

(Erase heading not required.)

Instructions regarding War Diaries and Intelligence Summaries are contained in F.S. Regs., Part II. and the Staff Manual respectively. Title Pages will be prepared in manuscript.

Place	Date	Hour	Summary of Events and Information	Remarks and references to Appendices
LICQUES	12-6-18		Bayonet fighting course for all Officers and Instructors continued at same times as yesterday.	
LICQUES	13-6-18		Instruction in Map Reading & Compass Work given to all Officers & Instructors by the C.O. from 9.30 am to 12.30 p.m.	
LICQUES	14-6-18		All Officers & Instructors carried out an Advance Guard and Attack Scheme under the C.O. at 9.30 am.	
LICQUES	15-6-18		Musketry Exercises and firing practices carried out by all Officers N.C.Os on LA SOLITUDE Range from 9.30 am to 12.30 pm.	
LICQUES	16-6-18		Baths allotted to Battalion from 2.0pm to 3.0pm. Draws received for Battalion to be attached to 118th Infantry Brigade to assist in training 2nd Bn 120th Infantry Reg: A.E.F. C.O. attended Conference at 118th Inf/Bde Headquarters.	
LISTERGAUX	17-6-18		Battalion moved from LICQUES to LISTERGAUX by march route. Arrival in new Billets at 2.0pm. Battalion affiliated to 2nd Bn 120th Inf/Reg: for American Brigade. Capt H AMON M.C. commenced Instructors returned from 9th Bdy Schools.	
LISTERGAUX	18-6-18		The C.O. and Capt H M TYER reconnoitred the WINNEZEELE Line which was to be occupied by the 120th Infantry Regiment and affiliated British Each Battalion in the event of a heavy hostile attack. Conference held at 118th Inf/Bde H.Qrs. Capt E.L. WEARE M.C. representing the C.O. as a Training Training of 2nd Battalion 120th Infantry Reg: commenced.	

WAR DIARY
or
INTELLIGENCE SUMMARY

(Erase heading not required.)

Army Form C. 2118.

Instructions regarding War Diaries and Intelligence Summaries are contained in F. S. Regs., Part II. and the Staff Manual respectively. Title Pages will be prepared in manuscript.

Place	Date	Hour	Summary of Events and Information	Remarks and references to Appendices
LISTERGAUX	19-6-18		Training continued. Capt P.F. DREW M.C. returned from 2nd Army Anti Gas School.	
LISTERGAUX	20-6-18		Training continued. Weather dull and showery.	
LISTERGAUX	21-6-18		2nd Bn 120th Infantry Regt. proceeded to NORTLEULINGHEM. At Musketry Practice. Adv. Company Commanders, C.S.M.'s, C.Q.M.S.'s and obligatory Instructors proceeded with Western Battalion and bivouaced in neighbourhood of RANGO for 2 days.	
GRASSE PAYELLE	22-6-18		Orders received for Battalion to take over 1st Bn 120th Infantry Regt. then affiliated to 13th R. Sus. R. Battalion moved to Billets at GRASSE PAYELLE. Signaller and runners took over from 13th R. Sus. R.	
GRASSE PAYELLE	23-6-18		Batts of RECRUES allotted to Battalion from 10am to 2pm. No Training carried out. Instructors returned from NORTLEULINGHEM.	
GRASSE PAYELLE	24-6-18		Battalion took over training of 1st Bn 120th Inf. Regt. Lt.Col A.E. ANDREWS, comg 120th Infantry Regimental Headquarters. Capt. H.M. TYLER took over duties of C.O. during absence of Lt.Col. ANDREWS.	
GRASSE PAYELLE	25-6-18		Training of Americans continued.	
GRASSE PAYELLE	26-6-18		Warning Orders received for Battalion to hold itself in readiness to proceed to ENGLAND. Warning Orders received for Battalion to hold itself in readiness to proceed to ENGLAND.	

Army Form C. 2118.

WAR DIARY
or
INTELLIGENCE SUMMARY

(Erase heading not required.)

Instructions regarding War Diaries and Intelligence
Summaries are contained in F. S. Regs., Part II.
and the Staff Manual respectively. Title Pages
will be prepared in manuscript.

Place	Date	Hour	Summary of Events and Information	Remarks and references to Appendices
GRASSE PAYELLE	29-6-18 to 29-6-18		Training still continued and preparations for expedition to ENGLAND commenced.	
GRASSE PAYELLE	29-6-18	6.30am	Word received from 118th Inf Bde instructing Battalion to entrain at 9WOLWICH at 11.0am	
			At BOULOGNE. Very hurried departure.	
		11.20am	10 Officers and 570 Other Ranks entrained at WIMEREUX carried on 30 vehicles at 30pm	
			Party conveyed by Major Price to OSTROHOVE Camp for the night. Bivouac alarm arrangement.	
BOULOGNE	30.6.18		Battalion left OSTROHOVE Camp at 9.15 am marched BOULOGNE harbour. Embarked on	
		10.30am	at BOULOGNE 12.30pm Arrived at FOLKESTONE at 3.30pm Entrained at	
			ALDERSHOT. Very calm crossing. Arrival at NORTH Camp Station at 8.0pm marched	
			to Camp at MYCHETT with other units of 20th Division. All in Camp by 9.45 pm	

[signature]
Captain
Comdg 11th Bn Royal Sussex Regt

www.ingramcontent.com/pod-product-compliance
Lightning Source LLC
Chambersburg PA
CBHW080911230426
43667CB00015B/2652